THE
DALIT TRUTH

RETHINKING INDIA
Series editors: Aakash Singh Rathore, Mridula Mukherjee,
Pushparaj Deshpande and Syeda Hameed

OTHER BOOKS IN THE SERIES
Vision for a Nation: Paths and Perspectives
(Aakash Singh Rathore and Ashis Nandy, eds)

The Minority Conundrum: Living in Majoritarian Times
(Tanweer Fazal, ed.)

Reviving Jobs: An Agenda for Growth
(Santosh Mehrotra, ed.)

We the People: Establishing Rights and Deepening Democracy
(Nikhil Dey, Aruna Roy and Rakshita Swamy, eds)

The Shudras: Vision for a New Path
(Kancha Ilaiah Shepherd and Karthik Raja Karuppusamy, eds)

Her Right to Equality: From Promise to Power
(Nisha Agrawal, ed.)

Being Adivasi: Existence, Entitlements, Exclusion
(Abhay Flavian Xaxa and G.N. Devy, eds)

RETHINKING INDIA

THE
DALIT TRUTH

THE BATTLES FOR REALIZING
AMBEDKAR'S VISION

Edited by K. RAJU

VINTAGE
An imprint of Penguin Random House

VINTAGE

USA | Canada | UK | Ireland | Australia
New Zealand | India | South Africa | China

Vintage is part of the Penguin Random House group of companies
whose addresses can be found at global.penguinrandomhouse.com

Published by Penguin Random House India Pvt. Ltd
4th Floor, Capital Tower 1, MG Road,
Gurugram 122 002, Haryana, India

Penguin
Random House
India

First published in Vintage by Penguin Random House India 2022

ISBN 9780670093014

Typeset in Bembo Std by Manipal Technologies Limited, Manipal
Printed at Replika Press Pvt. Ltd, India

www.penguin.co.in

MIX
Paper from
responsible sources
FSC® C016779

To Gurram Jashuva (1895–1971) and Boyi Bhimanna (1911–2005),
for inspiring, through their timeless masterpieces of literature,
the quest for the Dalit truth
and the vision of a just and humane society

Contents

Series Editors' Note

Psychologists tell us that the only true enemies we have are the faces looking back at us in the mirror. Today, we in India need to take a long, hard look at ourselves in the mirror. With either actual or looming crises in every branch of government, at every level, be it central, state or local; with nearly every institution failing; with unemployment at historically high rates; with an ecosystem ready to implode; with a health-care system in a shambles; with an education system on the brink of collapse; with gender, caste and class inequities unabating; with civil society increasingly characterized by exclusion, intolerance and violence; with our own minorities living in fear; our hundreds of millions of fellow citizens in penury; and with few prospects for the innumerable youth of this nation in the face of all these increasingly intractable problems, the reflection is not sightly. Our true enemies are not external to us, not Pakistani terrorists or Bangladeshi migrants, but our own selves: our own lack of imagination, communication, cooperation and dedication towards achieving the India of our destiny and dreams.

Our Constitution, as the Preamble so eloquently attests, was founded upon the fundamental values of the dignity of the individual and the unity of the nation, envisioned in relation to a radically egalitarian justice. These bedrock ideas, though perhaps especially pioneered by the likes of Jawaharlal Nehru, B.R. Ambedkar, M.K. Gandhi, Maulana Azad, Sardar Patel, Sarojini Naidu, Jagjivan Ram, R. Amrit Kaur, Ram Manohar Lohia and others, had emerged as a broad consensus among the many founders of this nation, cutting across divergent social and political ideologies. Giving shape to that vision, the architects of modern India strived to ensure that each one of us is accorded equal opportunities to live with dignity and security, has equitable access to a better life, and is an equal partner in this nation's growth.

Yet, today we find these most basic constitutional principles under attack. Nearly all the public institutions that were originally created in order to fight against dominance and subservience are in the process of subversion, creating new hierarchies instead of dismantling them, generating inequities instead of ameliorating them. Government policy merely pays lip service to egalitarian considerations, while the actual administration of 'justice' and implementation of laws are in fact perpetuating precisely the opposite: illegality, criminality, corruption, bias, nepotism and injustice of every conceivable stripe. And the rapid rise of social intolerance and manifold exclusions (along the lines of gender, caste, religion, etc.) effectively whittle down and even sabotage an inclusive conception of citizenship, polity and nation.

In spite of these and all the other unmentioned but equally serious challenges posed at this moment, there are in fact new sites for socio-political assertion re-emerging. There are new calls arising for the reinstatement of the letter and spirit of our Constitution, not just normatively (where we battle things out ideologically) but also practically (the battle at the level of policy articulation and implementation). These calls are not simply partisan, nor are they exclusionary or zero-sum. They witness the wide participation of youth, women, the historically disadvantaged in the process of finding a new voice, minorities, members of majority communities, and progressive individuals all joining hands in solidarity.

We at the Samruddha Bharat Foundation proudly count ourselves among them. The Foundation's very raison d'être has been to take serious cognizance of India's present and future challenges, and to rise to them. Over the past two years, we have constituted numerous working groups to critically rethink social, economic and political paradigms to encourage a transformative spirit in India's polity. Over 400 of India's foremost academics, activists, professionals and policymakers across party lines have constructively engaged in this process. We have organized and assembled inputs from *jan sunwais* (public hearings) and *jan manchs* (public platforms) that we conducted across several states, and discussed and debated these ideas with leaders of fourteen progressive political parties, in an effort to set benchmarks for a future common minimum programme. The overarching idea has been to try to breathe new life and spirit into the cold and self-serving logic of political and administrative processes, linking them to and informing them by grassroots realities, fact-based research and social experience, and actionable social–scientific knowledge. And to do all of this with harmony and heart, with sincere emotion and national feeling.

In order to further disseminate these ideas, both to kick-start a national dialogue and to further build a consensus on them, we are bringing out this set of fourteen volumes highlighting innovative ideas that seek to deepen and further the promise of India. This is not an academic exercise; we do not merely spotlight structural problems, but also propose disruptive solutions to each of the pressing challenges that we collectively face. All the essays, though authored by top academics, technocrats, activists, intellectuals and so on, have been written purposively to be accessible to a general audience, whose creative imagination we aim to spark and whose critical feedback we intend to harness, leveraging it to further our common goals.

The inaugural volume has been specifically dedicated to our norms, to serve as a fresh reminder of our shared and shareable overlapping values and principles, collective heritage and resources.

Titled *Vision for a Nation: Paths and Perspectives*, it champions a plural, inclusive, just, equitable and prosperous India, and is committed to individual dignity, which is the foundation of the unity and vibrancy of the nation.

The thirteen volumes that follow turn from the normative to the concrete. From addressing the problems faced by diverse communities—adivasis, Dalit Bahujans, other backward classes (OBCs)—as well as women and minorities, to articulating the challenges that we face with respect to jobs and unemployment, urbanization, healthcare and a rigged economy, to scrutinizing our higher education system or institutions more broadly, each volume details some ten specific policy solutions promising to systemically treat the issue(s), transforming the problem at a lasting structural level, not just a superficial one. These innovative and disruptive policy solutions flow from the authors' research, knowledge and experience, but they are especially characterized by their unflinching commitment to our collective normative understanding of who we can and ought to be.

The volumes that look at the concerns, needs and aspirations of the Shudras, Dalits, adivasis and women particularly look at how casteism has played havoc with India's development and stalled the possibility of the progressive transformation of Indian society. They first analyse how these sections of society have faced historical and structural discrimination against full participation in Indian spiritual, educational, social and political institutions for centuries. They also explore how the reforms that some of our epoch-making socio-political thinkers like Gautama Buddha, M.K. Gandhi, Jawaharlal Nehru and B.R. Ambedkar foregrounded are being systematically reversed by regressive forces and the ruling elite because of their ideological proclivities. These volumes therefore strive to address some of the most glaring social questions that India faces from a modernist perspective and propose a progressive blueprint that will secure spiritual, civil and political liberties for one and all.

What the individual volumes aim to offer, then, are navigable road maps for how we may begin to overcome the many specific challenges that we face, guiding us towards new ways of working cooperatively to rise above our differences, heal the wounds in our communities, recalibrate our modes of governance and revitalize our institutions. Cumulatively, however, they achieve something of even greater synergy, greater import: they reconstruct that India of our imagination, of our aspirations, the India reflected in the constitutional preamble that we all surely want to be a part of.

Let us put aside that depiction of a mirror with an enemy staring back at us. Instead, together, we help to construct a whole new set of images. One where you may look at your nation and see your individual identity and dignity reflected in it, and when you look within your individual self, you may find the pride of your nation residing there.

Aakash Singh Rathore, Mridula Mukherjee,
Pushparaj Deshpande and *Syeda Hameed*

Introduction

K. Raju

Across the country in Dalit localities today, statues of Dr Ambedkar—holding the Constitution of India in one hand and showing the way forward to the nation with the other—are a common sight. The Dalits not only own Ambedkar but also the Constitution, as they consider it as 'Ambedkar's Constitution'. This volume examines how far the constitutional promises made to the Dalits have been fulfilled and how far the Dalits have progressed on the way shown by Ambedkar. The Dalits are among the world's largest group of people with a long history of discrimination against them. In their quest for equality, as promised by the Constitution, they have been waging relentless battles against the caste system. The essays in this book are about those battles.

This book is set in contemporary times, when the political mobilization of the Dalits is following a trajectory that the founders of the Constitution would never have expected. Though the Congress party, in partnership with Ambedkar, had formulated the Constitution, and brought out policies, programmes and legislations aimed at their social, economic and political empowerment, the Dalits are drifting away from the Congress in a few states. Some critics argue that it is the Congress that is drifting away from the Dalits, with Manuwadi parties making inroads there. This volume tries to objectively examine the truth and falsities that are influencing the political mobilization of the Dalits.

This book has been influenced by my own career as a former civil servant and current Congress leader, and my life as a Dalit. In over three decades as a civil servant, I have had the opportunity to listen to the small and big voices of the Dalits, partake in their pain and celebrate their victories with them. As a Congress leader, I could closely fathom the realities of politics where the Dalits have a stake. It was with this in mind that I invited thinkers who have the courage of conviction to speak the truth to contribute essays for this book. The truth some of them speak may be unsettling to a politician, whether Congress or non-Congress. It is an attempt to engage with a variety of intellectuals on Dalit lives and politics, and to acknowledge the Dalit truth. Though I strongly believe that the Congress remains the best hope for Dalit emancipation, none of the essays in this book has been 'censored'—including those critical of my party.

The book's inquiry into Dalit lives takes you through to the Dalit truth. There are many things which are routinely said about truth: that it is naked and it hurts; that it cannot be hidden for too long; that it prevails. But one thing which is not often said is that it always bears the burden of the past with unflinching grace. It might reveal something ugly, dull or even obvious, but it always holds its head high elegantly since it has nothing to hide. Truth remains plain and solid in its transparency.

Yet societies have always had an unsaid preference for lies. Unlike truth, which can be uncomfortable, lies offer a tempting simplicity. They stand seductively in the corner, promising false liberation from the burden of untangling the complex web of the past. But the salve of lies is temporary. Along with being divisive, lies negate history so that the dominant classes, which are mostly responsible for fabricating them, continue their hegemony. The truth fights against forgetting, while lies encourage it.

To comprehend any socio-political phenomenon, the truth must be unravelled layer by layer, like the age-old metaphor of peeling an onion to reach the core. This metaphorical onion takes us through the layers of human and personal history to arrive at the nucleus. Over a period of time, these shiny layers of lies multiply. Each dominant regime contributes another layer of cover-up, making the quest for truth cumbersome. But the unalloyed truth remains buried underneath the palimpsest of time, mummified without decay.

And what is the truth of Dalit life? It is that in society's reparation attempts, there is exclusion hiding behind the pretense of inclusion. It is the dominant class's insecurity and obsession for power which makes them rob the Dalits of opportunities. The primordial lie, which forms the very basis of the Varna system, is that some are born 'higher' than the others. This leads to compulsive, draconian, ever-increasing lies, passed off as 'divine will', hiding the truth that the Dalits have been stripped of opportunities related to education, employment, wealth and dignity for centuries.

While this injustice has been at the heart of the Dalit truth, there is the *other* truth as well: that parallel to the stories of agony and despair of the Dalit life, there are also ones of extraordinary resilience, triumph and meaningful contribution to India and the world. The ability of Dalit individuals to overcome adversities is so profound that it can be held as an example for future generations. The Dalits, even while being crushed by society and the state, toiling under poverty, apply their remaining energies to the development of the nation. And what better way to teach inclusivity than to celebrate the contributions of *all* great Indians from *all* communities?

Take, for example, the first Dalit female graduate of India, and one of the fifteen women members of the Constituent Assembly, Dakshayani Velayudhan. A true Gandhian, she did not hesitate to contradict Gandhi's stand in favour of Ambedkar's on various occasions.[1] She had great determination for the Dalit cause and felt the need to lay a strong foundation for the nation. And yet, the loud lies of the dominant voices have muffled Dakshayani's truth to a great extent. Much before Dakshayani Velayudhan, another Dalit woman showed the world great courage and grit. Her name was Jhalkari Bai, and she showed exceptional strength and skills from an early age. In the famous battle against the British in 1857, she disguised herself as the rani of Jhansi and fought a fierce battle against British forces, facilitating the rani of Jhansi's discreet exit from the battlefield.[2] Lakshmibai's prowess is undeniable, but the fact that Jhalkari Bai's contribution was kept hidden for so long raises many questions.

In the history of our country, there are many instances when the truth of Dalit valour, wisdom and sacrifice was pushed under the tarp of caste-related lies. Consider Matadin Bhangi, the man responsible for awakening the conscience of Mangal Pandey. Matadin was the one who pointed out the hypocrisy of the social order which didn't allow Pandey to accept water from his hands due to his 'low caste' but compelled him to bite the end of the bullets smeared with cow and pig fat. Unfortunately, for centuries after 1857, Matadin's truth was purposefully hidden. Similarly, Udadevi and Makka Pasi, the Dalit couple martyred during the First War of Independence, were never remembered.

Ambedkar, one of the greatest figures in Indian history, is himself a story of success. The leading voice on the Indian Constitution, and a powerful leader safeguarding Dalit, women and minority rights, Babasaheb remains a beloved son of the soil. His understanding of people was truly unparalleled. He is cabined as a Dalit icon, but the truth is that his influence extends far beyond his caste, and even beyond India. He was a once-in-a-generation thinker, an advocate of a new social order that recognizes liberty, equality and fraternity as fundamental tenets of life.

Also, look at Babu Jagjivan Ram. He stands out as a key figure with his share of truths while bearing the burden of lies. A Dalit man from Bihar, he became a towering figure in the history of

India, not just as a Dalit icon but as an able administrator. He ensured the implementation of constitutional promises to the Dalits after Ambedkar resigned from Nehru's cabinet. His contributions to the Green Revolution were remarkable, helping bring food security for the first time to the hungry millions in Indians across the social spectrum. He served as defence minister during the 1971 Indo–Pak war and was instrumental in the creation of the 'Joint Command' of Bangladesh and Indian forces for the final assault which led to victory.

Damodaram Sanjeevaiah became the first Dalit chief minister of an Indian state, Andhra Pradesh (1960–62), when he was just forty years old. In 1962, Sanjeevaiah became the first Dalit leader to become the All India Congress Committee president (1962–63). He also served as Union minister for labour and employment (1964–66). As the Andhra Pradesh CM, he introduced 27 per cent reservations for OBCs in government jobs and educational institutions, long before the Mandal Commission came into the scene. As Union minister, he introduced the Payment of Bonus Act and pensions for the aged. He is remembered for his impeccable integrity and honesty. People of Andhra Pradesh fondly remember him as a chief minister who, after stepping down from office in Hyderabad, took a public transport bus to reach his humble house in his native village in the Kurnool district of Andhra Pradesh.

An Indian Dalit is a proud citizen who believes in egalitarian assimilation of cultures—an idea alien to the hubris of those in power. Dalits can never be accused of sub-nationalism. This sense of national integrity is one of their most remarkable contributions to India.

This book is our effort to strip the lies, the philosophical side-stepping and the self-serving excuses that have obscured the beating heart of the Dalit truth. The essays offer pathways of hope for the Dalits to realize the promises that we, the people of India, made to them when the Constitution was adopted on 26 November 1949. This book is a companion to the seekers of truth who wish to dismantle the architecture of lies designed to keep the Dalits in their place.

The book is divided into three sections. The first looks at the Dalits, the Constitution and representational politics. The second looks at why the Dalits, in some states, are drifting away from the Congress. And the third looks at Dalits outside politics. As you read through the contents, I encourage you to look for the truth that exists in each one.

Dalits, Constitution and Representational Politics

The adoption of the Constitution marks a political shift in any country, but in the case of India it was also a social shift. The Indian Constitution was a charter of social reform, a bold attempt to give freedom to the Dalits from a plethora of entrenched hierarchies. The Indian state, at the time of the framing of the Constitution, recognized the problem arising out of the social organization of the caste system. It made justice (social, economic and political), liberty, equality and fraternity the governing principles of society, overturning the principles on which the caste system was founded.

The drafting committee envisioned the Indian Constitution to be a transformative document that would enable the full and effective participation of every citizen in public life. The scholar Marc Galanter noted that 'the Constitution envisaged a new order both as to the place of caste in Indian life and the role of law in regulating it'.[3] In a society where caste privilege enabled the concentration of social, economic and political power, realizing a vision of equity required a constitutional commitment to address the historical disabilities imposed on minorities, including the untouchables. It is clear that the foundations of Indian democracy were built on the principles of equality, where caste would have no role to decide the fate of the people, whose lives and aspirations were crushed by it.

The first essay in the book is Sukhadeo Thorat's 'The Dalit Idea of the Nation, Inspired by Ambedkar'. Thorat explains the Ambedkarite idea of the nation, which involves a philosophic vision of hope for the oppressed and a concrete proposal to implement it. Thorat masterfully chronicles Ambedkar's efforts to incorporate his ideas of nation and nationhood into the Constitution. But the proposed economic framework to ensure economic equality and social democracy could not find a place in the Constitution. Thorat argues that without these components, the necessary conditions for inclusive nationhood have not been met. His essay addresses questions around Ambedkar's ideas of nation and nationhood, and how they can offer current policymakers solutions to the problems of poverty and caste discrimination. He observes that today, when both constitutional morality and the democratic fabric of the nation is being weakened, Dalit politics must rethink how to not only safeguard the existing progressive mechanisms that the Constitution has but also, for its own future, how to introduce radical measures into the Constitution dreamt by Ambedkar.

The second essay in this book is Raja Sekhar Vundru's 'Ambedkar's Representational Politics: Expanding the Possibilities'. Vundru focuses on the evolution and journey of representational politics of the untouchables in colonial and postcolonial India. This struggle, led by Ambedkar, exposed the majoritarian lies, while the truth for which Ambedkar fought remains relevant even today. And what is that truth? The truth is that the current electoral system, where a Dalit candidate is elected by all, has limitations in furthering the interests of the Dalits in a majoritarian polity. Therefore, the Poona Pact of 1932 has been the bone of contention among Dalit intellectuals. Gandhi had justified his opposition to separate electorates to the depressed classes for the sake of Hindu unity.

The Poona Pact, nevertheless, provided opportunities for the Dalits in education and employment, which had not been envisaged earlier. However, one must reflect on whether the

joint electorate system and political representation as it is now
have weakened Dalit leaders. Even Ambedkar was twice defeated
in the Lok Sabha elections and had to be elected to the Rajya
Sabha. Scheduled caste candidates had to rely on the votes of the
non-Dalits, particularly the upper castes. Dalit leaders have to
work for ruling-class parties, which continue to support them,
to be in positions of power. How can they safeguard the interest
of the most vulnerable? And when elections depend on financial
resources and guaranteed vote banks, one does need patrons. The
Congress party is possibly the only party to have some credible
Dalit leaders in positions of power. Independent India has seen
Dalit Presidents, chief ministers, ministers in the Central and state
governments, presidents of political parties at the national and state
levels, members of Parliament and state assemblies, chief secretaries,
secretaries to the GOI and state governments, collectors, DMs and
SPs—mostly due to the affirmative action diligently promoted by
the Congress governments at the Centre and in states. But have the
Dalit elected representatives been able to secure equity and justice
for the Dalits?

The judiciary has a crucial role in breathing life into the
constitutional provisions for advancing the rights of the backward
classes and enforcing the social contract between the state and its
citizens. The judgments of the higher judiciary in the first decade
reflected a glaring lack of understanding regarding the disabilities
suffered by individuals by virtue of their membership to a group. The
judiciary's 'caste-blind' attitude only served to perpetrate casteist
notions of merit and imposed unfair yardsticks of 'meritocracy' on
socially disadvantaged groups.

The constitutional right to reservations in government jobs for
the Dalits and adivasis under Article 16(4) is a fundamental right.
The Constituent Assembly had made its intention loud and clear by
including the right to reservations under right to equality, which is
a fundamental right. But for nearly two decades, the majoritarian
lies have influenced the Supreme Court to limit the reach of Article

16(4) by reducing it from a compulsory provision to a mere *enabling* provision. It was only in a dissenting opinion in 'T. Devadasan vs Union of India' (1964) that Justice K. Subba Rao ruled against the majority trend for the first time. He held that Article 16(4) is a facet of Article 16(1). By acknowledging that Article 16(4) was not an exception but one of the methods of achieving equality embodied in Article 16(1), the Supreme Court in later years signalled a fundamental shift in its understanding of equality.

Questions have been raised time and again regarding the social composition of the higher judiciary and its impact on judicial outcomes. Can an unelected higher judiciary that has historically selected upper-caste judges be trusted with safeguarding the interests of the Dalits and adivasis? Can a selection process that has repeatedly failed to elevate judges from SC/ST/OBC communities be considered fair? Does the glaring lack of representation in the higher judiciary shape outcomes that are prejudicial to the interest of the minorities? The National Commission to Review the Working of the Constitution, chaired by Justice M.N. Venkatachaliah, had noted that there were in every state, an adequate number of persons from the SC, ST and OBC communities who possessed the qualifications, integrity, character and acumen required for appointment as judge of the superior judiciary; and that in the face of 'weighty opinion' against reservation in the higher judiciary, a necessary way should be found to increase the representation of SC, ST and OBC judges.[4]

It would be interesting to examine the social profile of the purveyors of the abovementioned 'weighty opinion' and weigh in their arguments. The repeated attempts to weaken the statutory provisions against atrocities, dilute executive action regarding reservation and a tendency to either dilute or read down judgments pronounced by larger benches pertaining to reservation have highlighted the need to have a more representative judiciary. History teaches us that the failure to be inclusive only breeds prejudices and exploits stereotypes.

Kiruba Munusamy's essay 'Caste and Judiciary in India' gives a vivid description of the battle between truth and lies on the question of reservation before the Supreme Court. The defenders of the caste system are not prepared to accept the truth of inequality perpetuated by the caste system. As recently as 7 February 2020, in 'Mukesh Kumar vs the State of Uttarakhand', the Supreme Court ruled that the state government cannot be directed to provide reservations for appointment in public posts and is not bound to make reservations for SCs and STs in matters of promotions. In other words, reservation was denied status as a fundamental right. By leaving reservations up to the political judgement of the state government, the ruling essentially demoted reservations from an essential mechanism for equality to a mere optional benefit.

Munusamy's essay helps you understand the structural biases, stereotypes and unequal social order in the judiciary against the marginalized and weaker sections that lead to decisions like this. Munusamy argues that these biases begin from the judicial appointments themselves. This calls for structural changes in the judiciary and transformation in the mindset of upper-caste judges. After reading the essay, ask yourself whether a verdict like the one offered in 'Mukesh Kumar' was coincidental or inevitable.

Caste discrimination is so deeply ingrained in our society that it needs to be addressed at every step, and this has not been done— neither by the society nor by the polity. Exploring the theme of the history of caste, Suraj Yengde, in his essay 'Leveraging International Institutions to Address Casteism', argues that caste no longer shall be viewed as Indian society's internal matter. He asserts that Dalits should capture cultural and academic spaces and develop relations with global cultures and politics. He gives a clarion call to the Indian government and opposition political parties to demonstrate their commitment to the Constitution and love for the Dalits and Ambedkar by submitting to international political checks.

Can Dalit issues one day become central to the discussions at UN Security Council meetings on international peace and security?

Unless these processes are channelized, the author feels that no amount of Ambedkar affection or building of Ambedkar statues would be justifiable by the stakeholders invested in Ambedkarite politics. Yengde strongly feels that the Indian caste system should be exposed on UN platforms to drive a sense of urgency among Indian intellectuals to join the voices for the annihilation of caste. The hope, actually, lies in the Constitution of India that has vested powers with the people of India to bring about this transformation. The battle shall be won on Indian soil.

Why Dalits Are Drifting Away from Congress?

The Dalits have been described as the *reed ki haddi* (backbone) of the Congress party, which is true as they have supported the Congress electorally for a long time. So why are they drifting away from the party now? Has the Congress neglected its spine? Before addressing this question, it may be pertinent to understand how the Dalits have come to be known as the 'reed ki haddi' in the first place.

Caste had become a political unit in pre-Independence India. And this was first recognized when a significant move was made in 1887 by Mahadev Govind Ranade of the Indian National Congress. He had established a National Social Conference to insist on the removal of exploitative practice of untouchability for social equality. In 1916, Dadabhai Naoroji moved a resolution in the Imperial Council for the upliftment of the untouchables. As far back as 1917, during the annual session of the Indian National Congress held in Calcutta, the following resolution was passed:

This Congress urges upon the people of India the necessity, justice and righteousness of removing all disabilities imposed by custom upon the Depressed Classes, the disabilities being of a most vexatious and oppressive character, subjecting those classes to considerable hardship and inconvenience.

In fact, the Congress, led by Gandhi, disagreed with Ambedkar on the issue of separate electorates (resulting in the Poona Pact), but the two agreed on many other strategies to counter the issue of caste discrimination. These included political reservation for the Dalits, allowing them entry into temples, inter-caste dining and marriages, eradication of untouchability, and providing education and new employment opportunities. Furthermore, Gandhi established the Harijan Sevak Sangh to pursue Dalit upliftment in the country and used the Congress as a platform.

The Congress was instrumental in bringing Ambedkar into the Constituent Assembly in 1946 (the seat in East Bengal which he had won against the Congress candidate became a part of East Pakistan, with the partition of India). Later, Ambedkar was nominated as the chairman of the drafting committee in a Constituent Assembly dominated by the Congress. It was an unprecedented contribution on the part of the Congress and Gandhi, with whom Ambedkar had fought fiercely. The Congress backed Ambedkar in bringing out the Constitution as a charter of social reform—a bold attempt to give freedom to the Dalits from centuries of oppression and subjugation.

The Constituent Assembly included several important rights in the Indian Constitution to ensure that principles of equality and social justice were the basis of all future developments in India. The fundamental rights, including Article 14, conferred equality before the law; Article 15 prohibited discrimination on the grounds of religion, race, caste, sex, place of birth and provided access to public spaces to all without discrimination; Article 16(4) served as a bedrock for the state to make provisions for the reservation of appointments or posts in favour of any backward class of citizens; and Article 17 prohibited untouchability. The directive principles, through Article 46, placed the responsibility on the state to make policies for the economic and educational progress of the scheduled castes, and to protect them from social injustices. These articles inspired the successive Congress governments to introduce schemes such as pre-matric and post-matric scholarships, establishment of welfare hostels, grant of house sites, and financial assistance for the construction of houses for the SCs and STs.

Allotment of government land to the Dalits and distribution of ceiling-surplus lands among them have transformed a small fraction of Dalit agriculture labour into peasants. Further, to enforce untouchability as a punishable offence, the Untouchability (Offences) Act, 1955, was enacted (later renamed the Protection of Civil Rights Act). When the Supreme Court struck down reservations for SCs and STs into educational institutions, Jawaharlal Nehru and Ambedkar moved the First Amendment to the Constitution in 1951 and safeguarded reservations for SCs and STs. Whenever certain judgments of Supreme Court posed impediments to implement reservations, more often than not, the Congress governments at the Centre moved quickly to amend the Constitution to pave the way for the smooth implementation of reservation.

The Scheduled Castes and Scheduled Tribes (Prevention of Atrocities) Act, 1989, was enacted under the Rajiv Gandhi government to empower the Dalits and adivasis, so that the state could punish the perpetrators of atrocities towards them. The 93rd Constitution Amendment Act was enacted in 2006 to provide reservation for the SCs, STs and OBCs in private higher-education institutions, whether aided or unaided by the state. In 2013, the Prohibition of Employment as Manual Scavengers and Rehabilitation Act was enacted, and self-employment schemes were proposed for rehabilitation.

Successive Congress governments also set up institutions to promote the economic and social progress of the Dalits. A special component plan was developed for the scheduled castes in 1975 for earmarking 16 per cent of plan funds, to accelerate the development of SCs and bring them on a par with the rest of the society. In 1985, the Ministry of Welfare was created, the progenitor of the Ministry of Social Justice and Empowerment. In 1989, the

National Scheduled Castes Finance and Development Corporation (NSFDC) was set up for financing, facilitating and mobilizing funds for the economic empowerment of persons belonging to the scheduled castes. In 2012, under the United Progressive Alliance (UPA) government, led by the Congress party, it was ordered that public procurement would include 4 per cent procurement by government agencies from SC/ST-run enterprises. In 2005–06, the National Fellowship Scheme for SC Students was initiated to increase the opportunities for SC students looking to pursue higher education like PhD.

While these changes have been momentous, only a small proportion of Dalit population could access these fruits of development. The majority of Dalits lead troubled lives as landless labourers, small-scale farmers, artisans in villages, manual labourers and hawkers working in the informal sector and living in slums in urban areas. Seventy-four per cent of Dalit households live in rural areas, where the per-household land area they own on an average is less than 0.3 hectares—most of them are landless according to the 2011 census. Untouchability continues to thrive. Atrocities against the Dalits are on the rise. Access to quality education is still a distant dream for the Dalits. Successful industrialists and entrepreneurs who are Dalits are, unsurprisingly, few and far between. Even after the implementation of agrarian land reforms, most of the Dalits continue to be landless agriculture labourers. Most of them continue to struggle on a day-to-day basis as unorganized workers. Educated Dalit youths face entry barriers to enter the private sector. Employment opportunities in the government sector are dwindling, and reservation in the private sector is a far cry. The Dalits' share of political power is very nominal, considering the portfolios allotted to them in the ministries of Central or state governments. Adequate budgetary resources are not being provided to bring the Dalits on a par with the rest of the society.

It is in this context that one must understand how non-Congress parties have succeeded in mobilizing the Dalits, giving them the hope of fulfilling their aspirations. How the BJP started attracting Dalit vote merits in-depth study. Why have historically marginalized communities that continue to endure caste violence started gravitating towards the Hindutva ideology? Understanding this trend and the shifting social contours that have fuelled the rapid rise of Hindutva is integral to understanding contemporary India. Are attempts to unite Hindus through aggressive cultural nationalism, aided by the wilful distortion of facts to cover the truth about the culpability of religion in perpetuating the caste system, succeeding in politically mobilizing the Dalits for the Hindutva cause?

To find answers to these questions, I encourage readers to approach the essays on the political mobilization of the Dalits. Each essay in this section supplies greater context to current trends in the political mobilization of the Dalits. Bhanwar Meghwanshi's essay 'Saffronizing the Dalits' traces the RSS's and the Sangh Parivar's shifting views on the question of caste, reservation and the legacy of Ambedkar. The Hindutva narrative's success in appropriating cultural symbols and crafting caste histories has yielded rich political dividends. Meghwanshi attributes this phenomenon to the left-of-centre parties' unwillingness to engage with the Dalits—their lack of commitment to nurturing a new generation of Dalit leadership has had the eventual effect of pushing the Dalits towards right-wing forces. The essay offers powerful suggestions on how to counter the lies deployed by the RSS–BJP, and how to empower Dalit–adivasi communities to reclaim their own radical history of fighting oppression.

What is the Dalit truth about their mobilization? Ambedkar noted that the relationship between the *touchables* and the *untouchables* resembled that between different clans in a primitive society. Neither could the untouchable claim rights that the touchables were bound to respect nor demand justice outside their clan. The fixed and non-negotiable nature of the relationship imposed an inferior status on the untouchables and was embodied in a code of social conduct. Political mobilization that fails to acknowledge this fundamentally unlevel playing field and fails to challenge the inferior social status accorded to the Dalits tries to bury the truth.

Ambedkar closely studied the question of why institutions like slavery and serfdom had vanished in other societies, while untouchability survived in India as a near-invincible force. He noted that class composition in other countries was founded on social and economic considerations, and since these were not sacrosanct and yielded to time and circumstances, institutions like slavery and serfdom had ceased to exist. On the other hand, untouchability had its foundation in religion and hence continued to enjoy divine sanction. To truly accomplish the abolition of untouchability and the inclusion of Dalits in public life, one must accept that inequity is not merely a social phenomenon subject to the changing sands of time; it is embedded in religious dogma itself.

Move then to Professor Badri Narayan's essay 'Hindutva and the Future of Dalit–Bahujan Politics in India'. Narayan sheds light on the impact of neo-liberalism on Dalit political mobilization, particularly the role of an aspirational Dalit middle class. He writes that the desire for religious acceptance among a section of Dalits is also fuelling the rise of Hindutva. According to Narayan, the RSS's socio-cultural projects, coupled with their promise of dignity and religious equality, have drawn several Dalit sub-castes within the Hindutva fold. But are these promises founded in true commitment to social reforms, or are these an opportunistic ploy for political gains? Narayan poses relevant questions about whether the aspiring Dalit middle class can ignore the falsehoods underlying the promise of greater social and economic equality without rejecting religious orthodoxy. Narayan goes further and examines the reasons for the declining electoral fortunes of Bahujan Samaj Party (BSP), as well as of the mainstream parties like the Congress, and highlights the need to put forth a vision that speaks to the diverse aspirations of the Dalits in a rapidly changing world.

Recall that in July 2016, in the town of Una in Gujarat, Hindutva vigilantes stripped, flogged and lynched four Dalit youths for the 'crime' of skinning a dead cow. The obvious truth is that it is not a crime to possess the skin or hides of dead cows. The videos of the lynching spread across the country, and Dalits, many of whom earn their livelihood from skinning dead animals and selling their hides to leather traders, rose up in protests across the state. A larger movement of non-cooperation rose from here, led by Jignesh Mevani. This marked a turning point in the Dalit movement that highlights the plight of the Dalits while remaining entirely non-violent.

In his essay 'A Blueprint for a New Dalit Politics: An Open Letter to the Dalits', Mevani delves into the urgent need to forge a broad anti-caste coalition that goes beyond identity-based associations to defeat the Hindutva forces. He advocates for anti-caste movements to look beyond identity-related issues and envisages a social democratic *mahagathbandhan* that forges an alliance between Muslim, Dalits, OBCs and leftist movements. As noted, the emergence of political movements like the Bhim Army and the Vanchit Bahujan Aghadi is a step in this direction. He emphasizes the importance of intersectionality and urges Dalits to avoid being pigeonholed into narrow ideological battles, and to also fight for material issues. He warns against the danger of a retreating state that neglects its welfare functions and exhorts the Dalits to fight for public goods and services. Finally, he reiterates the commitment to guarantee every individual a life of dignity and access to opportunities to grow beyond their circumstances. Mevani's essay represents a view into the pragmatic concerns of real Dalit policymakers operating in India today.

In 'New Phase in Dalit Politics: Crisis or Regeneration?', Professor Sudha Pai expertly frames the major Dalit political issues of our time. Her essay sheds light on the profound shifts within the Dalit communities due to globalization and cultural modernization. The widening gap between middle-class Dalits and marginalized sub-castes has led to greater fragmentation, particularly on ideological lines, between the Ambedkarites and Hindutvawadis. In Pai's view, this shift has led to the decline of traditional Dalit parties like the BSP and the Republican Party of India, and propelled the rise of the BJP among the Dalits. The persistence of caste violence, coupled with the aspiration for a greater stake in economic progress, has led to the emergence of new Dalit movements, like the Bhim Army, Una Dalit Atyachar Ladat Samiti and Vanchit Bahujan Aghadi. These movements have extended solidarity to protests against major national issues like the CAA and NRC, and are helping forge a broad coalition of forces committed to the idea of pluralism. Most importantly, they are challenging the inherent lies in the Hindutva ideal of social harmony that promises social equality but is built on social subservience. Lastly, she weighs in on the possibilities offered by the Azad Samaj Party's foray into electoral politics and its impact on reviving the Dalit movement in Uttar Pradesh. Pai's essay will arm the readers with a contemporary insight that can help them understand and interpret the events happening today.

The four essays mentioned earlier highlight different strategies deployed across the country, by different political parties, to draw the Dalits into their fold, with varying degrees of success and sustainability. It is too early to say which of these approaches will succeed in mobilizing the Dalits on a long-term basis across the country. Having laid the basic foundations to Dalit empowerment, it is time for the Congress to critically evaluate its approach towards the Dalits and evolve a strategy that would enable the party to regain their confidence. It is important for the Congress to recognize that Dalits are not a homogeneous group. There are many sub-castes within the community, each with its own social and cultural moorings. In terms of economic well-being, too, there are perceptible differences. While celebrating the socio-historical legacy of each sub-caste, the Congress party should make sure that adequate space is given to all the sub-castes within the party.

Similarly, it should be ensured that the fruits of development are equitably accessed by all the sub-castes among the Dalits.

The Congress needs to make sure that Dalit leaders, from the village level to the national level, are given space within the party, in such a way that they are part of all decisions that navigate the party forward. Issues concerning the Dalits should be discussed in party forums at all levels. When the party is in power, at the Centre or in states, the Dalits should have a significant share of the political power, in terms of the portfolios of ministries/departments assigned to them. Every Dalit family shall be endowed with a permanent house to stay in, with access to piped drinking water, electricity and good roads connecting their localities. The party has to support a comprehensive developmental policy architecture for the Dalits to secure for them access to: quality education from KG to PG; quality health services; skill development for employment; education in Ivy League colleges in the US; investment and marketing support for enterprise development; and greater share of employment in the private sector, etc. It should be a non-negotiable objective that in a given time frame, Dalits' share of the nation's wealth should be proportionate to their share in the population.

Dalit elected representatives in the assemblies or in Parliament should be encouraged to articulate the reality of Dalit lives and to highlight challenges in securing equality in all spheres of lives for the Dalits. The Congress party representatives should not shy away from pointing out the maladies of the caste system and the need for realizing a caste-less society.

Dalits Outside Politics

The final section of this book deals with Dalits outside politics. The Dalits should not only be seen through the prism of politics. They have left an indelible mark in various fields outside politics. Take, as an example, cricket. It was Palwankar Baloo who led the first all-India cricket team to many victories in 1911, and many times after that. Anindya Dutta's *Wizards*[5] and Ramachandra Guha's *Spin and Other Turns*[6] provide excellent background on the man who was— as Guha wrote—'the first great Indian spinner'. Yet, Baloo's story has many more turns. His truth was that even though he was the most deserving for captaincy, he was never made the captain of the team because of his caste. Since Gandhi's support for the so-called 'untouchables' was reaching its peak in those years, the selection board for the cricket team yielded and made Baloo the vice-captain. Still, there are some gifted Dalit sportsmen who continue to challenge discrimination. At the Tokyo Olympics 2020, it was Vandana Kataria, who became the first woman Indian hockey player to score a hat-trick at Olympics. She and her family had to suffer humiliation when a few upper-caste individuals from her village staged a dharna before her house, demanding the banning of Dalits from representing India at Olympics.

Sumit Kumar from Kurad village of the Sonipat district in Haryana is an Indian midfielder who was part of the bronze medal-winning team at the Tokyo Olympics 2020. Apart from being a Dalit, Sumit belongs to a landless agriculture family, but he did not let his unprivileged background prevent him from attaining his goal.

Gurram Jashuva (1895–1971) and Boyi Bhimanna (1911–2005), both Dalits, were legendary poets in the Telugu literary world and Padma Bhushan awardees known for their timeless masterpieces of poetry and literature. Both had the distinction of having risen above oppressive caste-based discrimination. Though issues like fighting against untouchability, Dalit rights, etc., have been common themes in most of their works, their literature was not confined to these; they forayed into all aspects of life for the well-being and development of their fellow Indians, of their country as a whole, inspired as they were by the principles of universal humanism. The brilliance of Gurram Jashuva's poetry won him great acclaim and many accolades as a universal poet. Boyi Bhimanna's literature spanned all aspects of human life and ideas—beauty, romance, governance, nationalism, humanism, spiritualism, etc.

The Dalit struggle can be seen in artistic endeavours, too. In his essay 'Dalit Cinema in India', Pa. Ranjith explains cinema's tacit acquiescence to the caste order. He attempts to answer historically significant questions: Why has Dalit life not been adequately featured in cinema? Is it that Dalits don't have cultural values of their own? You cannot but admire Ranjith's successful efforts to challenge existing narratives on Dalits and put new ones in place in Indian Cinema. He narrates how our society has fabricated a narrative which, in the name of narrating Dalit stories, attempts to disturb public peace. Casteism enabled such lies to thrive for a long time. Indian cinema chose to stay away from narrating Dalit stories. Ranjith shares his anguish at how young assistant directors who worked with him and wish to make their own films have found it hard to interest producers in their stories, because of their association with him. Ranjith's analysis holds a mirror to that side of our society which unsettles us the most.

Pa. Ranjith, who entered the film world with a photo of Ambedkar on the first page of his first script, has made invaluable contributions to Dalit cinema in India. The opening scene of *Kabali*, directed by Ranjith, shows superstar Rajinikanth in a prison, reading the book *My Father Balaiah*. It is a book written by Professor Y.B. Satyanarayana, of Osmania University, which poignantly espouses education for Dalits for their emancipation. *Kabali* was a superhit film, and the opening scene inspired many translations of *My Father Balaiah* into various languages.

The truth is that since time immemorial, the Dalits have been making rich contributions to the arts and cultural traditions of India. But due to the lies of the varna system, the Sanskrit word 'pandit', meaning a 'learned person', has been handed down by virtue of birth. Many Dalits have broken this myth. One such immensely talented 'pandit' was the musical giant Ilaiyaraaja, a

Dalit man whose music transcended boundaries, not just of castes but of nations. Reading these essays will help you peel back the layer of the lie that Dalits are uncultured and untalented.

You might also look at the economic toll such lies have taken on the Dalits. The truth is that the Dalits are born equal to everyone else. Generations of Dalits have proven that merit or intrinsic capability is not alien to them. But to prove this again and again, Dalit individuals have to overcome massive barriers—social, psychological and economic—erected shamelessly by the dominant caste.

Current thinkers have carried forward the legacy of Ambedkar by proposing new methods to remove those barriers. Free, fair and equal education is one means of overcoming the barriers. R.S. Praveen Kumar's essay 'Education and Dalit Liberation' highlights the critical role of residential education in the pursuit of social justice. As a case study, it takes a close look at the experiment of the Telangana Social Welfare Residential Schools. While reading this essay, imagine how many more successful Dalits we would have seen in this world, what contributions they could have made to society, had they been given a chance.

The economic boom following the liberalization programmes of 1991 have, without a doubt, helped the Dalits. Today, entrepreneurs like Bhagwan Gawai, who began as a construction-site worker and went on to become the CEO of an energy company based in Dubai, or the highly successful woman entrepreneur Kalpana Saroj and businessman Ratibhai Makwana, among many others, are symbols of the formidability of the Dalits and Indians. The Dalit Indian Chamber of Commerce and Industry is making great leaps. Marginalized communities, such as religious minorities, the Dalits and tribal communities, were expected to achieve more in the 1991 liberalization in India. However, the truth is that only a minuscule section of Dalits benefited due to privatization and globalization. While Ambedkar put forth radical ideas on Dalit upliftment in the 1940s, new ideas are required in the markedly different economic context of today. Entrepreneurship is one opportunity that has opened up. How can the community which has been on the margins for centuries be encouraged to start their own enterprises? Priyank Kharge and Neeraj Shetye, in their essay 'Annihilating Entrepreneurship Casteism', attempt to address this question while presenting a new approach to boost entrepreneurship as a career among the SC and ST communities.

In his 1947 document *States and Minorities*, which Dr Ambedkar had initially prepared as a draft constitution before he was chosen to chair the drafting committee, he wanted to incorporate a democratic and socialist form of economic structure into the Constitution. He wanted the Constitution to grant ownership of agricultural land, education, health and insurance to the state. Ambedkar argued that there was a direct linkage between fundamental rights and economic structures in society, and believed that an economy based on private ownership of property would not guarantee fundamental rights to the marginalized and unemployed. But Ambedkar's socialist form of economic structures could not be incorporated into the Constitution. Today, along with economic progress, the gap between the rich and the poor is widening. The Dalits' share of ownership of the nation's wealth is far lower than their share in the population. What needs to be done to secure to the Dalits their legitimate share in the nation's wealth? How close are we to achieving Ambedkar's dream? Will the Dalits' quest for equality meet with success anytime in the near future?

As a conclusion to your journey of finding the Dalit truth, I encourage you to read Budithi Rajsekhar's essay, 'Redesigning the Dalit Development Paradigm'. No amount of lies can obscure the truth about the Dalits' rightful share in the economy. Rajsekhar sheds light on how much we can change by changing our approach to the development paradigm that has defined the Dalit community's economic empowerment for decades. He highlights the fault lines, resting on five misconceptions in the current approach to Dalit development, and articulates five remedies to secure to the Dalits their rightful share in the nation's wealth. He argues that it is time to change the narrative from 'not bothered' to 'we care for the Dalits'.

Conclusion

Dr Ambedkar observed that if the problem faced by the untouchables was the denial of political or economic rights, it could be solved by legal and constitutional methods. Any struggle, to secure political or economic rights for the Dalits, that fails to fight for the annihilation of caste would only further the concentration of caste capital in the hands of a few communities.

On the occasion to commemorate Dr Ambedkar's 125th birth anniversary in 2016, Rahul Gandhi, while addressing a rally in Nagpur on 11 April, highlighted that as a nation we have a choice between two competing ideologies: one that perpetrates the regressive Manuwadi values; and the other that stands against those very ethos. Both ideologies offer a different vision of social cohesion and progress. While the former imprisons individuals to a rigid caste hierarchy, the latter offers every individual the ability to make choices that are independent of rigid social norms and traditions. It paves the way for crores of Indians to escape a life of dehumanization and indignity.

Today, caste has survived not only socially but its manifestations can be seen in every framework. If one denies the existence of caste, then one is contributing to the discriminatory systems that have thrived on the denial of identity and expression to the Dalits. What India needs today is an all-round attack on caste and its manifestations. We have definitely progressed since 1947, but that progress is not on the desired scale. Every inch of progress made by the Dalits has come through decades-long struggles and sacrifices.

Often, narratives about caste hierarchies are framed around the idea of privilege or the lack of it. While they highlight the structural and institutional barriers to the progress of the Dalits, there's also the risk of their perpetuating the notion that addressing caste inequality is inimical to the interests of dominant groups/ upper castes. Studies have highlighted the economic cost of caste and gender discrimination on the Indian economy. However, our public conscience is yet to acknowledge that discrimination has a personal cost for everyone. A society that dehumanizes some groups and normalizes violence in all its forms, erodes our collective humanity. Social trust is a key determinant of a country's social and economic success, and it is about time that caste is acknowledged as a major impediment to India's ambition of becoming a global power.

Political parties have a special responsibility towards the larger goal of the annihilation of caste. The days of tokenism are over, as the Dalits in contemporary India need full-time dedication from all stakeholders so that they understand the enormity of the problems and take action to resolve them. Development cannot happen without dignity. Progress cannot happen without acknowledging the persisting social discrimination against the Dalits. Our lives, as citizens, must start every morning with this reality in mind. Most importantly, we all should understand that an inclusive society, which fosters empathy and compassion, can help every individual to realize their true potential.

The Dalit Idea of the Nation, Inspired by Ambedkar

Sukhadeo Thorat

The Promise of the Constitution

The Indian Constitution reflects the aspirations and collective will that the emerging nation state, breaking free from colonial clutches, formulated for its people. In 1950, the people of India, through their representatives in the Constituent Assembly, developed a progressive idea of a nation that could deter internal antagonisms and cultivate unity. This idea of India is what the Constitution embodies and guards.

The Preamble to the Constitution defines the nation and its goals as a 'Sovereign, Socialist, Secular, Democratic Republic'. It is a 'Republic' and 'Sovereign' in the sense that the people of the nation are supreme; the ultimate power—the power to rule through their elected representatives—rests with them. It is 'Socialist' in the sense that it is based on the belief that everyone has an equal right to the country's wealth, which is to be shared equitably; and in the sense that the government should own and control the main economic and social sectors. It is 'Secular' in the sense that it accords

1

freedom to all to follow their religious beliefs and teachings, within the framework of the Constitution, but at the same time the state's governance is not to be determined and/or influenced by one particular religious ideology. It is 'Democratic' in the sense that the nation's governance is slated to be controlled by representatives who, in turn, are elected by the people of the country.

The Preamble also lays down certain goals and promises to secure certain rights to all citizens, including *Justice*—social, economic and political; *Liberty* of thought, expression, belief, faith and worship; *Equality* of status and of opportunity to all, irrespective of religion, caste, race, colour, ethnicity, gender and region; and finally, *Fraternity*, assuring the dignity of the individual, and the unity and integrity of the nation.

This idea of India had been the guiding force behind successive governments over the first six decades of the nation, despite many errors and mishaps in the governing process. The goals of social justice, social, economic and political liberty or freedom, equality and fraternity, along with national unity, were pursued ardently. While the state managed to attain some success in this process, it was clear there still was a long way to go. The constitutional dream that Ambedkar saw required much more concentrated effort on our part.

Erosion of Constitutional Values

In that historical phase, despite economic and social blunders on the part of various governments, there was hardly any indication of the state trying to undermine the very foundational constitutional idea of the nation. While there were failures to properly implement the plans and dreams of post-coloniality, the goals of a new India were still the beacon of inspiration and motivation for the governments. However, during the last few years, both the state and civil society have tried to indirectly, or even directly, undermine the founding principles of India.

What we see today is our nation at the cusp of becoming a Hindu Rashtra, which excludes Muslims from its understanding of itself and violently appropriates Dalit and other backward castes in its fold. This state of the country has rendered minorities and erstwhile oppressed groups both helpless and hopeless. It has resulted in the erosion of both our accepted idea of the nation as well as the goals which the Constitution pledges to achieve and which it mandates the state to promote.

Firstly, sovereignty is no more regulated by the rule of law, as a humanist political philosophy demands. Such a picture of sovereignty untamed by law is authoritarian in both spirit and practice. We see the centralizing power of the state that has managed to undermine democratic practices, if not the laws. Secondly, the minimal welfare schemes that were the last socialist hope for the poor of this country are being replaced by the strengthening of big corporations by the present government, which has allowed neo-liberalism to thrust its claws deeper into our society, giving rise to rapid inequality, dispossession and economic precarity. What we see today is that the role of the government and public sector is being reduced, and that of the private sector is being promoted, without any alternatives for the deprived groups and the poor. Privatization means de-reservation. The state does not recognize the impact of its silence about the alternatives for the marginalized, such as affirmative action in the private sector for the Dalits, Adivasis and other backward castes.

Thirdly, promoting a secular state entails that the teaching of any particular religion will not form the basis of governance by the state. In contrast to this principle, we see a growing Hinduization of the state, with attempts being made to apply Hindu religious values and practices in selected public spheres of governance. From time to time, statements are made by some in favour of making the Vedic religion as the basis of state governance.

Fourthly, democratic institutions and various arms of the state are being gradually and systematically taken over by followers of the Hindutva ideology. Some forces repeatedly go to the extent of advocating the Manusmriti as a basis for governance. The fundamental principle of a democracy is that the political party winning a majority in elections forms the government and works to fulfil the promises it had made to the people during its election campaign and in its electoral manifesto. However, in the last few elections, we have observed a decline of the political majority and a rising trend towards the imposition of a communal majority whose interests are to be served by the government more than that of other groups.

Finally, the harmony between the state and the people has been on the decline. The autonomy of civil society is being dismantled, while civil-society organizations affiliated to the party in power are encouraged and supported.

Further, violence is increasingly being resorted to for resolving issues. There's selective recourse to law enforcement on the part of majoritarian groups, with lynch mobs taking centre stage. This has made a mockery of justice, and a communal mob rule persists on the streets. Even more disturbing is the trend to impose restraints on the fundamental rights of people by curbing their freedom of speech, expression and beliefs, including the freedom of the news media, both print and television. Efforts are also being made to regulate individual freedoms in terms of the choice of food, clothes and interpersonal relationships. Such compromise of liberty is a quintessential feature of illiberal governance.

The ideology that governs the nation currently prioritizes some groups over everyone else. It challenges the nation's unity and integrity, resulting in the victimization of religious minorities. At last, the idea of fraternity as a moral guideline no longer obtains, which is reflected in the rising conflicts among various castes as also in the majoritarian attacks on minorities, disrupting social harmony across the country.

Ambedkar as an Inspiration

The Constitution has been a horizon of hope for the Dalits in India since Independence. Ambedkar ensured that the ills taking place against them before Independence did not recur in post-colonial India. The erosion of constitutional values, therefore, affects the Dalit community substantially and adversely. Today, Dalit politics is concerned with saving the Constitution.

The actualization of the constitutional idea of the nation, therefore, remains the political horizon that Ambedkarites and other humanists fight towards. Immense faith is reposed by the Dalits and other principled humanists in Ambedkar, and their vision of the nation is shaped by Ambedkar's ideas. In this respect, we should make a distinction here between two categories for analytic purposes: the constitutional idea of the nation and the Ambedkarite idea of the nation.

The constitutional idea of the nation is the conception of nation/nationalism stemming from the Constitution and its Preamble, as elaborated above. This idea of the nation is being undermined today. The Ambedkarite idea of the nation is the conception of nation/nationalism emerging not only from the present structure of the Constitution but also from Ambedkar's idea that we ought to take substantive measures to make such a nation, to make it into a reality. In the following sections of this essay, we discuss the Ambedkarite idea of the nation. It provides a viable political goal for future Ambedkarite politics. Simultaneously, given the fact that this idea of the nation already includes the principles that the constitutional idea of the nation defines, a struggle towards achieving it must necessarily ensure the recognition and application of those principles.

The distinguishing feature of Ambedkar's position is that like others in the Constituent Assembly, he also supported the parliamentary form of democracy, and some sort of socialist economy and secularism, as the basis of our sovereign republic.

However, Ambedkar's stance went beyond the consensus of the early parliamentarians, as he attempted to understand the very conditions for a viable political democracy. Ambedkar is unique in this respect. Therefore, we discuss three main aspects of nationhood that his thought delineates. These include: 1) the idea of the nation and the necessary conditions for its realization; 2) the necessary conditions for political democracy; and 3) methods for the effective representation of religious and social minorities.

Realizing Ambedkar's Idea of the Nation

Ambedkar dealt with the concept of nation and nationalism for the first time in his book *Thoughts on Pakistan*, which was reprinted as *Pakistan or the Partition of India*.[1] According to one prevalent view, which is represented by Savarkar and his followers, the nation is primarily a matter of geography, culture and language. The commonality of language, race, territory and culture, or religion, makes the nation. Ambedkar's views differed from this notion. He argued, 'A nation is not a country in the physical sense, whatever degree of geographical unity it may possess. A nation is not a people synthesized by a common culture derived from a common language, common religion or common race . . . Nationality is a subjective psychological feeling. It is a feeling of corporate sentiment of oneness which makes those who are charged with it feel that they are kith and kin . . . It is a feeling of "consciousness of kind" which binds together those who are within the limits of kindred. It is longing (a strong feeling of wanting together) to belong to one's own group . . . This is the essence of what is called a nationality and national feeling.'[2] Ambedkar's notion of the nation was much more ethically oriented than the religiously and metaphysically oriented ones of his contemporaries.

He further observed that there was a difference between nation (or nationality) and nationalism. They are two different states of the human mind. Nationality means 'consciousness of kind' and 'awareness of the existence of ties of kinship'. (Kinship here means the fact of 'being related to family, a feeling of being close to a member of the family, because you have similar origins or attitude.')[3] Ambedkar writes, 'Nationality is a social feeling of a corporate sentiment of oneness. It is a feeling of consciousness of kind, like-mindedness, possessing things in common in life of communication, participation and of sharing with all those who constitute one nation. In this sense, a nation is a society where there is an unlimited scope for "social endosmosis". Nation is . . . a mode of associated living, of conjoined communicated experience.'[4]

He subsequently argues, 'The point is that nationality is not primarily a matter of geography, culture or language . . . The nation is not a physical thing in which certain objective characteristics, such as commonality of language, race, territory, etc. persist. Nation, on the contrary, is a spiritual reality binding people into a deep comradeship.'[5]

Nationalism, on the other hand, means the desire for a separate national existence for those who are bound by this tie of kinship. In this context, Ambedkar observed, 'There cannot be nationalism without the feeling of nationality being existent. But the converse is not always true. The feeling of nationality may be present and yet the feeling of nationalism may be quite absent. This is to say that nationality does not flame in nationalism. For nationality to flame in nationalism, there must arise the "will to live the nation". Nationalism is the dynamic expression of that desire.'[6]

In this context, it is quite clear that a common land, language, culture and religion are partly necessary conditions for the existence of a nation, but this commonality is not enough to make the country a nation in the concrete sense of the term. A feeling of oneness, that we are all kith and kin, really binds people together. This oneness is possible only through constant communication, participation and open sharing among all those who constitute one nation. The relevant message from Ambedkar is thus that fraternity is a necessary condition for the existence of a nation in the concrete sense of the term. Fraternity encourages a mental attitude of fair play and equality towards one's compatriots. The lack of fraternity in social relations undermines all efforts to strengthen the nation. Hence, if there is a lack of fraternity, we would remain a nation in the making and never be able to achieve the substantial status of a nation.

From the point of view of the Dalits or ex-untouchables, the Hindu social order, namely the caste system, remains a great obstacle to the idea of nationhood. The caste system is, in fact, antagonistic to the concept of nation or nationality. Caste divides people and leads to a sense of isolation and segregation. Above all, it creates an anti-social feeling and foments rifts and antagonism between the low castes (or untouchables) and high castes. The lack of fraternity in social relations undermines the feeling of oneness, which is a prerequisite for a healthy nation. So the idea of a nation for Dalits is one which is free of discrimination, isolation and segregation. This necessitates sincere and sustained efforts on the part of both the state as well as the high-caste members of civil society. The reality, however, is just the opposite. The upper castes do not seem to be making any effort to build relations based on equality and fraternity. Therefore, for the ex-untouchables, the idea of a concrete nation remains a distant dream.

Necessary Conditions for Political Democracy

One of the most important pillars of the Indian nation is that it is a democratic republic. The state is governed by elected representatives of the people, which is something that signifies a negation of hereditary rule. In Walter Bagehot's view, 'Democracy is government by discussion' and not by 'fisticuffs'. Abraham Lincoln, too, propounded the fundamental concept of democracy as 'a government of the people, by the people, and for the people'. Ambedkar, on his part, defined democracy as 'a form and a method of government whereby revolutionary changes in economic and social life of people are brought [about] without bloodshed'.

Socialist Goals for Constitutional Dream: Ambedkar's Proposal for Economic Democracy

For Ambedkar, however, the critical condition for the successful functioning of a political democracy was the absence of glaring economic inequalities. He asserted that there cannot simultaneously be a class which enjoys all privileges and a class that suffers from disabilities and discrimination. This deep division between classes becomes the greatest hindrance in the success of a political democracy. Economic inequality between classes lays the foundation for discontent and violence.

Although parliamentary democracy provides a solution for nurturing economic equality within its political framework, Ambedkar differed from this traditional solution and offered an alternative.[7] He argued that the economic structure supportive of a political democracy should be made a part of the Constitution. Most democratic countries left economic policies to be framed by the legislature within the framework of a system based on the private ownership of property. In his view, this method had serious limitations. He observed, 'The inadequacy and the futility of the plan has been well established. Therefore, the successful invocation by less powerful of the authority of the legislature is a doubtful proposition. Having regard to the fact that even under adult suffrage all legislators and government are controlled by the more powerful, an appeal to the legislature to intervene in economic spheres is a very precarious safeguard against invasion on liberty of less powerful.'[8]

Ambedkar argued that it was equally essential to prescribe the shape and form of an economic structure if a democracy was to live up to its principle of 'one man, one value'. In fact, at the very outset, during the adoption of the resolution on the 'Aims and

Objectives' of India's future Constitution, moved by Jawaharlal Nehru on 13 December 1946, Ambedkar argued for economic remedies to realize those objectives. He opined,

> I find that this part of the resolution, although it enunciates certain rights, does not speak of remedies. I find a complete absence of remedies . . . I must confess that . . . this resolution is to my mind very disappointing . . . There are certain provisions which speak of justice, economic, social and political. I should have expected some provision whereby it would have been possible for the state to make economic, social and political justice a reality and I should have from that view expected the resolution to state in most explicit terms that in order that there may be social and economic justice in the country, that there would be nationalization of industry and nationalization of land. I do not understand how it could be possible for any future government which believes in doing justice, socially, economically and politically, unless its economy is a socialistic economy.[9]

Subsequently, in a memorandum titled 'State and Minorities',[10] submitted to the Constituent Assembly in 1947, Ambedkar outlined an economic system which would enable political democracy to be accessible to the poor and marginalized. He maintained that an economy based on private enterprise and in pursuit of personal gain would compel people to relinquish their fundamental constitutional rights in order to sustain their livelihoods, as such a system would delegate powers to private (non-state) persons to govern others. Therefore, Ambedkar proposed an alternative economic framework to ensure economic equality. He proposed state ownership in agriculture, and in key and basic industries, including the insurance, education and health sectors, while leaving other activities to the private sector. The unique feature of this proposal was that it did not leave it to the will of the legislature to establish socialism but proposed the establishment of state socialism by law under the Constitution, thus making it unalterable by any act of either the legislature or the executive. In order to provide stability to socialism under parliamentary democracy, he suggested the establishment of state socialism by constitutional law, without abrogating parliamentary democracy. He believed that this was the only way of achieving the triple objectives of establishing socialism (or economic equality), retaining parliamentary democracy (or liberty) and preventing a dictatorship.

Prescribing an economic framework along with a political structure in the Constitution was not as per the norms of the British system of parliamentary democracy. It was a new initiative that Ambedkar undertook, by suggesting an innovation in constitutional jurisprudence. He justified this initiative as follows: '[The British] never realized that it was equally essential to prescribe the shape and form of the economic structure of society, if democracy is to live up to its principles of "one man, one value". [The] time has come to take a bold step and define both economic structure as well as political structure of society by the law of the Constitution. All countries like India which are latecomers in the field of constitution making should not copy the faults of other countries. They should profit by the experience.'[11] However, Ambedkar did not receive support for his proposal of constitutional socialism by the Constituent Assembly.

Nonetheless, Ambedkar brought the provision for social and economic justice through the Directive Principles of State Policy, which place the responsibility on the state to follow certain principles for pursuing the goal of social and economic equality through the implementation of various laws and policies. In a later interpretation, learned judges of the Supreme Court emphasized the significance of the Directive Principles for social and economic transformation.

While the fundamental rights primarily aim at ensuring political freedom to citizens, the Directive Principles aim at securing social and economic freedoms through appropriate state action. In particular, the state is expected to strive to 'minimise the inequalities in income, and eliminate inequalities in status, facilities and opportunities, amongst individuals and amongst groups of people'. The state is obliged to secure for the common man an adequate means of livelihood. The ownership of the material resources of the community are to be distributed in a manner that best serves the common good of the people. Further, the operation of the economic system should not result in the concentration of wealth and means of production in the hands of a few people, as it is detrimental to public interest. This indicates how the goal of economic and social equality is sought to be achieved through the Directive Principles as an alternative to the socialist system suggested by Ambedkar. It was a weak alternative, not enforceable in a court of law; yet it was one accommodation in the Constitution that Ambedkar had to be content with.

Socially Just Law and Socially Conscious Religion: Ambedkar on Social Democracy

The precondition for the success of political democracy is the absence of social inequality. Ambedkar propounded equality in status, facilities and opportunities, and the principle of non-discrimination, irrespective of caste, ethnicity, religion, gender or race, which formed the core of the fundamental rights. He did not stop there and went on to propose a ban on the practice of untouchability within the framework of the fundamental rights, making it punishable by law. In 1955, the Untouchability (Offences) Act was passed. It was later renamed the Protection of Civil Rights Act, 1979.

In Ambedkar's view, the roots of democracy do not lie in the form of government, parliamentary or otherwise. A democracy is more than a form of government. It is primarily a mode of associate living. He stated, 'The roots of democracy are to be searched in the social relationships, in the term of associated life between the people who form society. The society means that there is unity of purpose (by community), desire for welfare, loyalty to public ends, and mutuality of sympathy and cooperation.' Any society based on a particular caste excludes members of other castes, as its members have no common experience to share and have no bond of sympathy with others. What is the moral order that a caste system holds? Ambedkar observed, 'There are no rights in the Hindu society which the moral sense of man could recognise. There are privileges and disabilities and the privileges for a few and disabilities for the vast majority.'[12] Thus, in the Hindu social order, a social conscience (or a secular public conscience), supportive of equal rights and equal status for all, is nearly absent. The denial of equal rights to the lower castes is thus the outcome of the absence, or limited presence, of a social conscience in favour of equality.

When the community as a whole is opposed to giving equal rights to the ex-untouchables, the solution is the development of a moral conscience supportive of equal rights. In *Annihilation of Caste*, Ambedkar wrote:

People are not wrong in observing caste. In my opinion, what is wrong is their religion, which has inculcated this notion of caste. If this is correct, then obviously the enemy, you must grapple with, is not the people who observed caste, but the Shastras which teach them this religion of caste. The real remedy is to destroy the belief [of people] in the sanctity of the Shastras, because Shastras continue to mould the belief and opinion of the people. We should realize that the acts of the people are merely the results of their belief inculcated in their mind by the Shastras and that people will not change their conduct until they cease to believe in the sanctity of the Shastras on which their conduct is founded.[13]

Ambedkar recognized the crucial role of Buddhism for developing a social consciousness supportive of equality, liberty, fraternity and social democracy. Here, Ambedkar's views on the role of Buddhism in promoting social democracy—that is, social relations based on equality and fraternity—are extremely relevant. In the context of Indian traditions, equality could be achieved through Buddhist teachings.

Ambedkar's reading of Buddhism had not only social implications but also political implications. Considering that the 'religion of the Buddha gives freedom of thought and freedom of self-development to all', Ambedkar observed that 'the rise of Buddhism in India was as significant as the French Revolution'. In that sense Buddhism was a democratic religion, and Ambedkar eventually found in it the societal values he had tried to promote through political democracy. In his historic speech of 25 November 1949, after the submission of the final draft of the Indian Constitution to the Constituent Assembly, which was passed on 26 January 1950, he pointed out that by becoming a parliamentary constituency 'again', India was returning to its Buddhist roots. Such an 'invention of the tradition' shows that even in his interpretation of the historical impact of Buddhism on India, Ambedkar remained deeply interested in the political ideas of social justice.

Safeguarding Political Democracy: Ambedkar's Critique of Communal Majority

Ambedkar also applied his mind to the issue of the 'minority' in a more systematic way and suggested some innovative proposals for the protection of minorities from the communal majority. He expounded these views in a memorandum titled 'Communal Deadlock and Ways to Solve It', submitted to the government in 1945. He was immensely concerned about the political consequences of the communalization of the Indian polity, as he firmly believed that in India, the majority was not a political majority but a communal majority. Therefore, he drew a useful distinction between the two, arguing that the communal majority is born, not created, and is thus permanent and fixed in its attitude, inherently capable of posing a danger to the minorities at any time. The political majority, on the other hand, is not fixed and is impermanent, as it is constantly being made, unmade and remade.[14]

He observed, 'Unfortunately, for the minorities in India, Indian nationalism has developed a new doctrine which may be called the Divine Right of the Majority to rule the minorities according to the wishes of majority. Any claim for the sharing of power by the minority is called communalism while the monopolizing of the whole power by the majority is called nationalism.'[15] He was, in a way, prophetic in his articulation. What he envisaged in the mid-1940s has often been reflected in the nation's experiences with caste and the religious base of electoral democracy after Independence, with serious implications for nationalism and nation-building. Therefore, he had suggested the introduction of proper safeguards against the communal majority.

Ambedkar suggested the concept of a *relative majority* to overcome the dominance of the communal majority vis-à-vis the minority and suggested a method to accord a relatively high weightage to the minorities in the legislature in terms of the number of seats. Even among the minorities, he suggested that high priority should be given to those who were educationally and economically more backward as compared to others. In other words, he suggested a scheme that moderated the majority's power and ensured a 'balanced representation of majority and minority'. In order to reduce the dominance of the communal majority, Ambedkar recommended the implementation of the principle of 'unanimity', whereby the minority would also have an equal say in decision-making. Further, he proposed the principle of 'faith or confidence' for elected members of the legislature belonging to the majority community, who were occupying executive positions. He stated that the prime minister and all the ministers from the majority party should enjoy the faith and confidence of the whole house.

Following this principle of faith, he proposed the election of the prime minister, and of members of the PM's cabinet of ministers, from among the majority party, by the whole house. Similarly, he proposed that the majority party's cabinet ministers from the minority community should be elected by members of each minority community in the legislature.

These creative ideas indicate that Ambedkar was looking for a suitable check on communal majority, while also ensuring space and agency for the minority in political governance. His apprehensions about the danger posed to the minorities under the rule of a communal-majority government unfortunately seem to be coming true today. This makes it imperative for us to draw lessons based on his proposed solutions for safeguarding the minorities.

Effective Representation of Religious and Social Minorities

Ambedkar's views on and efforts to secure political representation for the scheduled castes (SCs) and scheduled tribes (STs) are equally important. While justifying a notion of the minorities, the principles justifying their representation and the electoral method to be used for it remained important agendas for Ambedkar, we know from history that his proposals were not allowed to be fully actualized in the early days after Independence and also at the time the Constitution was being made by the Constituent Assembly. He had proposed a separate electorate, had suggested an alternative to separate electorate in the form of a 'qualified Joint electorate for sending the real representative of the dalits and adiwasis'. However, this was not supported by even those who sat alongside Ambedkar in Parliament. They hadn't committed themselves to the full force of social justice as he did.

The only suggestion here to those activists from the Dalit community who will fight tooth and nail to save the Constitution is this: a Dalit conception of nation/nationalism can be more expansive, as mentioned earlier, than the constitutional one and yet remain within the confines of constitutional morality. But it demands not only visionary rethinking in terms of Dalit politics and its principles but also political influence and moral integrity to reach a consensus that a humanist project requires. It would be in the interests of the Dalits to build a national narrative on the importance of such political representation and then progressively to try to attain it in the future.

Summary

The above discussion tries to articulate the Ambedkarite idea of nation. It has been argued that Ambedkar remains the solitary inspiration and ray of hope for the Dalits as someone who gave a viable perspective to their problems, by intersecting them with a particular idea of nation and nationhood that would provide practical solutions for the contentious issue of caste discrimination. Ambedkar was the central figure who incorporated various provisions into the Constitution that the Dalits not only approve of but also cherish.

Ambedkarite politics is centred on the idea of a nation as a sovereign, socialist, secular, democratic republic and the goals of justice (social, economic, and political); liberty of thought, expression, belief, faith and worship; equality of status and of opportunity to all irrespective of religion, caste, race, colour, ethnicity, gender and region; and finally, fraternity, assuring the dignity of the individual and the unity and integrity of the nation. However, the major concern for the Dalits relates to the non-inclusion into the governing structure of some remedies proposed by Ambedkar for the political, economic and social empowerment of the Dalits and other deprived groups.

These omissions include the economic structure that Ambedkar proposed for the alleviation of poverty in general and in specific relation to the Dalits. He had proposed the introduction of state socialism, with state ownership of agricultural land and key industries; he advocated bringing the social sectors, like education, health and insurance, under the domain of the state, which he referred to as the 'economic system of Constitutional State socialism with parliamentary democracy'. The economic equality ushered in by state socialism would also, Ambedkar believed, facilitate the participation of both the Dalits and the poor in the political democracy while offering them access to fundamental rights.

But this economic structure of state socialism proposed by Ambedkar was not accepted by the Constituent Assembly. And the consequences are there for everybody to see. While poverty levels remain high, the Dalits and the poor are not able to effectively participate in this democracy. Space in the political arena is determined more by a person's wealth and less by worth.

The second omission in the Constitution is related to social democracy. In theory, all citizens of the country, including the Dalits, are entitled to citizenship rights, but in practice, despite the enactment of laws, the Dalits have been deprived of citizenship and fundamental rights in the full sense. The idea of the nation remains incomplete in practice because the necessary conditions for inclusive nationhood have not been met. It is clear that a common land, language, culture and religion are necessary conditions for nationhood, but this commonality is not sufficient for ensuring an inclusive nation. The feeling of oneness, that we are all kith and kin, binds people together, but the lack of a sense of fraternity in social relations undermines the efforts towards the strengthening of the nation. In view of this lack of fraternity, India remains a nation in the making. From the point of view of the ex-untouchables, the caste system remains a great obstacle to nationhood, as it is antagonistic to the concept of nation or nationality. The roots of democracy lie not in the form of government, parliamentary or otherwise, but must be sought in social relationships, and among the people who constitute society. However, since the Dalits continue to remain segregated and isolated, they are unable to become a part of the larger society.

Another limitation of the Constitution is the lack of safeguards for the minorities against the communal majority. Ambedkar foresaw the danger the minorities could face under a regime of the communal majority. He proposed three safeguards against a possible communal majority government: (1) balanced representation; (2) the principle of unanimous decision in important matters; and (3) the principle of faith or confidence. The Dalits are also extremely unhappy about the lack of an appropriate electoral method to ensure real representation for the SCs in the legislature. Ambedkar had proposed a qualified Joint Electorate as an alternative to a separate electorate for electing the real representatives of the Dalits in the legislature, which was not accepted. The negative consequences of that rejection are clear today.

The Dalits recognize that the constitutional promise made to them has been compromised in ways more than one can count. While certain provisions have actively been denied to them, there are others which Ambedkar had conceived but which were never allowed to be part of the national strategies in the first place.

Today, when the ruling party is destroying both the constitutional morality and the democratic fabric of the post-colonial vision, Dalit politics must rethink how to not only safeguard the existing progressive mechanisms that the Constitution has but also, for the sake of its own future, how to introduce in the Constitution the radical measures dreamt by Ambedkar. The Ambedkarite idea of the nation involves a philosophic vision of hope for the oppressed and a concrete proposal to implement it. Today, at this critical juncture of politics when Hindutva forces deploy the violence of Manu and market against the people of this country, the Dalit community and Ambedkarite politics must champion its antithesis as adumbrated by Ambedkar and show what substantive civic constitutional nationalism looks like.

Ambedkar's Representational Politics: Expanding the Possibilities

Raja Sekhar Vundru

India's representational politics emanated during the colonial period and transcended the independence struggle, reaching the constitutional framework in 1935 for several groups, including religious minorities, untouchables and backward classes. Eventually, in 1950, representation was restricted for only two distinct groups of untouchables and tribes. The constitutional framework provided a unique method of representation within the first-past-the-post electoral system, through reserved seats. The untouchables[1] of India, officially called the scheduled castes, or popularly addressed as the Dalits, have a very unique representational history, mainly brought about by the attempts made by Dr B.R. Ambedkar during the British colonial rule to increase the representation of Indians during 1909–46. The second group, the tribes, or officially, scheduled tribes, achieved it through the constitutional process; they have also been granted special tribal scheduled areas under the Constitution, keeping in view their unique geographical isolation and cultural identity.

The journey of representational politics of the untouchables had wide-ranging importance, as it emerged out of a great movement for self-respect, human dignity and political rights. It precipitated historical distance—between the Hindus and the untouchables, represented by Mahatma Gandhi and Dr B.R. Ambedkar respectively—for the representation of the latter in legislative bodies. To understand representational politics in India, the evolution of representation in colonial India needs to be assessed.

Political Representation of the Untouchables

With constitutional reforms in British colonial rule, since 1909, contributing to the representational landscape of the Indian population, with their myriad communities and religions, the untouchables too advanced their quest for representation as a community. But it made little headway till the 1911 Census, which enumerated the untouchables as a special category.[2] This was revealed by Ambedkar in his work *Pakistan or the Partition of India*: 'The Muslims have always been looking at the Depressed Classes with a sense of longing and much of the jealousy between Hindus and Muslims arises out of the fear of the latter that the former might become stronger by assimilating the Depressed Classes.'

In 1909, the Muslims took the bold step of suggesting that the Depressed Classes should not be enrolled in the census as Hindus. Once the untouchables became aware of their numerical strength, their political aspirations for representation took shape. All across India, associations of untouchables met and put forth their demands to the viceroy of India till 1918.[3] During the constitutional reforms process in 1919, the untouchables continued their political activities, which included getting several untouchable organizations from all over India to approach the Southborough Committee or the Franchise Committee; this was also Ambedkar's first political foray.[4] These demands made no impression on the British to set aside legislative seats by means of elections. The Southborough Committee recommended a meagre seven out of 791 seats in British India for the untouchables, that too by nomination process. The British government increased the nominated seats to twenty-four in the Government of India Act, 1919. M.C. Rajah became the first untouchable to be nominated for a legislative council seat in 1920 in Madras.[5] Later, in 1925, Ambedkar was nominated in Bombay. The untouchable political representation journey can be seen through the lens of five pacts, from the 1916 Lucknow Pact to the 1932 Poona Pact.

The Lucknow Pact of 1916[6] was an agreement between Hindus and Muslims, and sought representation in elected form in legislative bodies. It is also significant because the Hindus conceded concessions to the Muslims for their representation on the basis of (i) weightage; (ii) right to representation; and (iii) method of separate electorate as the election method. It was a pact between the Congress and the Muslim League, representing Hindus and Muslims respectively.

Ambedkar, in his evidence before the Southborough Committee[7] in 1919, laid out the principles on the basis of which he pursued representative politics for the untouchables. He did not consider the Congress–Muslim League's Lucknow Pact binding on the untouchables. He put across the principles of right to self-determination, the representation of the community by a separate electorate and seats to be reserved on the basis of population. Ambedkar stood by those principles, and, in the next two decades, he played a major role in shaping the electoral-representation landscape of the untouchables.

Even as the nominated untouchable representatives in various provinces focused on the emancipation of the untouchables by seeking civil rights and access to education, and fought against their exploitation through legislative and social-agitational modes, the arrival of the Simon Commission in 1928, to revise the constitutional arrangement for legislative bodies, furthered their cause. The Simon Commission received great opposition from the Congress. But untouchable organizations welcomed the commission in order to put forward their claim for representation; the Muslims and other communities also met the touring Simon Commission. The Congress called an all-party conference and, as an alternative, appointed a committee under Motilal Nehru to draft a new constitution. The Nehru report failed to absorb the aspirations of the untouchables, Muslims and Sikhs,[8] and was promptly rejected. When the British government contemplated a Round Table Conference in London, to be attended by all the representative groups, the untouchables sought the participation of at least eight of their representatives.[9] The British nominated two untouchables to the Conference, which was held from November 1930 to January 1931: Ambedkar, from the Bombay Presidency, and Rettamalai Srinivasan, from Madras.

Ambedkar was also aware of the Congress's position, which, as early as 1919, had denied communal representation except in the case of Muslims.[10] However, since the Congress had not participated in the first Round Table Conference, Ambedkar could secure the confidence of the British and make his case for representation with a separate electorate, which was accepted by the conference. However, on his first meeting with Gandhi in August 1931, upon his return from the conference, the latter made his position clear to Ambedkar: he was opposed to representation for the untouchables. With Gandhi representing the Congress at the second Round Table Conference in London (September–December 1931), a duel erupted, at the conference and in the press, between Ambedkar and Gandhi on the design of representation for the untouchables. It became the talk of the town.[11]

However, the minorities, including the untouchables, came together to oppose Gandhi's idea of limiting the representation of minorities only to Muslims and Sikhs. Gandhi tried to win over the Muslims to his side with the 1931 pact.

Drafted on 6 October 1931, the Gandhi–Muslim Pact, 1931, remained unsigned. Gandhi's proposal was: 'No special reservations to any other community save Sikhs and Hindu minorities.'[12] The Muslims were, however, not in agreement with that, unwilling to deny other minorities their due representation.

This was followed quickly by a pact between the minorities called the Minorities Pact, which was presented to the British prime minister on 12 November 1931. This was against the position of Gandhi, who opposed a separate electorate for all other minorities, including the untouchables, Sikhs, Indian Christians and Anglo–Indians.

The Minorities Pact, 1931, concerned 'Provisions for a Settlement of the Communal Problem, put forward jointly by Muslims, Depressed Classes, Indian Christians, Anglo-Indians and Europeans'. They sought representation on the basis of population weightage and election of representatives through a separate electorate.[13] The claims of the minorities reflected the parity they sought as political entities. In general, the claims[14] sought protection of their cultural rights; protection from discrimination; constitutional safeguards against discrimination; representation in services; representation in government cabinets by convention; right to manage their own cultural and educational bodies; and majorly, the demand that any governmental decision or policy affecting a minority community get the legislative approval of at least two-thirds of the members of that community.

The claims of untouchables were: the Constitution shall declare invalid any custom or usage by which any penalty or disadvantage or disability is imposed, and any discrimination made against any subject of the state in regard to the enjoyment of the civic rights on account of untouchability; that there should be generous treatment in the matter of the recruitment of the untouchables to public services and the opening of enlistment in the police and military services; the depressed classes in the Punjab shall have the benefit of the Punjab Land Alienation Act extended to them;

right of appeal shall lie with the governor or governor–general for redress of prejudicial action or neglect of interest by any executive authority, and seats in the legislative body shall be provided to the untouchables as per the 1931 Census and Simon Commission report.

By the end of 1931, Gandhi returned to India after a failed mission at the second Round Table Conference, launched the civil disobedience movement and was incarcerated. The British announced communal awards on the issue of electoral representation of the minorities, including untouchables. The Communal Award[15] of 4 August 1932 awarded reserved seats with separate electorates to all the minorities who were part of the Minorities Pact, including the untouchables and Sikhs. In the case of the untouchables, to accept Gandhi's claim that the untouchables were Hindus, the British granted the untouchables a second vote to participate in the elections in the Hindu general constituencies. Gandhi did not accept the communal award, even though he had signed an agreement before the British prime minister in London accepting the premier as the arbitrator.

The issue of separate electorates for the untouchables became a bone of contention. M.C. Rajah, then the senior-most untouchable leader in the country, and B.S. Moonje, a leader of the Hindu Mahasabha representing the Hindus, signed a pact known as the Rajah–Moonje Pact, denying separate electorates to untouchables and assimilating them in general constituencies by referring to them as joint electorates, with reserved seats for the untouchables.

The Rajah–Moonje Pact, 1932,[16] was signed on 1 March 1932 in Delhi. It had no relevance, since M.C. Rajah was not a representative of the untouchables at the Round Table Conference and was unrecognized. It, however, eventually supported Gandhi's position that the untouchables should not have separate electorates and should be part of the Hindu fold with joint electorates.

Gandhi announced a fast unto death against the 'statutory separation even in a limited form from the Hindu fold'[17] of the untouchables through separate electorates. However, he did not make an issue out of the communal award which had granted separate electorates to other minorities. His fast unto death led to a series of events that resulted in negotiations between the Hindus, representing the Congress headed by Madan Mohan Malviya (who accompanied Gandhi to the Round Table Conference), and Ambedkar on behalf of the untouchables, and the Poona Pact[18] was arrived at. Gandhi did not sign the pact. M.C. Rajah, the signatory of the Rajah–Moonje Pact, also became a signatory to the Poona Pact on 24 September 1932.

The Poona Pact, 1932, was signed between the Hindus and untouchables on 24 September 1932, and it had a major impact. Considering the untouchables as Hindus, it granted them reserved seats from Hindu general seats. Signed under coercion, because of Gandhi's fast, it was accepted by the British as an alteration of the communal award and was made a part of the Government of India Act, 1935.

The Poona Pact altered the separate electorate system for the untouchables to a two-stage election. At the first stage, it was similar to a separate electorate, except that a panel of four persons would be elected. At the second stage, one of the four would be selected from this panel for the reserved seat, based on a voting system including all the voters, including the untouchables. Ambedkar, the chief signatory to the Poona Pact, quickly sought a revision of this pact, changing the panel system of four persons to one-time polling (due to the cumbersome process and cost involved), with the condition that the winning untouchable candidate should get a minimum of 25 per cent of the votes from the untouchable voters. As the voters had a separate community-wise list (for communities in separate electorate process) during the pre-Independence period, the minimum cut-off based 'qualified joint electorate', as proposed by Ambedkar, would have been possible. But Gandhi rejected it. Ambedkar analysed the 1937 elections, altered on the basis of the Poona Pact, and published a scathing criticism of the method in his book *What Congress and Gandhi Have Done to the Untouchables,* published in 1945.

Ambedkar–Sardar Patel Contestation[19]

Ambedkar, who later became a member of the viceroy's executive council, could not alter the electoral system based on the Poona Pact and bring it back to the separate electorate system. He emphasized the futility of the Poona Pact system on several occasions, but in vain. In 1946, as India moved towards independence, the imminent spectre of Partition became a major issue for Gandhi and Sardar Patel. The latter negotiated with Ambedkar regarding his demand to adopt a qualified joint electorate method, and even considered the change. However, by September 1946, Patel made a turnaround and suspended all negotiations with Ambedkar. After Partition, in 1947, and Gandhi's assassination, in January 1948, on 30 December 1948, Patel proposed the abolition[20] of all reserved seats for all minorities, including the untouchables, to the dismay of Ambedkar and all the other untouchable leaders. With the death of Gandhi, who had been a witness to the five pacts, Patel had himself taken up the issue of the abolition of reserved seats. But this was thwarted by Ambedkar, who ensured that seats were reserved for the untouchables. The Constitution of 1950 provided reserved seats to the untouchables for a period of ten years, and the timespan was to be extended after a review.

When the British formed the Cripps Mission to frame a new constitution for India in 1941, it once again did not explicitly recognize the depressed classes as a separate element and remained vague with the usage of the term 'racial and religious minorities'.[21] It ignored the pleas of the depressed classes to have their independent voice recognized through political representation. Ambedkar opposed the Cripps proposals saying that 'the Scheduled Castes are bound hand and foot and handed over to the caste Hindus'. Two years later, when negotiations started again, the British made specific reference to the depressed classes.[22] The Wavell plan, declared in 1945, expanded the executive council but put forward only one representative per 50 million scheduled castes.[23] Ambedkar once again opposed this political arithmetic, and the Wavell plan failed.

Soon after that, the British formed the Cabinet Mission in June 1945 and made two announcements: one, that elections would be held in the winter of 1945 for the provincial and central legislative assemblies; and two, that a constituent assembly would be created after the elections for framing the new Constitution. Interestingly, the Central Legislative Assembly (CLA) had no reserved seats. The provisions of the Government of India Act, 1935, related to this were never implemented in the CLA, and thus it had only one nominated member from the scheduled caste category. Ambedkar opposed it once again in a meeting with the Cabinet Mission on 5 April 1946.[24] He produced evidence to show the committee how, in several cases, the Congress's scheduled caste candidates, who were outvoted by the Scheduled Castes Federation (SCF) candidates in the primary elections, were beaten in the final elections in 1946; and how the small number of scheduled caste voters were terrorized by the loot and arson ensured by the Congress candidates.[25]

Soon thereafter, in July 1946, the SCF, under Ambedkar's leadership, launched a satyagraha for the rights of the untouchables in Bombay, Poona, Lucknow and Kanpur. The Congress felt the need for rapprochement and asked Sardar Patel to meet Ambedkar, but they could not come to any settlement. Patel confined himself to criticizing Ambedkar for his attitude towards Gandhi in his writings and speeches.[26] Following the meeting, Ambedkar wrote a letter along with a detailed memorandum to Patel, proposing alternatives to the Poona Pact.[27]

Ambedkar's last attempt in this direction was at the Constituent Assembly, the entry to which was not easy for him.[28] On 15 April 1947, the All India Adi-Hindu Depressed Classes Association, on behalf of the scheduled castes, submitted a memorandum arguing that the system of joint electorates had deprived the scheduled castes of true and effective political representation and urged for the abrogation of the Poona Pact. The association also demanded that all representation in the legislatures should be done through separate electorates, and if not, then securing 40 per cent of the total number of scheduled caste votes should be made compulsory for a scheduled caste candidate to win in joint electorates. However, in its meeting on 21 July 1947, the subcommittee decided, by a majority of 28–3, that there should be no separate electorate for the elections to the legislature and that, as a general principle, there should be reservation of seats for the scheduled castes.

While arriving at this decision, the option of discussing various methods of joint electorates, as suggested by the All India Adi–Hindu Depressed Classes Association, was left open. The subcommittee also decided that the reservation should be for ten years, after which the position could be reconsidered.[29] However, the decision on the electoral method of representation of the scheduled castes and other minorities, based on the polling of a certain quota of votes from the community, grew contentious,[30] as the subcommittee got divided by seven votes on each side and had to refer this matter to the advisory committee.[31] This led to considerable discussion even before the Advisory Committee, but finally, K.M. Munshi, with the support of a large majority in the committee, moved a resolution that there should not be such a stipulation. This alternative method of electoral representation of a reserved seat was one of the options in terms of the substitution of separate electorates, but the proposal was defeated.

Ambedkar knew since the beginning that despite his strong efforts to bring in a settlement on the issue of the electoral method for the election of scheduled caste representatives, the Congress would virtually sweep aside any of his proposals. Facing a situation where the 'Harijan' members of the Congress in the Constituent Assembly were not speaking up for the rights of the untouchables, Ambedkar, at one point of time, even thought of disassociating himself from the Constituent Assembly.[32]

'You should however remember that in the Constituent Assembly of 292 or so I am one single, solitary individual. You should also bear in mind that no matter how great a man may have intellect or the capacity to argue and to defend, he is after all one man, a single individual. If the rest of 291 are determined not to listen to the reason, not listen to the argument but to oppose their opponent you can well realize my possible helplessness in the Constituent Assembly of 292 where I am, only one.'[33]

At last, on 28 August 1947, when Ambedkar's demand found the support of Sardar Nagappa, who brought in a minimum stipulation of 35 per cent of the votes for a qualified joint electorate, Patel nipped it in the bud and said,[34] 'Mr Nagappa wanted to move his amendment to fulfil a promise or undertaking or at least to show his community that he was not purchased by the majority community. Well, he has done his job, but other people took him seriously and took a lot of time.'[35]

As if this was not all, in May 1948 the Advisory Committee, led by Sardar Patel, decided to abolish reservations for the minorities, including the scheduled castes. It was at this stage that Ambedkar, the chairman of the Drafting Committee of the Constitution and also the law minister of India, decided to walk out of the Constituent Assembly, saying: 'I have laboured for three years preparing the Constitution on the cost of my health so that I could do something for the welfare of the Scheduled Castes . . . If seats were not kept reserved for the depressed classes in the Constitution, I would walk out of the Constituent Assembly so that in the pages of history it would remain written how the Hindus opposed the question of welfare of untouchables, when it came before them.'[36]

Ambedkar walked out of the meeting and did not attend the house until Congress agreed on the inclusion of certain provisions for the welfare of the scheduled castes. Later, on 16 November 1949, the Congress moved a resolution to substitute the word 'minorities' by the term 'certain classes' and exclude the scheduled castes from the ambit of the minorities permanently.[37] The amendment was

adopted, and with this came the special provision of reservation of
seats in the House of the People for the scheduled castes by Article
330 (1) of the Constitution. Clause 2 of this article says that the
number of seats reserved in any state for the scheduled castes or
scheduled tribes shall bear, as nearly as may be, the same proportion
to the total number of seats allotted to that state in the House of
the People as the population of the scheduled castes in the state, as
the case may be, in respect of which seats are so reserved, bears to
the total population of the state. The position taken by Ambedkar
to ensure the political safeguards for the untouchables despite the
loss of reservations for the minorities was the result of discussions
outside the Constituent Assembly.

During the constitutional process under the British, and later
under several agreements, a time limit was a specific clause for the
reserved seats. This time limit was in expectation and hope of the
amelioration and empowerment of the community or group under
question. In case of the untouchables, it was twenty years under
the Poona Pact, but any abrogation of time limit and extension
period was to be mutually decided. In the same convention, the
reserved seats for the scheduled castes were fixed a time limit of
ten years in the Constitution of India. The Indian Parliament has,
by consensus, extended the time limit for reserved seats till 2030.[38]

Non-Brahmin Seats and Reserved Seats for Backward Classes

The backward classes movement for political representation was
initiated in the form of a non-Brahmin movement in Madras
and Bombay Presidencies in British India. The domination of
the Brahmins as a caste, in all facets of administration, made the
non-Brahmins meet in 1916 in Madras and issue a manifesto now
known as the Non-Brahmin Manifesto.

The political movement of the non-Brahmins was energized
with the 1919 constitutional reform, as the government established

a commission to look into their political grievances under Lord Meston. 'The Meston Award' granted them only twenty-eight reserved seats out of ninety-eight elected seats in the Madras Legislative Council, despite a plea by the non-Brahmins that they were seven-ninth of the population. The Justice Party won the November 1920 council elections with an overwhelming majority by winning sixty-eight seats and formed the government. The Indian National Congress had boycotted the elections and participated in the non-cooperation movement. Out of the ninety-eight seats, the non-Brahmins had twenty-eight, the Muslims thirteen, the Indian Christians five and the Europeans and Anglo–Indians had six seats.

The non-Brahmin movement in the Bombay Province in western India was looking for a voice in the legislative councils and also sought reserved seats under the 1919 reforms. This resulted in seven reserved seats for the Marathas and thirteen other similar castes in 1920.[39] Under the 1935 act, the provincial legislatures had twenty-three seats reserved for the backward classes and tribes, and in Bombay, seven of the general seats were reserved for the Marathas.[40]

The Constituent Assembly deviated from the first draft of the Constitution, and after Partition in 1947, all reserved seats, for Muslims as well as other minorities, were abolished, and there was a proposal to abolish reservation for the scheduled castes, which was obtained under the 1935 act. But with the intervention of Dr B.R. Ambedkar, the reservations continued.[41] The reserved seats for the backward classes or the non-Brahmins were not taken into consideration. Since the 1951 elections, however, the domination of the Brahmins in legislative bodies reduced, with the advent of the Green Revolution and the rise and launch of the peasant castes into the political arena. This change had become visible by 1990. The backward classes movement, which was primarily restricted to electoral politics till the '90s, also became a pressure group seeking reservations in employment and education in state and (in 1990) central government institutions.

Ambedkar's Principle of Majority and Minority in Political Representation

Ambedkar held several views on the concept of majority and minority, also in the context of issues raised by the Muslim League, including the demand for Pakistan.

Ambedkar's initial views, at the time of the framing of India's Constitution, came up in his representation[42] to the Constituent Assembly in 1947. The remedial measures he proposed for the protection of the minorities from the tyranny of the majority were:

> The Prime Minister shall be elected by the whole House by single transferable vote. The representatives of the different minorities in the Cabinet shall be elected by members of each minority community in the Legislature by single transferable vote. The representatives of the majority community in the Executive shall be elected by the whole House by single transferable vote.[43]

The reasons Ambedkar cited for such a proposal, wherein the prime minister would be elected by the whole House, were:

(i) to prevent the majority from forming a Government without giving any opportunity to the minorities to have a say in the matter; (ii) to prevent the majority from having exclusive control over administration and thereby make the tyranny of the minority by the majority possible; (iii) to prevent the inclusion by the Majority Party in the Executive representatives of the minorities who have no confidence of the minorities; and (iv) to provide a stable Executive necessary for good and efficient administration.[44]

Ambedkar's views on this issue came to the fore again in 1955, a good eight years after Independence. He illustrated the effect of the caste system on single-member constituency-based elections:

(1) Voting is always communal. The voter votes for the candidate of his community and not for the best candidate. (2) The majority community carries the seat by sheer communal majority. (3) The minority community is forced to vote for the candidate of the majority community. (4) The votes of the minority community are not enough to enable the candidate to win the seat against the candidate put up by the majority community. (5) As consequence of social system of graded inequality, the voter of the higher communities can never condescend to give his vote to a candidate of a minority community. On the other hand, the voter of the minority community who is socially on a lower level takes pride in giving his vote to the candidate of the majority community. That is another reason why a candidate of a minority community loses in election.[45]

While seeking an answer to the question 'What right has the majority to rule over the minority?' Ambedkar classified majority as (a) communal majority and (b) political majority. Ambedkar explained the concept thus:

A political majority is changeable in its class composition. A political majority grows. A communal majority is born. The admission to a political majority is open. The door to a communal majority is closed. The politics of a political majority are free to all to make and unmake. The politics of a communal majority are made by its own members born in it. How can a communal majority run away with the title deeds given to a political majority to rule? To give such title deeds to a communal majority is to establish a hereditary Government and make the way open to the tyranny of that majority. This tyranny of the communal majority is not an idle dream. It is an experience of many minorities.[46]

The experience of the Dalit, adivasi and other minority communities under a political majority, which uses its power as a communal majority, is now becoming clear in Indian democracy. In case a political party wins an election on its party programme, it's invariably one caste or community that dominates the government and exercises power over all other castes and communities. The elected governments later come to be known as a government of that particular caste rather than that of a political party.

Ambedkar's remedy to this issue in electoral representation was multi-member constituencies with cumulative voting, as proposed in 1955.

Conclusion

The system of reserved seats, although it has continued as a mutual agreement between the scheduled castes and the Hindus since 1937, has been extended till 2030, including for the tribes. The reserved seats provided under the Government of India Act, 1935, was a result of a national movement, and it took into consideration the collective aspirations of emerging political groups who were granted reserved seats. The reserved seats were obtained by the minorities, such as the Muslims, Sikhs, Indian Christians, Anglo–Indians (Europeans); scheduled castes; non-Brahmins (in Madras); Marathas (in Maharashtra); people of backward areas and tribes; and interest groups from different industries, like mining and planting, landholders, university affiliates, labourers and women.

The reserved seats originally enshrined in the draft constitution of India[47] have not been taken up. Article 292 of the draft constitution provided for reserved seats for the Muslims, scheduled castes, scheduled tribes and Indian Christians, including Anglo–Indians, in Parliament and state assemblies.

The representative politics which Ambedkar took up had two specific patterns. The primary one had to do with the principles to establish representation, which are indisputable. These were the right to representation by virtue of population strength and the right to self-determination of a community or a group of people who are a minority and oppressed. After ensuring the acceptance of the principle of political representation, Ambedkar looked into the method of election as an important component of political representation. He always sought the separate electorate or qualified joint electorate method for untouchable reserved seats.

Ambedkar's principles can be applied to the issue of reservation for women as a political group and as an oppressed gender, seeking representation in Parliament and state assemblies, including the upper houses. That reservation for women has been successfully implemented recently in Panchayati Raj and municipal bodies is an indication that this is an idea whose time has arrived. The backward classes have shown their mettle in local bodies and need to be considered for reservation in Parliament and assemblies, too. This should include reservations in the upper house of Parliament as well as in the state legislative councils.

Political Representation for a political group has always been a negotiated pact historically, emanating from movements for representation over the last century. The Constitution of India, drafted by Ambedkar, is fully equipped to provide political reservations in the twenty-first century.

Caste and Judiciary in India

Kiruba Munusamy

Introduction

B.R. Ambedkar, while participating in a debate in the Rajya Sabha on 2 September 1953, argued that there are majorities and there are minorities, and we simply cannot ignore the minorities by saying, 'Oh, no, to recognize you is to harm democracy.' If one goes by Ambedkar's analysis, the term 'minorities' can be interpreted as the scheduled castes, scheduled tribes and backward classes, as well as religious, linguistic and ethnic minorities. He warned us that the greatest harm will come by injuring the minorities.

Dr Ambedkar, who had contributed most to the progressiveness of our Constitution, was a reformist too. The visionary was able to foretell the future of the minorities in view of the socio-political power that the ruling class held. However, this was not the first time that Dr Ambedkar had issued such a warning. During the presentation of the draft constitution in the Constituent Assembly, he said, 'I feel that it is workable, it is flexible and it is strong enough to hold the country together . . . if things go wrong under the new Constitution, the reason will not be that we had a bad Constitution. What we will have to say is, that Man was vile.'[1]

The state of democracy depends on how it protects the interests of its minorities. That responsibility does not lie only on the provisions incorporated in the Constitution but is shared by the institutions that implement them in letter and spirit. The institutions that ought to perform the constitutional duties of protecting and furthering the interests of the minorities are none other than the legislature, the executive and the judiciary. Of these three government organs, the onus of protecting the minorities is primarily on the judiciary, as envisaged in the Constitution.

As a watchdog of the constitutional order, the judiciary plays a crucial role by being independent of the other two organs of the government. It holds the power of judicial review, through which the court decides the constitutional correctness of a law or an order passed by the legislature and executive; and of judicial law-making, i.e. delivering decisions that have an effect of law.

Nevertheless, the framers of the Constitution had apprehensions about the powers that the Constitution would vest on the judiciary. Both the drafting and advisory committees saw the possible interference of the judiciary in the social reformatory laws enacted by the legislature in relation to the fundamental rights of life and liberty.[2] Realizing the excessive power that the judiciary could accrue, the constitutional adviser to the Constituent Assembly, B.N. Rau, had warned that 'the courts, manned by an irremovable judiciary not so sensitive to public needs in the social or economic sphere as the representatives of a periodically elected legislature, will, in effect, have a veto on legislation exercisable at any time and at the instance of any litigant'.[3] After deep deliberation and lengthy debates, the Constituent Assembly finally decided to delete the 'due process' clause and substituted it by the expression 'procedure established by law'. The exclusion was made with the intent to limit judicial power. Resultantly, Article 21 of the Indian Constitution reads: 'No person shall be deprived of his life or personal liberty except according to the procedure established by law.'

How Ambedkar Safeguarded Reservations from Judicial Overreach

The initial version of the current Article 16(4) was prepared by the Advisory Committee of the Constituent Assembly. As on 22 April 1947, it provided for the state to make 'provision for reservations in favour of classes not adequately represented in the public services'.[4] Ambedkar, who was then a part of the Advisory Committee, suggested the deletion of the words 'not adequately represented'. Instead, he wanted the clause to be rephrased to provide reservations 'in public services in favour of classes as may be prescribed by the State'.[5]

He argued that if the words 'not adequately represented' were retained, any reservation made by the state 'would be open to challenge in the court of law on the ground that the classes in whose favour reservation was made happened to be in fact already adequately represented'.[6] Ambedkar was thus opposed to the issue of reservation being open to 'judicial interpretation'.[7] In effect, he wanted to insulate reservations from any possibility of dilution by the judiciary.[8]

Later on, K.M. Munshi, who was also on the Advisory Committee, suggested rephrasing the clause of reservation to accommodate Ambedkar's concern. Instead of the words 'not adequately represented', the phrase 'classes which in the opinion of the State are not adequately represented' was added. Ambedkar accepted this change. The change gave primacy to the opinion of the state in making reservations.[9] The clause was ultimately presented to the Constituent Assembly by the Ambedkar-led Drafting Committee with one modification: instead of the words 'in favour of any particular class of citizens', the words 'in favour of any backward class of citizens' were inserted.[10]

Regrettably, Ambedkar's discernment in terms of the protection of the minorities under the new Constitution did not take too long to manifest. The framers of the Constitution were sceptical about the exercise of judicial powers only in respect to life and liberty. But ironically, the judiciary struck the first blow to the right to equality of the minorities.

The Judiciary's First Blow to Social Justice

Communal representation and reservations were integral even to the ethos of pre-British India.[11] Equal opportunity in education and employment for the non-Brahmins was also a pre-Independence demand. Since the late 1920s, various attempts had been made to reduce Brahmin preponderance and educate the non-Brahmins. Finally, the first Communal GO No. 613, on 16 September 1921, ensuring proportional representation, was passed.[12] For every fourteen seats in medical and engineering colleges, the order reserved seats on the following basis:

Non-Brahmin (Hindus): 6
Backward Hindus: 2
Brahmins: 2
Harijans: 2
Anglo–Indians and Indian Christians: 1
Muslims: 1

The GO also provided for a 20 per cent reservation for women (way back in 1921) in each category and allowed to admit a larger number of women candidates, if qualified and eligible for selection on merit.

While that being so, reservations in medical and engineering college admissions were quashed by the High Court of Madras[13]—months after the adoption of the Constitution—in petitions filed by Champakam Dorairajan and Srinivasan as violative of Articles 15 (1) and 29 (2) that prohibit discrimination by the state on the grounds of religion or caste and the denial of admission in the state-maintained educational institutions, respectively. Both the Brahmins were represented by Alladi Krishnaswami Ayyar, a Brahmin and a member of the Drafting Committee for India's Constitution. On appeal, the Supreme Court of India, by a unanimous decision,[14] upheld the high court order.

Thought the petitioners had not even applied, both were *not* denied admission and seats were promised if they were found qualified and eligible. It would not be an overstatement to say that the decision approving the casteist custom of denying education to non-Brahmins was emboldened by the presence of Alladi Krishnaswami Ayyar. Even if there was a chance for a different or a better understanding of discrimination and representation, the influence of the interpretation of one of the constitutional framers was strong enough to sway the judiciary. Given the Indian value system of position and power, the courts seemed to be unconcerned about the consequences of this decision.

Following education, reservation in public employment was held inconsistent with Article 13 (laws in contravention of the fundamental rights are void) and Article 16 (equality of opportunity in public employment).[15] The historical First Amendment to the Indian Constitution was made precisely to nullify the judicial decisions on reservation. Article 15 prohibited discrimination on the grounds of religion, race, caste, sex or place of birth; it originally consisted of three clauses, which were amended and Clause 4 was inserted by the Constitution (First Amendment) Act, 1951, as follows:

Nothing in this article or in clause (2) of Article 29 shall prevent the State from making any special provision for the advancement of any socially and educationally backward classes of citizens or for the Scheduled Castes and the Scheduled Tribes.

Judiciary's Shifting Views on Upholding Reservation as a Fundamental Right

As evident, Ambedkar strongly defended the provisions on reservation. Despite the first constitutional amendment, the Supreme Court, during the first two decades since 1950, interpreted Article 16(4) as an exception to Article 16(1),[16] and held that Article 16(4) was merely enabling and did not create a mandatory obligation on the state.[17] Justice K. Subba Rao's dissent in 'T. Devadasan vs Union of India' (1964) was a departure from this view.[18] He held that Article 16(4) was a facet of Article 16(1).

The dissenting opinion of Justice Subba Rao was later upheld in the case of 'State of Kerala vs N.M. Thomas'[19] (1975), where the court, by a majority of 4–3, held that Article 16(4) was a facet of Article 16(1) and not an exception to it. This position on reservation was defended strongly by judges such as S. Murtaza Fazal Ali,[20] V.R. Krishna Iyer[21] and O. Chinnappa Reddy.[22] The decision of 'N.M. Thomas . . .' was upheld by a larger bench of nine judges in 'Indra Sawhney vs Union of India'[23] (1992). Dealing with the issue of 27 per cent OBC reservation, 'Indra Sawhney . . .' was an authoritative holding on whether Article 16(4) is a fundamental right. Seven judges out of nine explicitly called Article 16(4) as a part of Article 16(1).[24]

It is to be noted that once a right is held to be a part of a larger right, it becomes an enforceable right in itself.[25] For example, the Supreme Court has given effect to so many rights within Article 21, which provides for 'right to life'.[26] Article 16(4) is therefore a fundamental right. Furthermore, in the Indra Sawhney case, only a minority of three judges called Article 16(4) 'enabling' for the backward classes.[27] For the scheduled castes and scheduled tribes in particular, only two judges called Article 16(4) 'enabling'. It is clear from the judgment that the view of Article 16(4) being merely an enabling provision is a minority view and cannot be used to prevent reservation policies.[28] As a result of the majority view in

'Indra Sawhney . . .', the state is bound to provide reservations, in particular to the SCs and STs.

However, later judgments have diluted the effect of the Indra Sawhney case.[29] These judgments are of smaller benches than that in 'Indra Sawhney'. For instance, in 'M. Nagaraj vs Union of India',[30] a constitution bench (five judges) said that Articles 16(1) and 16(4) operate in 'different fields', even though the Indra Sawhney judgment held that they operate in same field. The judgment in 'Nagaraj . . .' and other judgments, such as in 'Ajit Singh vs State of Punjab'[31] (1999), 'Mukesh Kumar vs State of Uttarakhand'[32] (2020), etc., called Articles 16(4) and 16(4A) as merely enabling, as though this was not the majority view in the Indra Sawhney judgment. These later judgments of smaller benches have interpreted the decision in the Indra Sawhney case to restrict the right to reservation under Article 16(4).[33]

The Supreme Court has also applied Article 335, which uses the phrase 'efficiency of administration', as a restriction on Article 16(4).[34] The court used the words 'efficiency of administration' as an artificial restriction on the right to reservation. It created a binary, as if reservation and efficiency are contrary to each other.[35]

Are There Hurdles in Courts for Dalits, Adivasis and OBCs?

Affirmative action, in its true spirit, intends to ensure and increase opportunities of under-represented groups. Instead of acting as a compelling force on the government in adhering to its social justice and equality commitments, as enshrined in the Constitution, the judiciary itself has become an institutional barrier for the historically oppressed classes by attenuating the efficacy of the reservation policy. It has, time and again, delivered body blows to India's social-justice paradigm. For example, proportional representation was confined to less than 50 per cent.[36] Similarly, on the non-availability of candidates, the carrying forward of reserved vacancies was invalidated.[37] Likewise, economic criterion was validated as a parameter for social and educational backwardness.[38] This led to the exclusion of the creamy layer from reservation.[39]

Furthermore, reservations in promotions,[40] the relaxation of qualifying marks and standards of evaluation[41] and consequential seniority[42] for the scheduled castes and scheduled tribes were denied. The collection of 'quantifiable data to show backwardness and inadequacy in representation' and the maintenance of efficiency were mandated for reservations in promotions.[43]

Reiterating its original decision of rescinding reservation, the Supreme Court has recently held that neither reservations in appointments nor promotions to public posts is a fundamental right, and the state is not bound to provide them.[44] Unsurprisingly, many of the above decisions have been nullified through various constitutional amendments.[45]

The judiciary, which has exhibited an anti-reservation tendency, has also been lax in the cases of violence against minorities. An analysis[46] of the National Crime Records Bureau (NCRB) data from 2006 to 2016 shows that the rate of crime against the scheduled castes and scheduled tribes has risen more than eight times (746 per cent) and over twelve times (1160 per cent) respectively. Yet, the rate of pending police investigations for crimes against SCs and STs has mushroomed by 99 per cent and 55 per cent respectively, while the pendency in courts has increased by 50 per cent and 28 per cent respectively. The worst is that the conviction rate for crimes against SCs and STs has fallen by 26 per cent and 21 per cent respectively.

The bitter reality is that the Supreme Court, regardless of the crimes committed, held that the SCs and STs (Prevention of Atrocities) Act, 1989 (SC–ST [PoA] Act), is misused by unscrupulous persons to oppress innocent citizens.[47] By removing the bar on the grant of anticipatory bail, mandating approval of the appointing authority, or senior superintendent of police, before an arrest and preliminary inquiry before FIR registration, the courts have diluted the very purpose of the act. Even when faced with the reality that law enforcement agencies are wilfully negligent and the criminal justice system has multiple loopholes because of which the perpetrators enjoy impunity, the courts have chosen to misconstrue 'low conviction' as 'false cases'.[48]

Decades before the SC–ST (PoA) Act, Ambedkar wrote, 'The police and the magistracy are the kith and kin of the caste Hindus. They share the sentiments and the prejudices of the caste Hindus against the Untouchables . . . There are innumerable cases in which this discretion has been exercised by the Magistrate to the prejudice of the Untouchables.'[49] From Keezhvenmani to Khairlanji, this has been the case.[50] The credibility of the victims and witnesses was questioned. The benefit of the doubt was placed in favour of the perpetrators. The victims were blamed for the violence against them.

Nevertheless, this is not a new tradition in the judiciary. In an earlier case relating to dowry harassment, the same bench of the Supreme Court (which diluted the Atrocities Act) took a similar stance by observing that the law is misused by wives to take revenge against their husbands and in-laws.[51] As per the NCRB data, there were 6208 dowry deaths in 2003; the number rose to 8172 in 2008 and 8455 in 2014.[52] Between 2006–2016, only one out of every seven cases resulted in a conviction. There was an increase of more than 150 per cent pending cases in eleven years, with 2,06,000 cases in 2006 and 5,15,000 in 2016.[53] The Supreme Court, disregarding these numbers but applying the 'low conviction is equal to false cases' formula, directed no registration of case and arrest until the Family Welfare Committees constituted thereunder submit a preliminary inquiry report. While the PoA Act misuse judgement was nullified through a legislative amendment,[54] the Supreme Court itself modified its dowry harassment misuse judgment.[55] What becomes clear is that victim–blaming has become common in the institution of judiciary, almost elevating the practice to an ideology.

Social reformatory policies and laws, such as affirmative action, the PoA Act and Dowry Prohibition Act have not been made overnight but are the results of centuries-old struggles and sacrifices of countless lives and attempts for an equal and just society. If the minorities who ought to be protected *by* the judiciary, in turn, have be protected *from* the judiciary's arbitrariness and insensitivity, the integrity of the judiciary becomes questionable. The judiciary is an arbiter of justice for whom? Is it simply to protect the privileges of the ruling class? And equally importantly, what makes the institution decide whom it functions for? These are precisely the issues that Ambedkar warned us about.

Protection of Minorities through Judicial Diversity

Firstly, the Indian judiciary has been dominantly comprised of the elite class for seventy years. It is high time the judiciary reflected the diversity and social composition of Indian society. Secondly, in a country where caste created citadels of power, the ruling classes held a monopoly over decision-making for centuries. As expressed by Justice Rathnavel Pandian, the right of entry into a superior judicial office is not the exclusive prerogative of any privileged class or group of people. It is neither inheritable nor a matter of patronage. If the vulnerable sections of the people are completely neglected, we cannot claim to have achieved real participatory democracy.[56] Therefore, dismantling the Brahminical structure of the judiciary through proportional social representation and the reformation of judicial appointments is a must to effectuate the moral right of the historically oppressed, minorities and weaker sections.

At present, judges to the Supreme Court and high courts are selected through the collegium system consisting of five senior-most judges and are directly appointed by the President in consultation with the chief justice of India (CJI) to the Supreme Court and in consultation with the governor and chief justice of the state to high courts. However, the collegium does not have to give reasons for selection. Thus, to bring transparency to the appointments, the legislature passed the National Judicial Appointments Commission (NJAC) Act, 2014, with the CJI as chairperson and five other members from the legislature and executive, together with the Constitutional (99th Amendment) Act, 2014, amending the method of appointment in the Constitution. But the Supreme Court struck down both the acts as unconstitutional.[57] While the collegium—introduced with a view to expanding representation—has not resulted in any change, the NJAC does not offer any deliberate improvements beyond transparency. Thus, it is imperative to develop alternative ways that will bring diversity and inclusivity in the judiciary.

How Judges' Appointments Hamper Justice in India

The Indian judiciary has been retaining its basic Brahminical structure. From the time of the adoption of the Constitution of India, judges of the Supreme Court have largely been the products of socially prestigious and economically advantaged families.[58] A comparison of the first list of Supreme Court judges from 1950–67 with the list of sitting judges of the Supreme Court[59] reveals that except for a scheduled caste and an OBC judge, the structure has not changed.

In 1982, of the 325 high court judges only four were from the scheduled castes.[60] In 1983, of the nearly 400 high court judges, only six were members of the scheduled castes, and there was no judge from the scheduled tribes.[61] By 1993, only thirteen out of 547 judges were from the scheduled castes. In 2002, the Supreme Court had one scheduled caste judge out of twenty-six judges and one scheduled tribe judge,[62] while the high courts had 25 SC/ST out of 625 judges.[63] Of the thirty-three Supreme Court judges at present, only one is from the scheduled castes, that too after a decade since the retirement of Justice K.G. Balakrishnan in

2010; over 80 per cent are Brahmins and upper castes.[64] It is also known that Justice B.R. Gavai, who was appointed to the Supreme Court in 2019, became the first judge belonging to the scheduled castes to be appointed in almost a decade. And there continues to be no chief justices of high courts who belong to the SC and ST communities.

This data shows how caste factors have played a role in the appointment of judges. The social background of judges has a direct correlation with the decision-making process. The values and beliefs influenced by the personal background and life experiences of the judges impact the exercise of discretion in the decision-making process and have a consequent effect in the decisions reached. A study of the Indian Supreme Court judges reveals that almost all the judges come from a homogeneous socio-economic background, with similar social and life experiences.[65] Many of them are second-generation judges and have had either a practising lawyer or a politically involved parent or a family member. The primary problem in having such a homogeneous judiciary is how it affects judicial behaviour.

The more socially alike the judges are, the more unanimous the judgments. During the first decade after Independence, 93 per cent of Supreme Court decisions were unanimous.[66] This is so even today, and the few dissenting judges either agree with the majority decision, but for different reasons, or such judges tend to change their voting behaviour in due course. Another problem we often encounter with the judiciary is that its foresight is far from the societal reality. The judges do not get to think or know the impact of the judicial decisions, or line of decisions, they make.

An individual's narrow social world can restrict their understanding of social structures and the handicaps they impose on certain groups. There is a need for varied voices, which bring along with them varied perspectives from their own experiences in life. No one can speak for the other better than the person who has lived that experience. The collegium system can have its own social markers and therefore blinders, too. It is one of the most opaque systems, which was not envisaged even by the makers of the Constitution. As T.M. Krishna puts it, 'Even a judge with an impeccable record, who believes that he is dispassionate, can see things based only on his life experience. Hence the more socially privileged he is, the more limited his life experience. Therefore, it is necessary that, in a democracy, we have people with different life experiences as part of the higher judiciary. The system must structurally compensate for social blinders. In Indian society, the trajectory of an individual is inextricably connected to his or her caste.'[67]

And this possibly makes the judges of the Supreme Court express views such as: 'For how many generations will reservations continue?'[68] 'This may be a beginning; all reservations may go and only EWS may remain, but these are all policies.'[69] 'It was for the Government to take a decision on dismantling caste and reservations.'[70] This was while hearing submissions for extending reservation to the Maratha community in public education and employment under the Maharashtra State Reservation for Socially and Educationally Backward Classes (SEBC) Act, 2018, in the case 'Jaishri Laxmanrao Patil vs Chief Minister'.[71]

In the author's view, the judges were asking the wrong questions. The questions should have been:[72] 'When will caste-based discrimination come to an end?'; 'Why are the backward classes not represented in the higher positions of state services, including the judiciary?'; 'Why is reservation not being implemented in letter and spirit?'; 'Why are the backlog vacancies of these classes not filled?'; 'What is the sanctity of economically weaker sections reservation when economic backwardness was not accepted as a standalone ground for providing reservation in "Indra Sawhney" (1992)?'; 'How can the Union government recruit directly to higher positions in civil services through lateral entry, bypassing the constitutional provisions?'; 'Why are public enterprises being privatized on such a large scale?'; 'Why is there no reservation in the private sector?'[73]

P. Shiv Shankar, who was the Union law minister in the 1980s, raised several pertinent issues regarding the composition of the judiciary when he made a speech on the occasion of the silver jubilee of the Bar Council of Andhra Pradesh in Hyderabad. P.N. Duda complained to the Supreme Court that Shankar had committed contempt, but the Supreme Court declined to take any action for contempt.[74] The points raised in Shankar's speech as questioned in the case were:

> The Supreme Court composed of the element from the elite class had their *unconcealed* sympathy for the haves i.e. the Zamindars . . . [italics supplied]
> (a) '. . . Anti-social elements, i.e. FERA violators, bride burners and a whole horde of reactionaries *have found their haven* in the Supreme Court.' [italics supplied]

P. Shiv Shankar and B. Shankaranand as law ministers in the late '80s went on to change the composition of the Supreme Court for the first time. George F. Gadbois's book, *Judges of the Supreme Court of India*, concluded on the basis of empirical data that between 1950 and 1989, 92.2 per cent of the Supreme Court comprised male Brahmins and other forward castes. Not much has changed since. A testimony to this is the fact that Chief Justice K.G. Balakrishnan is the first and only CJI belonging to the scheduled castes out of forty-seven chief justices of India.[75] Gadbois writes:

> As forty years drew to a close, there began a major change in the caste composition of the Court. Following the appointment of N. D. Ojha in January 1988, there was not a brahmin among the next dozen appointees. The explanation for this turnaround was the fact that B. Shankaranand of the

Scheduled Caste community, and P. Shiv Shankar of the OBC community, were law ministers in 1988 and 1989. By the end of 1989, a spate of appointments had increased the number of judges to twenty-five. Only seven were brahmins. These appointments are evidence of caste being a selection criterion. Evidence that it was a criterion earlier when the first Scheduled Caste and OBC judges were appointed is impeachable.[76]

A Case for Reservations in the Higher Judiciary

While subordinate posts have reservations, the higher judiciary does not. As a result, it took thirty years for the first scheduled caste and another eight years for the first OBC to reach the Supreme Court. Justice A. Varadarajan, a member of the scheduled castes, was appointed as a Supreme Court judge in 1980 and later, in 1988, Justice S. Rathnavel Pandian, an OBC, was appointed as a Supreme Court judge.[77] It is noteworthy that both the SC and OBC judges were from the High Court of Madras. But the question here is: How was Tamil Nadu able to do so, and why other states could not? It is because there was effort in Tamil Nadu to commit to a politics and principle of social justice and reformation. As a result of this policy decision, the state became more diverse and inclusive in judicial appointments than any other in the country. Such state efforts heightened the consciousness of representational rights, leading to a lawyers' protest in 2016 against the list of names recommended for the appointment of judges. The protesters demanded that in the list of names, of people who could be recommended for appointment to the post of high court judges, there shall be no one from the Brahmin, Mudaliar, Gounder and Pillai communities; and that persons belonging to hitherto-unrepresented communities should alone be recommended hereafter for appointment.

The core of these demands—the representation of the most underrepresented groups—is an eventuality of the culture of social justice championed by the state in Tamil Nadu. Therefore, the takeaway is that wilful commitment of the state in invoking the reservation policy is inevitable to ensure the representation of minorities in judicial appointments.

Also, though much required, the All India Judicial Services (AIJS) is a stillborn concept, with the idea itself facing strong opposition from the higher judiciary—in spite of the fact that Parliament amended Article 312 in 1976 to incorporate a provision for its establishment. Article 312(1) says that Parliament can pass an act to provide for the creation of the AIJS while Article 312(3) says the AIJS cannot include a post inferior to the rank of district judge. Yet, four decades after Parliament passed the amendment, the AIJS remains just an idea. The Law Commission of India, in at least three reports—the 14th (1958), 77th (1978) and 116th (1986)—recommended the creation of the AIJS. Even the Supreme Court, in its judgment in the 'All India Judges Association vs Union of India'[78] case, recommended that the feasibility of establishing the AIJS be examined.[79]

The UPA government prepared a comprehensive roadmap for the constitution of the AIJS, and the same was cleared by a committee of secretaries in November 2012. However, the opposition to the plan has come mainly from within the judiciary, with several high courts[80] and some state governments opposing it on the grounds that inadequate knowledge of regional languages[81] could make the judges' job extremely difficult. But when the issue was taken up for discussion at the 2013 Conference of Chief Ministers and Chief Justices, there was no unanimity. The Madras, Andhra Pradesh, Bombay, Delhi, Punjab and Haryana, Gujarat, Karnataka, Madhya Pradesh and Patna high courts opposed it. Consensus eluded the issue at the 2015 Conference of Chief Ministers and Chief Justices, too. This has allowed successive governments to keep the issue in cold storage.[82]

In 2000, while the NDA was in power, the Parliamentary Committee on the Welfare of Scheduled Castes and Scheduled Tribes, headed by Kariya Munda, suggested in a report to the government that the latter take steps to amend Articles 217 and 124 of the Constitution to give adequate representation to the deprived sections in the higher judiciary.[83] It stated, 'Judges take oath that they [will] uphold the Constitution and the laws. But the Supreme Court and a few high courts, by claiming power over the Constitution, practise untouchability and are disobeying the Constitution with regard to Article 16(4) and Article 16(4A).'[84] Even the National Commission for Scheduled Castes, in a report on reservation in the judiciary, submitted to the President in 2013, pointed to the insensitivity of the judiciary towards SCs/STs, stating unequivocally:

> . . . despite suggestion of the Ministry of Home Affairs, the Supreme Court has so far not attempted to frame suitable recruitment rules for reservation of SC/STs. It is deplorable that framing of codified recruitment rules have not been finalized during the last 61 years. Judges take oath to uphold the constitution & the law of the land but even Hon'ble Supreme Court has failed to follow the Constitutional provision under Article 16(4) & 16(4A).[85]

If adequate representation could not be attained on its own even after seven decades of independence, it is high time that explicit provision is made for such reservation and representation for the backward classes among the judges of the Supreme Court and high courts.

Enhancing Diversity in India's Justice System

Apart from judges having courtroom experience, we need judges who can understand the purposes of laws and the implications of their decisions, and empathetically approach the cases before them. According to Article 124(3) of the Constitution of India, the qualification for appointment as a judge of the Supreme Court is:

At least five years as a Judge of a High Court; or
At least ten years as an advocate of a High Court; or
In the opinion of the President, a distinguished jurist.

Although the term 'jurist' was not defined in the Constitution, it can be interpreted as a legal scholar or an expert of law, such as professors who have expertise in a particular area of law. Justice Felix Frankfurter, of the Supreme Court of the United States, was the first radical judge to openly speak about the impact of judicial decisions of the Supreme Court on the American government and society at large. He advocated judicial restraint throughout his tenure which postulates that courts should not interpret the Constitution in a way that imposes limits on the authority of the legislative and executive branches. He has expressed his harsh self-doubt and agony concerning the practical consequences of judicial decisions. This was because he was a law professor first and a justice later.[86] A further and liberal interpretation of 'expert of law' would include rights-based lawyers.

Justice V.R. Krishna Iyer, who introduced the concepts of Legal Aid Movement, safeguards against custodial excesses and made bail a fundamental right, was an activist–lawyer who went to jail for his underprivileged clients. It is evident that the pioneering decisions that he made were heavily informed by his time in activism. Scholars and activists who have witnessed the barriers faced by the minorities in the justice-delivery system are more likely to pronounce orders that are shaped by their understanding of the social disabilities faced by such groups. Thus, it is critical to reconsider the aristocratic yardsticks of eligibility and to allow the appointment of persons who have dedicated their entire career to the cause of justice.

Conclusion

It is time to confront the elite institutionalism in the judiciary and challenge the citadels of power that oppose any reform. The marginalized sections of this country have always had faith in the judiciary. It is primarily because they believe that the Constitution is made by 'Our Babasaheb Dr Ambedkar',[87] and so the judiciary has all the moral and constitutional responsibilities of serving justice to them. And a judiciary that is progressive, anti-caste and anti-majoritarian understands its duty to conserve that public confidence in the justice system. A diverse, inclusive and representative judiciary will only make justice more accessible and equitable. Our judiciary should be well aware that protecting minorities' interests is the only way to safeguard a country's democracy and, indeed, its very existence.

Leveraging International Institutions to Address Casteism

Suraj Yengde

Introduction

'We don't talk about it. It occasionally happens in India, and it is changing. God, why do you bring these things here?' said one of the students during my studies in the UK. These echoes were heard in South Africa and the United States. The 'it' referred to the issue that no one wants to touch or engage with: caste. Caste has come to my face whenever I tried to assert my Dalit identity. Every non-Dalit who is bitterly embarrassed with the mention of caste outside India takes this as an assault on their deification of Indian nationhood. Whatever India constitutes for them is an appreciation of their lived experience, which is about diversity and culture. A privileged-class, dominant-caste individual can only relate to the media image of India, which is a PR set-up of 'Incredible India'. Thus, the non-Dalits rarely pay sympathetic attention to Indian Dalit or tribal life. My claim to my Dalithood is taken as an affront against India's unity, as if Dalits do not constitute India and caste is not persistent in the country.

Caste has the ability to mutate. This gives it an opportunity to expand without resistance. The idea of caste stabilizes the social pressures through claims that it is a rational and historical condition. Therefore, caste has managed to transcend in various quarters outside its original location. Caste in India originally developed in Brahminical Hinduism and later moved into other religions. Today, there is hardly any religion that can claim caste neutrality in the subcontinent. Along with this, caste's tendency to adjust with culture, religion, social habits and belief has given it a further lifeline. There is hardly any commonly acceptable position against caste. Each society invested in the hierarchy has taken a stand in favour of caste. That is why caste has managed to give global acceptability to a local practice.

Almost all the caste groups across the world have the validity of history and tradition. The diaspora from the subcontinent has taken caste to a heightened status of dogma, where it is preserved without being overtly discussed in the host society.[1] The practice and norm are retained in their original form by virtue of the internal structure of South Asian society—mostly family and community. Caste is thus an Indian problem with a global presence. So an approach to end caste has to be initiated with the originator of caste—Indian society—so as to create a template for the rest of the world.

In this essay, I will present a brief history of how caste came to rise in our popular imagination. Building on this, I will offer insights into the theoretical construction of caste, followed by the various disciplinary approaches that attempted to understand the problem of caste and propose a way out for caste-related isms from the structural ideals instituted through various institutions. The institutionalization of caste has produced two contradictions: 1) the dilemma over underscoring the historicity of caste, and 2) encouraging cultural parameters that uphold caste and caste-related virtues.

The study of caste and caste-related factors are mostly confined to the academic repertoire premised on Western academe. The broader disciplines that engage with the issue of caste are mostly in the social sciences, followed by economics and literature. Disciplines such as anthropology, sociology, political science, history, literature, comparative literature, developmental economics and welfare economics have attempted to estimate the impact of caste in our society.

But by only academizing the experience of caste, the discourse has remained frozen. It was only open to fixed analyses, with their inflexible dicta. Caste, therefore, was a settled phenomenon that would only proffer creative apparatus to control the body politic and macro societal operation. It was meant to regulate society and divide it for better governance. Castes were not meant to be oppressive in their original avatar. However, through the brute force of the ruling class to control the most productive labour, it was made rigid and inflexible.

This is an explanation held by one school of thought. As much as this approach strengthened the academic canonical thinking, it did not expand further. It did not aim to uproot the edifice of caste upon which most of our thinking, caste-wise, developed over centuries. Thus, the character of caste was casteized on every level of macro-sociological functioning of Indian society. The apparatus to challenge casteism was localized, and thereby the doors to take it to a global level were shut by the Indian state and other international diaspora based outside India, be it in east and southern Africa or in North America.[2] It is through this contextual departing point that I will look at the possible roles of international institutions to address casteism.

Formation of Caste Studies

Caste studies as a disciplinary academic approach was strengthened in the religious texts of the Vedas, which sponsored casteism, and, more particularly, the Rigveda. The Purusha Sukta's verse 12 made a definitive mention of the Brahmans as the superior mouth (profane head), followed by the Vaisya and the Shudra:

The Brahman was his mouth, of both his arms was the
Rājanya made.
His thighs became the Vaiśya, from his feet the Śūdra was
produced.[3]

Kautilya's *Arthashastra*, popularly known as a scientific treatise on
economic, political and military policies, was one of the earlier
texts that regimented the corporeal bodies and prescribed various
kinds of punishments towards people. The infamous Book III
of the *Arthashastra* recommends draconian punitive actions. The
punishments get more severe as we descend to the lower rungs
in the social hierarchy. Punitive legalities govern in the case of
remarriage of women (chapter IV), dividing inheritance (chapter
V) and in the rescission of purchase and sale of land (chapter
XV), particularly in relation to persons of the 'fallen caste' or
'persons born of outcaste men, and eunuchs'.[4] The Manusmriti,
a legal text composed by Sumathi Bhargava around 200 CE and
developed over several centuries, strengthened the control over
the casteized communities and women, relegating them to a low
social status.

In modern canonical knowledge production, B.R. Ambedkar
was to theorize the origins of caste and then deploy that armory
against the condescending socio-legal atrocities through the Indian
Constitution and the Hindu Code Bill, which granted autonomy to
women and oppressed caste groups to own property, inherit wealth
and assert reproductive rights. Therefore, it becomes imperative to
take stock of the history of such theories up to the colonial era that
crystallized the operations of caste.

Given the historical evidence of the development of caste
theory, especially in India, one wonders how to de-hagiographize
the institution of caste so that we reach to the bottom of casteism
and use various methods to uproot the causes for it.

I suggest four methods that will help us in leveraging
international institutions:

1. UN route
2. Academic institutions
3. Think tanks
4. Civil society solidarity

UN Route

Although for its own political benefits the colonial government did extend help to the Dalits under the leadership of Ambedkar, its overall goal to emancipate the Dalits was limited, owing to its self-serving investment in India's politics and overwhelming control of Brahminical interests that acted against the Dalits. Ambedkar's demands to free the untouchables from the clutches of Hindu control created a rift with dominant caste Hindus who were at the helm of the Congress party. Under the leadership of M.K. Gandhi, the feud between Gandhi and Ambedkar heightened. Ambedkar felt betrayed by Gandhi during the 1932 Poona Pact and the succeeding years when dealing with the Congress government.[5] This policy of suppressing a Dalit agency continued in the post-Independence national framework.

The pre- and post-Independence eras have been mired by the duplicitous agenda of the Indian government's task on tackling human rights abuses at home. Nehru undertook the UN-level fight against apartheid in South Africa and even co-sponsored resolutions imposing sanctions on South Africa.[6] Nehru also issued Indian travel documents to South African revolutionaries like Oliver Tambo and Yusuf Dadoo. This was an ideal anti-colonial legacy that Nehru wanted to preserve the world over.[7] He, however, did not take up India's caste issue on any international forum. As, referring to caste segregation in India, Ambedkar once observed, 'South Africa is replicated in every Indian village.'[8] The All India Scheduled Castes Federation passed a memorandum prepared by Ambedkar in 1947, which stated that the 'tyranny and the constant and shameless resort to violence by Hindus, makes the position of the Scheduled Castes far worse than the position of Indians in South Africa'.[9] South African prime minister D.F. Malan went to the level of challenging the Nehru government over the treatment of India's untouchables.[10] Referring to the South African Blacks, Malan retorted that at least 'they were better off than Black people in the USA as well as untouchables in India'.[11]

The Indian government ensured that the embarrassing and poignant question of caste was not raised. It went to the level of doing a back-door agreement with the apartheid government, whom it had chosen to shame and publicly fight against by becoming the frontrunner of post-colonial solidarity.[12] This became a hymn of a sacred foreign policy doctrine. Successive prime ministers of various hues and colours successively adopted this as a mantra and aggressively worked against the protection of human rights of the Dalits.

Brahminism—which was not only casteist but racist, as it maintained an unequal recognition of Africans as of 'lower-caste Indians'—was exported in India's foreign-policy visions.[13] The Indian Foreign Service officials were almost all Brahmins and from other dominant caste groups.[14] This elevation of the dominant castes ensured that the issue of caste remained anathema and that it would not be exposed on international platforms.[15]

Ambedkar's UN Route

B.R. Ambedkar, on the contrary, was committed to making caste an issue of international concern. He saw this as the only way to get required justice for the Dalit community, which was put on the receiving end by the Indian National Congress and Jinnah's Muslim League. Up to the Lahore Resolution, the Dalits were confident that a minority alliance between the Dalits and Muslims would help both the groups to fight in the Hindu-majority country.[16] However, after the Lahore Resolution, this partnership was out of the question and thus, Ambedkar started actively seeking international alliances.[17]

Pursuant to this, Ambedkar ensured that he took in confidence the British political class and general public that was invested in India. His 1946 trip to England, to advocate for international relief for the Dalits, has been analysed by Jesús Cháirez-Garza in his paper 'B.R. Ambedkar, Partition and the Internationalization of Untouchability, 1939–47'.[18] Cháirez-Garza argues that after his failure to secure rights from the imperial government, Ambedkar embarked to meet with the leaders of the British parliament. Prominent among them was the Conservative Party leader Winston Churchill. Ambedkar also made representations to the leadership of various political parties and MPs from the Labour Party, Conservative Party and the Fabians.[19]

Ambedkar's diplomatic move to garner international support was stopped by the influence of M.K. Gandhi, who preferred to not 'negotiate' with Ambedkar for fear of losing on 'both fronts'.[20] For Ambedkar, the call of the Indian nationalists for self-determination—'Swaraj'—while defying the purpose of minority rights protection, was betrayal and unbecoming of a nation state. Thus, he chose to approach the UN after his failure to receive adequate support from the Opposition and the government.[21] This time, Vallabhbhai Patel, along with other Congress leaders, approached Ambedkar to negotiate.[22] Gandhi continued to distrust Ambedkar's efforts. In a reply to a letter by Carl Heath, a member of the Indian Conciliation Group who was an ardent follower of Gandhi, the latter did not exhibit sympathy to Ambedkar's cause of internationalizing the struggle of the untouchables. Referring to Ambedkar, Gandhi added, 'with men like him the end justifies the means', and he refused to meet or entertain Ambedkar's pressing demands.[23]

The cause of Ambedkar was, however, echoed by Churchill and Jan Smuts, prime minister of South Africa, at international meetings and the United Nations.[24] Smuts used the issue of untouchability to silence the hypocritical Indian government delegation led by Maharaj Singh, former governor of Bombay, who pressed for the rights of Indians in South Africa at the UN. Both Churchill and Smuts, colonial warlords, used untouchability for their own politics. The untouchables, however, remained the suppressed subjects, in spite of their sound political presence. Ambedkar got a seat in Nehru's first cabinet as a law minister but was not given the important portfolios he had hoped for. In his resignation letter, Ambedkar elucidated various reasons for his exit.[25] He was tokenized in the administration without having been given any substantive powers.

Ambedkar had not taken the case of the untouchables to the UN in 1947. His reasoning was premised on trusting the Constituent Assembly and the future Parliament of India, which he hoped would accord required rights to the untouchables. He was wrong, and thus his bitterness grew towards the ruling dispensation. Ambedkar also perhaps did not pursue the UN route aggressively, because he was hoping to get into the Constituent Assembly so he could channel the Constitution towards this goal. However, provisions made in the Constitution for the scheduled castes did not impress him. He bluntly stated in the resignation letter that:

> . . . the provisions made in the Constitution for safeguarding the position of the Scheduled Castes were not to my satisfaction. However, I accepted them for what they were worth, hoping that the Government will show some determination to make them effective. What is the position of the Scheduled Castes today? So far as I see, it is the same as before. The same old tyranny, the same old oppression, the same old discrimination which existed before, exists now, and perhaps in a worst form.[26]

This was a damning self-indictment of the leader of the scheduled castes who had hoped to secure their future in a Brahmin–Baniya-ruled independent India. Getting Ambedkar into the Constituent Assembly worked mutually for Ambedkar and the

Congress party. However, the causes Ambedkar espoused were subdued and could not see the light. The internationalization of the Dalit cause and the intervention of the UN on the caste issue would have been an embarrassment for India. Perhaps there was some unwritten, silent agreement between the Congress and Ambedkar when he threatened to take India to the UN, which would work in delegitimizing the leadership of dominant caste Hindus in a recently independent nation. And this would also mean taking down the third-world, coloured people's internationalism that Nehru wanted to champion. These questions remain with us, but the indifference of the UN towards the issue of caste continues.

Lessons Learnt: Further Actions

To resolve the matter of untouchability and caste-related atrocity in India, there isn't any other legitimate body, apart from Indian courts, that can serve justice to the Dalit population. However, internationally, there are two prominent bodies that have jurisdiction to address the Dalit's plight: first, the United Nations and its various treaty bodies; and second, the International Court of Justice and the International Criminal Court.

The United Nations as an international lawmaking intergovernmental body carries the definitive weight to help get the attention of the world to caste-based issues. They have some measures in place that relate to caste-based discrimination.[27] But due to the Indian government's hostility towards any discussion on caste-related issues at the UN, there has not been any significant progress in making caste a mainstream point for mediation on human rights abuses.[28]

An ugly feud between Dalit activists and the Indian government was seen during the World Conference Against Racism, Racial Discrimination, Xenophobia and Related Intolerance at Durban in 2001. The Indian government refused to acknowledge caste

as a category that could be considered within the framework
of discrimination at Durban. It dismissed the demands of the
Dalits for recognizing caste discrimination on the global scale.
Due to the government's diplomatic foul play, caste now features
alongside other analogous forms of discrimination, which deprives
it of its unique position as a historical, religion-supported form
of oppression.

The United Nations, too, has had a chequered history.
Conceived in the post-World War II era, it had a vested interest
in retaining the colonial order that was now losing its grip. After
fighting the Great War, the imperial economies saw devastating
losses. They could not hold their foreign colonies together amid
growing protests from nationalist movements in the colonies.
Therefore, to retain control, the United Nations devised pacifist
and human rights-centric policies.

This gave the framers of the United Nations, which had a
Judeo–Christian ethic, an upper hand to intervene in countries that
did not adhere to the principles of UN-defined human rights.[29] The
rights lens was built upon moral constraints and punitive measures.
Philosophically, those values were anti-human and oppressive.
They were meant to promote peace and restraint. However, the
promoters of human rights also saw that peace as a non-violent
doctrine would not be applicable in societies whose cultural
and political conditions did not align with the Judeo–Christian
formulation of human rights.

Thus, the conflicts that arose in this regard have been met with
equally invasive and destructive methods led by the preachers of
human rights. It is in this light that one has to consider the UN
as an instrument that could be utilized for advancing our goals
of protecting the lives of the Dalit population—the sixth largest
autonomous group in the world if it chose to have a country of
its own. But with the limitations of the UN in sight, one should
find ways to work through those blind spots with scepticism and
constantly look for alternatives.

This would give political credibility to the struggles of the Dalit rights movement. Juridical proceedings should be part of international activism wherein international laws are invoked and a possible action, with international judicial apparatus, is considered. Many international legal instruments, such as the International Criminal Court, and almost all the conventions and treaties of the UN human rights body are available, and yet caste-related atrocities, the silent genocide, are committed with impunity.[30] In the past ten years, close to half a million crimes were reported against the Dalits.[31] The statistics are an indictment against any institution that has failed to uphold the human rights, dignity, safety and security of its citizens.

With the available avenues, the United Nations body could be a catalyst in putting pressure on the Indian government, which has been apathetic to the suffering of the Dalits in India. The Indian government needs to fully embrace the ideas of Ambedkar, who, in his lifelong struggle, tried to get the Dalits recognized by the world governments because in a country ruled by the oppressive majority, the minority communities cannot secure their rights. He strongly emphasized the jurisdiction of the UN over the scheduled castes in India. Acknowledging its past mistakes, the Indian government should follow the ideals of the founders of our democratic republic and open itself up to the humanitarian scrutiny of the world that is beyond politics. India's excessive focus on Kashmir as a foreign-policy dictum has come at the cost of human rights abuses of the scheduled castes.

Academic institutions

Academic institutions of foreign countries play the role of a catalyst in cementing social and cultural relationships with the host country. Academic institutions also carry the reputation of being cultural powerhouses of the country. The intellectuals and researchers in these institutions add immense value to the future projects of bilateralism and knowledge exchange and partnership.

Many of these academic institutions can be potentially leveraged to elevate the cause of caste-related topics. But due to the absence of focused research agenda on caste, such institutions have remained distant from proffering important and timely interventions on the issues affecting caste subjects.

A dedicated chair in research institutes would help push for a composite agenda of caste studies. An endowment to the chair by the government or through private philanthropy would effect the desired change in narrative-building and compilation of facts for wider public consumption.

In addition to the investment in the chair, doctoral-level scholarship initiatives for Dalit students to pursue higher education would enable capacity-building among Dalit students. A Dalit student is the most important resource for the Dalit community's liberation. If exposed to worldly knowledge and quality education, s/he can gain access to cutting-edge research projects and laboratories that would offer an opportunity for our knowledge to expand.

Dalit students should also be exposed to exchange initiatives and au pair programmes. Exchange initiatives concentrating on marginalized students could help the students to expect more from their lives. The confidence gained in an overseas environment and knowledge acquired through various cultures can create awareness and sensitivity towards the world.

Their exposure to global cultures and ways of life at a young age could help change the narratives surrounding their own experiences as 'low-born' or stigmatized people. Instilling confidence in Dalit students should be a priority. For this to take effect, an international Dalit students' committee needs to be established, which would support, promote and advise Dalit students in their research and learning, and expose them to diverse global situations by placing them in conversation with other similarly oppressed groups, so that they can derive strength and inspiration from each other.

Through this exposure, the Dalits can be educated about the other groups' struggles and exposed to their social realities. This cross-cultural education will help both groups to develop newer connections and build solidarity. This appreciation of other cultures would persuade students to gain maturity and harness an independently informed world view.

The government should create special foreign scholarship programmes for students from the Dalit and adivasi backgrounds. MoUs with various foreign governments and educational institutes from diverse fields could help this work. Students who are trained from a young age to aspire to study in a foreign country will be a good investment in establishing concrete partnerships and expanding diplomatic efforts. Students from STEM, law, the social sciences, humanities and journalism would play an important part in building the international institutional agenda. An international network of student bodies sensitive to the issues of caste and social justice from diverse ethnicities and nationalities would help to organize discussions and debates about the progress of the Dalits and other oppressed caste groups.

The academic institutions would help create more experts who would offer advice on dealing with issues of importance. To tackle the challenges at hand, a set of independent experts placed in academic institutions or think tanks would help to push for more credible public debates among an international network of students.

Think Tanks

Think tanks are the bedrocks of any policy. The snowballing of credible think tanks has advantaged the work of lobbying groups and legislators engaged on critical tasks. To support the work of the two institutions mentioned earlier—the UN and academic organizations—think tanks could become an ideal convening space for people from various disciplines and background willing to contribute to the cause of liberation.

A strong policy on liberty and equality needs to be devised, backed by evidence comprising empirical data. This work can be handled by think tanks. In the age of globalization, focusing on policy directives and their global impact has been one of the tasks of governments and non-governmental bodies worldwide. Drawing from global experiences and applying it to local contexts can be a possible way out for handling the macro issues at hand.

It is with this prospect that those think tanks that are solely devoted to the promotion of caste-related issues and the welfare of the oppressed peoples need to be prioritized. Currently, there is no international-level autonomous institution acting as a think tank that has professional researchers, writers, policymakers and academics to concentrate on the caste question.

Caste has adjusted into the structures of our society. It has become invisible and yet has continued its stronghold upon our mindset and policies. It is through institutionalized casteism that psychological and administrative casteism takes effect. This gives rise to casteist policies, much like the 'racist policies' that are exclusionary in every measure and aimed at strengthening the 'racist power'.[32] Such power measures empower the citizenry as well as institutions to invoke caste more proactively against the caste subject. The structures of system play a part in ensuring its tight grip over oppressed bodies.

Therefore, to upend the structures of the power, a think tank project will probably help in crafting new policy measures to keep in check every policy-level intervention on behalf of the government. Such policy think tanks would be tasked with bringing domestic and international perspectives to caste narratives. What kinds of organizations or states could be potential allies for the cause of taking up caste-related issues at the international level? Think tanks could be a bridge for local policymakers, international governments and private donor agencies. Various development-related projects and their implementation need to be validated at every level. Think tanks could be an independent social and political public audit that will cater to the needs of the oppressed caste subjects.

A team of independent experts from the disciplines of social sciences, social policy, political science, economics, environment, health, science, military and technology would help to frame the research objectives effectively to get a wholesome picture of caste humanity. A collaborative, cross-disciplinary approach in crafting research thematics would help diversify goals and strategies in reaching critical solutions.

Strategizing around political issues is of paramount importance for research dynamics to play well. Think tanks can help us understand the potentialities and possibilities with which Dalit issues can be dealt at an international level. State and non-state think tanks can lobby with diverse constituencies and be the power brokers at the centres of decision-making. To address the causes affecting the poor and marginalized peoples, a strategic location and development of thought need to be channelized. Think tanks are about evidence-guided interdisciplinary research that can help us prepare better for taking on the complexity of caste. Thus, we need to set agendas that bolster ideas and put them into action. Think tanks can transform ideas into action by facilitating critical conversations at conferences, workshops and seminars on caste-specific topics.

Think tanks can also help us process credible information based on research to connect, or not, with other groups of importance. The Dalit community is severely under-resourced as far as building global solidarity is concerned. Due to the overwhelming influence of NGOs, a progressive, cross-border agenda has not been fully formed. The other oppressed groups barely know of caste-like systems and about the Dalits who are working proactively to end such oppression. This information could potentially be relevant in their context. Around the world, be it Africa or elsewhere, caste-like systems have persisted. Colonial anthropology has elevated the understanding of caste. Now, we need to revisit this issue and start a healthy debate around it.

Since caste mostly falls in the ambit of the post-colonial, Global South framework, a determined focus to probe civil society functions through these areas of approach could work well. A concentrated focus on politicizing the Dalit experience and atrocity, and making these issues of concern for international peace and security could be a step in the right direction—it can make the international community aware of the Dalit experience. This fits with the mandates of the Indian Constitution. Article 51(a) has clear instructions to the state: promote international peace and security.[33]

The role of think tanks as influential negotiators needs be instrumentalized. The right approach for Dalit liberation has to be tied in with global actors in similar situations; yet, we can't divert our attention from the unique existential caste factors that make up the conditions for Dalit oppression. In this regard, civil society groups are important partners in taking the issues of caste to other important social and political forums.

Civil Society Solidarity with Similar Oppressed Groups

This is an important field that requires political parties and social movements to play a proactive role. Civil society, without a social-movement agenda, cannot proceed to further its longer-term agenda.

Globally, there are recognized non-governmental organizations who have vast experience in dealing with the state and other institutions. These need to be tapped for creating a robust alliance and partnership. In total, there are 4045 NGOs officially recognized by the United Nations under the ECOSOC's (Economic and Social Council) 'General' consultative status.[34] Not one of these international NGOs has caste as its central focus.

Many organizations which deal with issues related to race, gender and descent-based discrimination can be effective allies. One could take on the issue of Dalit rights in their advocacy and simultaneously build cross solidarity for the Dalits to stand for other groups. A programme needs to be drafted that aligns the Dalit civil rights struggle with other groups worldwide that are fighting for the land rights of the landless people, against unlawful incarceration, state oppression and lack of representation in positions of power. Global social movements have an internationally relevant agenda—against privatization, neo-liberalism and militarism. Dalit groups that align with these mandates need to add their voice and support to the issues that impact human rights violations of any groups without paying heed to any political calculations. The minorities of Europe—the Roma and other persecuted groups, the indigenous, religious and national minorities, and the sexually oppressed groups—are potential allies with whom the Dalits can build solidarity.

In addition, a concentrated movement has to be developed, demanding for reparations from the Dalit perspective. A global movement for reparations is in operation, seeking repatriation for the losses incurred by oppressed groups. The reparations go beyond monetary compensation. There are moral, ethical and humane acknowledgements that the oppressor groups need to make. It's the first step towards correcting historical injustices. The Dalits need to align with other groups fighting for the rightful restitution of their dignity and respect. The Dalit experience needs to be repaired. A mass-scale healing needs to be emphasized, as well as education campaigns to enable Dalit groups to acknowledge their past. A potential alliance could be developed with and along the lines of the Global Reparations Movement based in Guyana at the Caribbean Community (CARICOM) secretariat that caters to the needs of groups seeking reparations. These groups include people from different parts of the world, from the Caribbean, Latin America and Australasia to Africa and the USA.[35]

Conclusion

The Dalit community needs a strong diplomatic undertaking of their issues. Government as well as non-governmental institutions can play a huge part in this. The cultural and academic spaces should be captured by the Dalits—these can be deployed in developing relations with other cultures and peoples. In addition to this, the role of the media is highly crucial. The narratives of Dalits and their experiences need to be sensitively approached and written to establish a conversation with global culture and politics. Dalit-related academic, cultural and literary organizations should be given adequate opportunity to interact and develop relations with other groups, besides having their own voice to raise their concerns at the UN. The casteist strategy of not acknowledging the persistence of caste at the UN level has exposed the double standards of the Indian government. By not having a discussion on caste at the international level, the Indian government has made itself complicit in the atrocities committed on the Dalits. The possible justification for this is to claim that 'caste is an internal matter', a historical misjudgment that continues to date.

The Indian government and Opposition political parties should demonstrate their commitment to the Constitution and love for the Dalits, and for Ambedkar, by submitting to international political checks. This would demonstrate their commitment to the protection of human, civil, social, cultural and economic rights of the Dalits. In every important conversation at the United Nations Security Council and meetings on international peace and security, Dalit issues should take centre stage. No UN-level protocol should pass without accounting for the historical and present plight of the Dalits. Unless these processes are actualized, no amount of tributes and statues in the name of Ambedkar can justify the inaction of the stakeholders invested in Ambedkar's politics.

Saffronizing the Dalits

Bhanwar Meghwanshi

Introduction

The Rashtriya Swayamsevak Sangh (RSS) is a product of a careful deliberation by the *savarna* (upper-caste) Hindus. RSS apologists have argued that it was a mere coincidence that the first group of youths and children assembled at the RSS *shakha* in Nagpur by the founder of the organization, Keshav Baliram Hedgewar, were Brahmins. However, the shakha was founded on the ideas of the gurukul, which only enabled the inclusion of the Brahmins. It was because of this calibrated selection that the RSS became an organization of, for and by the savarna Hindu male. It was neither inclusive nor did it adopt a national character; it stood on the foundations of the Hindu caste system. Hedgewar organized the Sangh in a manner that ensured the dominance of the Brahmins, which continues.

Hedgewar worked towards strengthening the organizational structure of the RSS, especially the militaristic wing focused on building the physical strength of the Hindu upper-caste male. Hedgewar neither left behind a body of significant work or speeches, nor have his biographers been able to give us any significant insight into his thought process. From the available literature, we can clearly discern the influence of his mentor B.S. Moonje, president of the Hindu Mahasabha, and Bal Gangadhar Tilak. Savarkar's idea of radical Hindutva, his intention of safeguarding Brahminical supremacy and establishing a Hindu Rashtra, were instrumental in shaping the ideological framework of the RSS.

The RSS's real thoughts are revealed in the writings of its second head, Madhavrao Sadashivrao Golwalkar, through works like *We, or Our Nationhood Defined*, *Bunch of Thoughts*, and other writings and speeches. What's apparent is that Golwalkar was a strong supporter of the caste and varna systems, as well as the Manusmriti. The RSS had attempted to distance itself from Golwalkar's controversial thoughts in *We, or Our Nationhood Defined*,[1] a book that defends racism and Nazism, and praises Hitler, by conveniently dismissing these views as his personal opinions. However, *Bunch of Thoughts*, which contains controversial opinions on the caste and varna systems, is still available at RSS offices and literary centres. Praising the varna system, Golwalkar writes in *Bunch of Thoughts*:

> Our old social order laid down a specific duty for each group and guided all the individuals and groups in their natural line of evolution just as the intellect directs the activities of the innumerable parts of the body. The highest scope for development of the individual was secured in the process of his best service to the Virat Purusha (Corporate Person) of society. Such was the highly complex and organised structure of society that we had envisaged as the practical ideal and strove to realise it in life. This state, looked at from a distance, appears as a bewildering diversity but, in fact, denotes the highest evolved state of society that ever existed on the face of the world.[2]

Unlike B.R. Ambedkar, Periyar, Jawaharlal Nehru and other ardent defenders of social justice, Golwalkar does not deem the caste system as a reason for the weakening of the social fabric. He justifies the discriminatory social hierarchy by stating:

> If a Brahaman became great by imparting knowledge, a Kshatriya was hailed as equally great for destroying the enemy. No less important was the Vaishya who fed and sustained society through agriculture and trade or the Shudra who served society through his art and craft.[3]

Golwalkar's views on caste, the varna system and the Manusmriti began inviting widespread criticism, and this was challenging for the RSS, given that he and Savarkar were their main ideologues. After Mahatma Gandhi's murder, distancing themselves from Savarkar became a political and social necessity for the RSS. They did this by claiming that he was a member of the Hindu Mahasabha and not the RSS. But the same could not be said about Golwalkar.

And so, the RSS hit upon a different plan to accomplish this 'social-distancing' project. By disingenuously expunging some of his controversial writings and speeches, the RSS, through Sahitya Sindhu Publications, Bangalore, published Golwalkar's works under the title *The Complete Writings of Shri Guruji*. Despite this whitewashed version of Golwalkar that was presented to the world, his problematic views on caste, the varna system and the Manusmriti were retained. According to Golwalkar:

> Smritis, and the varna system advocated by them, are a creation of God. It is due to its divine creation that we even see some disruptions, but despite that, we do not worry since what is divine creation will, despite human intervention, re-establish itself . . . the varna system in our religion is a cooperative enterprise. What is termed as a guild today and was referred

to as caste in the past have the same form. There is nothing
untoward in the four varna system that obtains from birth.[4]

Appropriating Ambedkar

Despite aggressive efforts by the RSS–BJP to appropriate
Ambedkar in recent times, Hedgewar and Golwalkar neither
praised nor supported him in his lifetime. The RSS was
established in 1925 and largely operated in Maharashtra and
Central India, areas where Ambedkar was spearheading his
movement for social transformation. Despite recent propaganda
on social media platforms highlighting the supposed friendship
between Ambedkar and Hedgewar, there is no evidence that
either the RSS, its sarsanghchalak or ordinary workers supported
popular Dalit movements, such as Mahad Satyagraha and the
burning of the Manusmriti in 1927, and the Kalaram Temple
entry movement in Maharashtra in 1930. In fact, we know
that Ambedkar was a staunch opponent of both Hindutva and
a society based on the thoughts of Manu.[5] He warned against
the grave dangers of Hindu Raj and argued that it should not be
established at any cost.

Golwalkar was a lifelong opponent of Ambedkar, whose views
on the caste and varna systems were diametrically opposite to his
own. Ambedkar not only burnt the Manusmriti but aimed to
destroy the philosophical basis and system from which it emerged.
He tried to actualize this by playing an active role in the making of
the Indian Constitution.

Golwalkar did not shy away from criticizing the Constitution,
calling it a foreign import. Sharing his thoughts on the Constitution,
Golwalkar wrote:

> We forgot our self and the fact that we are Hindus, in the
> absence of the soul that combines these two, we created a
> constitution that will create conflict.[6]

The RSS's mouthpiece, *Organiser*, carried an editorial that stated:

> The worst thing about the Indian constitution is that there is nothing Indian in it. It does not talk anything about ancient Indian constitution, laws, institutions, vocabularies or metaphors. We do not find any trace of the unmatched constitutional journey of ancient India. Manu wrote his laws way before Lycurgus of Sparta or Solan of Persia. Manusmriti is appreciated worldwide till date. It is easily and universally acceptable to Indian Hindus, but it does not hold any value for our constitutional pandits.[7]

The RSS's endorsement of the Manusmriti shines through time and again. After the Constitution of India was adopted, the *Organiser* published an article titled 'Manu Rules our Hearts'. It argued that despite the promulgation of the Constitution, it was the Manusmriti that ruled the hearts of the Hindus. According to the article:

> Despite the proclamation of Dr. Ambedkar in Mumbai that the days of Manu are over, it is true that even today Manusmriti and other Smritis' rules and dictums influence the daily lives of Hindus. Even a liberal Hindu finds themselves entangled in the rules of the Smritis and is helpless in completely disentangling themselves from it.[8]

Additionally, on 11 December 1949, the RSS, the Hindu Mahasabha, the Ram Rajya Parishad and other Sanatan institutions organized a protest rally at Ramlila Ground in Delhi against the Hindu Code Bill presented by Ambedkar.[9] The rally saw calls of 'Hindu Code Bill down down (*murdabad*)' and 'Law Minister Dr Ambedkar down down (*murdabad*)'. Effigies of Ambedkar were burnt, and Karpatri Maharaj, a prominent Hindu monk involved in the agitation, made a casteist remark against Ambedkar, stating that an untouchable should refrain from interfering with matters reserved for the Brahmins.[10]

Apart from his opposition to reforming Hindu personal law, which was aimed at uplifting and empowering women, Golwalkar even opposed the reservations guaranteed to the Dalits and adivasis by the Constitution. He argued that such reservations would destroy the age-old amity in Hindu society. For him, India's social justice programmes, as enshrined in the Constitution, would create interpersonal enmity within the Hindu community. Golwalkar wrote:

> Dr. Ambedkar had provided for special rights of the scheduled castes for a period of 10 years from the establishment of the Republic in 1950. But this period is constantly being increased. Unrestrained reservation, based solely on caste, will force them to develop selfish feelings that arise from being a separate community. This will impede their solidarity with the rest of the community. It is therefore apt that reservation be based on the economic situation of the individual. This will contain conflict and restrain the feelings of envy among those who think that only untouchables are enjoying the benefits of reservation.[11]

He further argued:

> It is not desirable to lower the educational standard for jobs; people with lesser ability will lower the standard of the area they work in. This will risk their and other people's lives.[12]

In a speech in Delhi, Golwalkar mocked the democratic process, dismissing the guarantee of universal adult franchise thus: '. . . this is nothing more than offering rights to cats and dogs.'[13]

In 1949, Golwalkar criticized the then structure of the union of India:

> Our constitution is nothing but a heavy and unharmonious aggregation of different articles borrowed from different western constitutions. There is nothing in it to call it our own. The constitution is nothing but a mixture of incomplete tenets in the declarations of the United Nations and the League of Nations and some specialities in the British and the American constitutions.[14]

Golwalkar's views on caste, varna, race, reservation and the Constitution are not only antithetical to the values enshrined in the Constitution but also undermine B.R. Ambedkar's struggle against social, economic and political inequalities, and the spirit of fraternity envisaged in the Preamble to the Constitution.

The RSS continues to harbour similar views regarding the Constitution. In 2017, Mohan Bhagwat, the sarsanghchalak of the RSS, stated: 'The Indian constitution should be amended to suit the Indian moral rules. Many parts of the constitution are based on foreign ideas. We should ponder over this after 70 years of freedom.'[15]

The Atal Bihari Vajpayee-led NDA government had initiated a review of the Constitution.[16] Recently, another BJP leader, Subramanian Swamy, approached the Supreme Court with an appeal to remove the terms 'secular' and 'socialist' from the Constitution.[17] Prime Minister Narendra Modi also famously wrote *Jyotipunj*, one of the sections of which was a hagiography to Golwalkar.[18] It is therefore not surprising that he followed his guru's thought process in amending the Constitution (102nd Amendment to the Constitution, 2018), which provided for reservations for the economically weaker sections (EWS).

The BJP government has eroded and diluted the constitutional provisions through various policy decisions, including recruitment through lateral entry, and the privatization of public-sector undertakings and education.

BJP–RSS's Changing Attitude towards the Dalits

The BJP and RSS have been working to rectify their anti-Dalit image. This entails subsuming the Dalit identity into a larger Hindu identity. Despite their initiatives, the RSS has been unable to change its anti-Dalit image due to recurring violence against the Dalits by members of dominant castes and the failure of the RSS to condemn such violence.

By studying the work of RSS's ideologues, talking to its cadres and reading articles and books published by writers belonging to the Sangh and the BJP, one can discern the RSS–BJP's anti-Dalit and anti-adivasi attitude. They have problems with reservation, the Constitution and democracy; they believe in the rule of the Manusmriti and wish to create a Hindu Rashtra.

But this is not possible till the time the Dalits, adivasis and other backward classes (OBCs) join the Hindutva bandwagon. Until they leave behind their identities for that of a proud Hindu, they are of no use to political Hindutva. It is towards this end that the RSS has begun to strategically alter its anti-Dalit image.

This began with Madhukar Dattatraya, also known as Balasaheb Deoras, who succeeded Golwalkar as the RSS sarsanghchalak after his death in 1973. It was during the tenure of Deoras, perhaps the most low-profile sarsanghchalak of the RSS, from 1973 to 1994, that active work among the Dalits was initiated under Seva Bharati, the Sangh's non-governmental organization devoted to the purpose. The ensuing shifts of stance included placing Ambedkar among the Sangh's *pratahsmaraniya* (literally, one who is venerated in the morning prayer), and floating—on Ambedkar's birth anniversary in 1983—a purpose-built vehicle, the Samrasata Manch, to woo middle class Dalits who yearned for social recognition from the upper castes.[19]

At the Pune spring (Basant) address in 1974, Deoras went to the extent of saying, 'If untouchability is not a sin, then there is no sin in this world.'[20] Deoras was a political figure and played an important role during the inception of the Jan Sangh and its first elections. Later, due to differences, he was inactive within the RSS for seven years. Deoras realized the need for the RSS to increase its social base. It was thus important to transform the image of the political avatar of the RSS, the BJP, from an urban Brahmin–Baniya party to a common person's party. Towards this end, he transformed the Ram Janmabhoomi and Babri Masjid movement into a political movement and then tasked a Dalit *swayamsevak*, Kameshwar Chaupal, to lay the foundation stone of the Ram Mandir in 1989.

Despite these gestures, the RSS could not tide over its anti-Dalit image, with its leaders, workers and other affiliated organizations voicing their anti-Dalit views time and again. The current sarsanghchalak, Mohan Bhagwat, has adopted a twin-pronged strategy to work on this issue. First, by offering Dalit leaders some share of power and wooing them into the BJP. Many known Dalit leaders and activists who were openly opposed to the RSS–BJP's communal politics were accommodated in the BJP. They were made MLAs and MPs in order to earn the trust of the community.

Secondly, the Sangh has also inducted many Dalits and other backward classes as *pracharaks* at the lower levels of the organizational hierarchy. At its upper echelons, it remains a Brahmin organization, with none of its seven sarsanghchalaks coming from the Dalit, adivasi or OBC communities. This is likely to continue in the foreseeable future. Nevertheless, this ploy of the RSS seems to have been effective to an extent, as they have been able to entice the new generation of educated Dalits and adivasis.

The protests linked to the institutional murder of Dalit researcher Rohit Vemula, and the unprecedented situation following the reaction of the Dalits and adivasis who had gathered on the streets after the 2 April 2018 judgment on the Scheduled Castes and

Scheduled Tribes (Prevention of Atrocities) Act, compelled Mohan Bhagwat to organize feedback sessions on a grand scale. Following a discussion with grassroots workers, pracharaks, *vistaraks* and other affiliate organizations, the Sangh decided to strategically shift its views, especially against reservation.

The RSS realized that if it did not assuage Dalit and adivasi anger, it would risk losing the support of these communities and risk the electoral fortunes of the BJP. Accordingly, they appropriated adivasi and Dalit heroes, their places of worship, their gods and goddesses. Despite their internal ideological leanings, the RSS publicly re-articulated its thoughts on caste, reservation and the Constitution. Mohan Bhagwat went so far as to claim that the Sangh no longer agrees with the thoughts of Golwalkar![21]

A collection of Mohan Bhagwat's speeches, interviews and articles, titled *Yashasvi Bharat* (Glorious India), was published by Prabhat Prakashan.[22] The RSS chief has made a volte-face on many issues covered in this volume, as will be demonstrated shortly. But is the RSS really changing or is this merely a clever obfuscation to serve its political ends? How does a sarsanghchalak who was advocating the amendment of the Constitution till 2017 suddenly propound opposite views in 2018? And more importantly, does this hint at a wholesale transformation in the RSS, BJP and its other affiliate organizations? These questions remain unanswered.

Let's now try to examine the contemporary thoughts of the Sangh on the Dalits, the adivasis and the Constitution. As Mohan Bhagwat said in 2020:

We, in a democracy, have accepted a constitution, a constitution that has been drafted by our own people. This constitution is a consensus among our people. It is thus our duty to follow the discipline laid down by the constitution. Sangh has always believed in this. We appreciate all the thought behind the constitution and all the symbols of a free India.[23]

A staunch opponent of reservation, he was asked about the Sangh's opinion on reservation. His answer demonstrates the strategic change in the RSS:

> The Sangh duly supports reservation enshrined in the constitution. The Sangh supports and will continue to support all kinds of reservation clauses in the constitution that are aimed to remove social inequality. The duration of the reservation system should be decided by those for whom it was mandated in the first place. When they feel that there is no longer a need for this system then we will see. Till such time the reservation should be in place. This has been a well-thought-out opinion of the Sangh that it has held since the inception of the question. There is no change in that.[24]

Despite these claims, the actions of the government have been distinctly different. Direct recruitment at the level of joint secretary by the Union government,[25] an amendment to the rules of the Union Public Service Commission (UPSC), the constitutional amendment granting reservation to the upper castes based on their economic status, and the move towards the privatization of public-sector units and the contractualization of employment in the public sector, all hint towards a systematic move to end reservation.[26] A speech given by Subramanian Swamy in Jodhpur, Rajasthan, is very important in this context, testifying to that strategy. Swamy publicly argued that 'to end reservations totally is madness, but the BJP government will take reservations to the level where its existence or lack of it will be the same'.[27]

Hindutvawadi organizations have always been opposed to the Scheduled Castes and Scheduled Tribes (Prevention of Atrocities) Act and allege that it has been openly misused. The Supreme Court's ruling on the act, which the Dalits and adivasis see as a panacea to the countless atrocities they suffer, was welcomed by these groups. But when the judgment provoked protests by the

Dalits and adivasis, they were attacked in most BJP-ruled states. Rajasthan's Jalore, Barmer and Jodhpur districts saw organized attacks on Dalit and adivasi protestors, allegedly by members of the Sangh.[28] Despite their recalcitrance on the Atrocities Act, and there being a divergence between their claims and their acts, the RSS changed their opinion, arguing:

> There is a situation of atrocity due to obvious social backwardness and the arrogance of caste. The Atrocities Act came into force to counter this situation. It should be implemented but not misused. There are two things, both of which are true: it is not implemented properly, and it is abused. It is for this reason that the Sangh believes that this law should be implemented properly and not misused.[29]

Questions have constantly been raised on the absence of the Dalits, adivasis and other backward classes in the higher echelons of the RSS. Quite understandably, the RSS has consistently avoided this question. Or, to be more precise, the RSS has a well-formulated response, namely that it neither inquires into the caste of the person nor does it have a quota system for giving space to the Dalits, adivasis, OBCs and minorities in their organization and its affiliate organizations. But does the RSS really not inquire into a person's caste? Or are they merely obfuscating the issue? The latter seems more to be the case.

In the years I spent in the RSS, I acutely and painfully experienced that people *did know* about each other's caste. Sharing the same kitchen, every swayamsevak is fully aware of the social and economic backgrounds of their peers. Given this fact, it is a lie to assert that the RSS does not believe in caste. Although public events do not involve inquiries into the caste of the person, personal interactions are replete with such instances and consequent exclusionary practices. To cite just one notable example, how is it that *all* the six sarsanghchalaks the RSS has had so far are from the upper castes? It wouldn't have been so if the RSS were truly inclusive of all castes. Why did other caste groups not get an opportunity to assume leadership within the RSS?

The RSS has begun to understand that people will start asking tough questions about leadership and demanding their due share. Anticipating and proactively countering such questions, it has already begun to proffer answers. Mohan Bhagwat says:

> When I was a student studying in Nagpur, all the leaders of the Nagpur Sangh were Brahmins. One could only see Brahmins in the Sangh of the '50s. Because you ask and from what I see and observe, today's sangh in each zone comprises members of different caste groups. Even at the all-India level it is not merely one caste. This will keep expanding and you will see a working committee that comprises all castes and is a reflection of the entire Hindu community.[30]

Has the RSS really changed? Publicly, their beliefs have taken a turn on every matter. They have altered their opinions on different issues ranging from the question of women, the Dalits and the third gender to inter-caste marriage, reservation, Atrocity Act, Ambedkar and Muslims. They have sidelined *Bunch of Thoughts* and accelerated their quest to present a different image of themselves. Bhagwat says:

> As matters concerning *Bunch of Thoughts* things that have been said are both context- and situation-specific. They are not eternal. The eternal thoughts of Guruji have been published under a collection titled *Shri Guruji, Vision and Mission*. By removing all that concerns the current context we have presented those thoughts that are eternally relevant. Times change, the situation of the institution changes, our thoughts and its pattern change. If you consider Sangh as a closed organization then *Bunch of Thoughts* does raise doubts.

I argue that one should rather consider and experience what
the workers of the sangh are doing today, what their thoughts
are and how they think them. This will dispel all the doubts.[31]

The Remaking of the Dalit Consciousness

Confronted by a rise of the Dalit consciousness, the RSS first
began to bring out publications about caste histories, semi-
mythological books on local gods and goddesses, saints, sadhus
and caste heroes, and saffronized versions of works by Bahujan
ideologues, to cater to a primarily Dalit audience. For example,
the Rajasthan folk god Ramdev Pir, considered to be a symbol
of Dalit upliftment and communal amity, was portrayed as a
protector of cows (*gau rakshak*) and the sun of Hinduism (*Hindua
suraj*). Stories about his supposed martyrdom while protecting
cows from Muslim invaders are peddled as history. This is a
twisted representation of facts.[32] Then there is the portrayal of
Ravidas, the sixteenth-century mystic, as a staunch devotee of
Krishna and the attempt to depict him as a martyr who laid down
his life to save Hindu dharma.[33]

The RSS has also been involved in a project of writing (or more
appropriately, re-writing) a history of various Dalit sub-castes. BJP
leader Bizay Sonkar Shastri has written three books: *Hindu Balmiki
Jati* (The History of Hindu Valmikis), *Hindu Chamar Jati* (The
History of Hindu Chamars) and *Hindu Khatik Jati* (The History of
Hindu Khatiks).[34] These books were launched by Mohan Bhagwat.
The common themes of the books is that the scheduled castes were
religious warriors during the Mughal era. They were Kshatriyas who
refused to convert to Islam, and hence were relegated to the task of
cleaning. Their supposed readiness to take up such an occupation
rather than leave Hinduism is valorized. This accomplished two of
the RSS's objectives: the Dalits are being convinced to accept their
status as proud Hindus; and the Muslims are being held responsible
for the caste system, the practices of untouchability and the Dalits'

descent into an inhuman and degrading system of work. The wilful design to cultivate animosity towards Muslims is an integral part of the Hindutva project.

The RSS has also initiated multiple projects among the Dalits and adivasis that peddle soft-Hindutva spirituality. An army of storytellers, trained and paid for by the RSS, go on *yatras* to Dalit–adivasi villages. Bhajan Mandlis across villages are instrumental in amplifying these new myths. Additionally, unemployed youths from marginalized communities are being associated with cow shelters. Furthermore, several small Ram and Hanuman Mandirs are being constructed, and the task of offering prayers is being assigned to local Dalits. Devotee movements have been launched to ensure that people turn towards vegetarianism. Those who had converted to Islam or Christianity are being reconverted through *shuddhikaran* rituals (rituals of purity). Those reconverts readily bought into the communal agenda.

The RSS has been organizing inter-dining events, celebrating occasions like Ambedkar Jayanti, Ravidas Jayanti and Sabari Kumbh to back the claim that it respects Eklavya, Ravidas, Sabari Mai, Ambedkar and Birsa Munda. These actions are attempts to appropriate the legacy of Dalit icons. The collective appeal of this symbolic socio-cultural reengineering on the Dalit consciousness (especially the Dalit sub-castes) cannot be exaggerated.

The then BJP government in Maharashtra deliberately slowed down the process of republishing Ambedkar's essays[35] and speeches but has fast-tracked the process of installing his statues and memorials.[36] On the one hand, in the name of celebrating Constitution Day, the Constitution has been reduced to a text to be worshipped, but on the other hand the constitutional spirit is being destroyed. Numerous publications misrepresenting Dr Ambedkar's friendship with the RSS are being promoted, while others portray Gandhi, the Congress party and the communists as his staunch enemies.[37] This is an ongoing project of the Sangh, to radically alter the consciousness of the Dalit–Bahujan youth.[38]

To destroy Dalit unity, the RSS has also initiated a sustained discourse on the pride of the sub-caste groups, pitting minority and small Dalit groups against majority Dalit groups. These groups were given political representation through the BJP. Right from offering election tickets to enhancing representation in the cabinet, the RSS and the BJP have successfully pitted Dalit sub-castes against each other. This experiment is being conducted right from the level of the gram pradhan to that of the country's highest office. The only condition is that it solely promotes swayamsevaks to these few positions of power. Educated and capable members of the Dalit community are falling for this agenda to fulfil their political ambitions. The Opposition parties are yet to formulate a coherent strategy to counter this.

Road Map for a Secular Polity

The RSS–BJP have adopted cultural and social strategies in order to push their political agenda. Although the RSS calls itself a cultural, apolitical organization, it has always been politically active. It openly supports the Ramrajya Parishad, the Hindu Mahasabha, the Bharatiya Jana Sangh, the Janata Party and the Bharatiya Janata Party. Even today, in the BJP, an organization minister is nominated from and by the RSS. In the national, assembly and local-body elections, out-of-uniform RSS workers play a significant role. The RSS has been, and will be, very interested in those forces and groups who shape the politics of the country. It is beyond politics, but not above politics. It assumes the position of the adviser to the king.

In order to understand and counter the politics of the RSS, one has to understand its socio-cultural tools. Finding alternatives to the RSS strategy of infiltration and consciousness-shaping is critical to counter its sectarian agenda. In the name of service, it has embedded itself in the dwellings of the marginalized; in the name of promoting education and health in tribal areas through the Vanvasi Kalyan Ashrams and the Ekal Schools, it has co-opted adivasi youth in its programmes.

Additionally, one has to keep unmasking the political ambitions, interventions and actions of the RSS. One also has to highlight the fact that under the garb of being a cultural organization, the RSS controls India's political and administrative machinery. It is also noteworthy that despite being discriminated against and relegated as second-class functionaries, adivasis and Dalits are being attracted to the RSS–BJP.

The Opposition needs to understand and counter this process of Sanskritization of the Dalits. The desire for upward social mobility (not economic empowerment alone) and respect has drawn a large number of Dalits to the RSS. The emerging Dalit middle-class elite, which consists of educated, industrious and white-collar workers, in order to demonstrate their socio-cultural superiority, to occupy a higher social status and to distance themselves from the ordinary Dalit, join the RSS–BJP.

The RSS insidiously exploits this aspiration among the Dalits. In order to increase its membership, the RSS is methodically accommodating educated, articulate and capable people into its various organizations. The saffronized youths are even being promoted publicly as examples to attract more people.

At the same time, other political parties continue to patronize those Dalit families who have been their trusted and loyal members for several generations. This despite the fact that these Dalit families are not connected to their communities and occupy their positions primarily because they benefited from the politics of representation. Most damningly, the parties are not ideologically engaged or socially active with these communities except during election time. Can any political party in India, save the BJP and the Communist Party of India (Marxist), claim to have a well-funded and well-networked ideological organization that can counter the RSS? Does the presence within these Opposition parties of representatives sympathetic to the RSS explain their muted response to the RSS?

The secular–progressive parties must offer an inspiring vision that appeals to the growing consciousness among the Dalits and the adivasis. They have to be included as equal participants and not merely as followers.

The knowledge systems of the Dalit–adivasi communities, their icons and heroes must be duly recognized and platforms provided for amplifying their works. Only then can an alternative to the RSS–BJP emerge. The failure to offer an alternative vision will push the Dalits towards Hindutva and delude them into considering their sacrifices to be a revolution. A growing number of Dalits have started to read and understand Ambedkar. This is an apt opportunity for progressive forces to include the Dalits through the path of the Constitution. This is not merely a question of an instrumental political alliance but also of Dalit liberation. The politics of Hindutva is a path to un-freedom. Freedom from discrimination cannot be realized without the annihilation of caste. The language of social harmony employed by the RSS is a thinly veiled attempt to maintain the status quo of an unjust social order. Let our Dalit brothers and sisters not be swayed by the promise of assimilation that will continue to rob them of dignity and respect.

Hindutva and the Future of Dalit–Bahujan Politics in India

Badri Narayan

Dalit–Bahujan politics in India can be aptly described by the popular Hindi proverb, 'Elephants tread ahead, while their shadows loom behind.' The forces unleashed by liberalization in the early 1990s dramatically altered the social and economic aspirations for a generation of Indians. These changes have had a profound impact on Dalit communities across India. However, sections of the Dalit movement failed to adapt to these changes and continue to engage with Dalit issues in the same form as in pre-1990 India.

Often, when theoretical analyses fail to make sense of social processes, folk wisdom, particularly *maslas* (or popular sayings) help in creating a framework within which we can reconceptualize existing paradigms. During my field work, I would often hear this popular proverb 'jaisa ann, waisa mann', loosely translated as 'you are what you eat', or, more specifically, 'your heart, mind and ideology are the product of what you absorb'. This famous rural proverb suggests that food, money and economy play a crucial role in shaping our ideology in life. Even though social *sanskaras* (norms) deter drastic changes on an individual level, the deep and transformative influences of India's neo-liberal economy on society and human identity are starkly visible. India's political economy has very substantively changed the face of the politics of democracy and empowerment, because of the deep changes it has effected in the nature of social communities in India.

The introduction of economic reforms in India dramatically increased the power of the market and redefined the role of the state. For various reasons, this coincided with the beginning of identity-based politics. Various movements and parties emerged with the avowed goal of empowering the marginal and vulnerable sections of society, including women, the Dalits, other backward classes (OBCs), transgenders, etc. This bottom-up desire for political–economic empowerment was amplified by the consumerist spirit that liberalization unleashed and even encouraged. The needs and aspirations of the Dalits enhanced manifold. The prevailing climate affected everyone equally—it didn't matter whether they were dominant castes or not; whether they were the poorest of the poor or in the middle classes; whether they were living in urban or rural India. To once again borrow from a popular saying, neo-liberalism enabled both the lion and the deer together; it freed and legitimized the lion's hunger and yet gave the deer courage to go where the lions lived.

This neo-liberal economy produced a huge middle class. The total number of people in the middle class, which stood at 1 per cent of the population in 1990, grew to 5 per cent in 2004.[1] In the next eight years, the middle class doubled from 300 million to 600 million.[2] Economists have extrapolated that a consumer who spends between US$2–10 per capita, per day is classified as belonging to the middle class. According to this indicator, approximately half of India's population is now in the middle class.[3] The fastest growth in this class has been in the lower middle class, which spends between US$4–6 per day.[4] The Dalits, most backward castes and other marginal communities form the bulk of this lower middle class in India. Over 40 lakh Dalits, in central and state governments and public sector enterprises (PSEs) together, earn lakhs of crores of rupees as salaries every year.

This neo-liberal economy not only provided economic mobility to a section of marginal communities but also reshaped their politics. It not only created a new set of aspirations but also indirectly created a new framework of assertion and expectations. Neo-liberalism subtly tamed the ferocity and dynamism of Dalit movements, and instead channelized their energies into milder and more sanitized forms of dissent. Driven by petition politics, Dalit movements moved away from the boldness of the Dalit Panthers and instead were co-opted into 'civil' society.

Thus, 'civilized' Dalit movements increasingly started operating within a set of rules that were set by hegemonic forces. Instead of radical mass movements, Dalit movements started adopting calibrated language and methodologies—symbolic protests, such as candlelight vigils, dharnas at public places in capital cities, advocacy efforts with governments and even international organizations based on reports prepared by civil society organizations, or going to the media, particularly social media, to articulate their demands, etc. The efficacy of this form of protest is doubtful, since it circumscribed the vitality of Dalit movements. This has made sections of the Dalit community more pliable to compromises, accommodations, negotiations and various kinds of alliances. Dalit leaders, who have rejected more radical forms of protest and embraced more acceptable forms of soft political protest, have become a diversion to the social, political and economic empowerment of the Dalits.

The interplay of these factors created space for the rapid rise of Hindutva in India. This was further bolstered by new modes of political communication, innovative redeployment of political mobilization strategies from the freedom struggle and greater ideological clarity. The Bharatiya Janata Party (BJP) and, more crucially, the Rashtriya Swayamsevak Sangh (RSS) cleverly identified the cleavages and vacuum created by the Dalit leadership (political and social) that emerged because of neo-liberalism.

For example, mainstream Dalit leaders and national parties have consistently failed to adequately recognize the intense generational aspiration for religious equality and dignity among the Dalit sub-castes. Their entire approach and discourse have been based on the concepts of human rights and political and economic equality. This worked well in the first few decades after Independence, and parties competed to outshine each other. For example, in Uttar Pradesh, the Bahujan Samaj Party (BSP), which was formed in the 1980s, coinciding with the rise of the Dalit–Bahujan movement, outpaced the Indian National Congress (INC), the Communist parties and the Republican Party of India. The BSP gradually swallowed the Dalit base of these parties and established itself as the pre-eminent Dalit–Bahujan party in north India through the use of the political language prevalent at the time.

However, due to an overdependence of political parties on these normative categories, an emotional distance crept in between Dalit movements and the community. What these mainstream leaders and parties failed to understand was that after centuries of exclusion and oppression, there had always been a very strong desire among the marginalized communities to bypass what B.R. Ambedkar famously called the 'graded inequalities of the past'. Dominant castes within the Dalit community often monopolized the benefits emanating from the state's social justice and welfare programmes. For these excluded sub-castes aspiring for upward social mobility, religious acceptance and equality are unstated, non-negotiable tenets of social dignity.

Acknowledging this deep-seated longing for social inclusion and upward mobility among these sub-castes, the BJP–RSS have been spearheading various programmes for religious inclusion. They have worked systematically to alter the terms of negotiation and focused on delivering what the Dalit and other marginal communities coveted most, thereby developing a form of subaltern Hindutva.[5] Their various programmes of *vidya* (education), *pravachan* (sermons) and *seva karya* (welfare work), under the RSS's *samajik samrasta* (social harmony) campaign prepared the emotional ground among the Dalits for Hindutva. Slowly and methodically, Hindutva started appropriating and absorbing the Dalit movement within its own fold.[6] Interestingly, the Sangh has also tried to appropriate Ambedkar by arguing that he was the greatest icon of samajik samrasta, as argued in *Rashtra-Purush Baba Saheb Dr Bhimrao Ambedkar*, written by Sangh ideologue Krishna Gopal and Shri Prakash in 2014.[7] This multi-layered process adversely affected traditional Dalit–Bahujan parties like the BSP as well as mainstream national parties like the INC.

The BJP and other Hindutva political outfits routinely organize caste conferences (community organizations' summits), strategically reinventing and reshaping narratives of identity. The histories and heroes of these communities are celebrated and incorporated within the Hindutva fold. Leveraging the stories of Eklavya (the archer who sacrificed his thumb for dharma, whom they call 'Dharmaparayan Dalit' or a Dalit who follows his dharma) and Valmiki (the author of the Ramayana), among others, the BJP–RSS have tried to portray the Dalits as martial races,[8] as the 'rashtrarakshak' and 'dharmrakshak'.[9] The Dalits are taught that their ancestors fought against the Mughals and other Muslim rulers, and were turned into slaves only when the Hindus lost against Muslim rulers.[10] By propagating such myths, the RSS–BJP claim that the Dalit community has traditionally produced 'Dharmaparayan Dalit Mahapurush' (great dharma-following Dalit men) and that as a community the Dalits are totally committed to Hindu cultural values.[11] Their groundwork, along with their methodical appropriation of Ambedkar, blocks radical Ambedkarite consciousness from taking root among the Dalit community, and especially among the sub-castes.

Additionally, various BJP governments have complemented these socio-cultural efforts to win over the Dalit sub-castes by targeting them through government schemes like the Ujjwala Yojana and the Awas Yojana. This social re-engineering has helped the BJP fracture the Dalit votes and has enabled them to win election after election.

Shifting Locations: Why Dalits Moved Away from Congress

As we know, the INC as India's main centrist party remained influential among the Dalits till the late 1980s. Their role in the freedom struggle, coupled with their promises of Harijan–Dalit emancipation, was instrumental in drawing the Dalits post Independence. The actualization of India's constitutional ethos by successive Congress-led governments, through various emancipatory schemes and developmental programmes, helped retain this voter base. The provision for reservation and various legislations against untouchability and atrocities provided relief and mobility among a section of Dalits in India. Even today, Dalits in rural India remember the contribution of various developmental programmes implemented by the Congress.

However, this loyalty was abruptly shaken in 1977, when Babu Jagjivan Ram, an eminent leader and one of the icons of the Dalit community, left the Congress and formed his own party, and later joined the Janata Party. The disillusionment was clearly visible among rural Dalits. For example, Bhullar, a fifty-year-old Dalit of the Sahabpur village near Allahabad, said, 'We all wanted to see him as PM. Congress did not make a Dalit PM in India and we again realized that being Dalit is a big curse in Indian society.'[12] Kanshi Ram tapped into this dissatisfaction and argued that Dalits in national parties were accorded the status of *chamcha* (sycophant) and that they wouldn't get their political dues unless they developed their own independent parties.

This impression was cemented by the Congress party's traditional approach in promoting leaders from the Dalit and adivasi communities. There is a perception that most assertive and aggressive leaders from these communities are not promoted in political parties; only subdued leaders who wouldn't ruffle the status quo are given space within the party's fold. They are neither very aggressive in championing Dalit causes, nor are they especially sensitive to issues of social justice. Nor has any of them undertaken a mass-contact programme to engage with, uplift and empower the Dalit community. It is because of these multiple factors that Kanshi Ram (and later Mayawati) emerged as new hope among the disillusioned Dalits and managed to get their overwhelming support. A large section of the Dalit community shifted from the Congress and gravitated towards the BSP, especially in Uttar Pradesh.

Even then, the Congress retained some influence among a section of the Dalits in various parts of India, since the BSP did not have a pan-India presence. The saffron turn of the Dalits in India will not only weaken the BSP but also the Congress party because unlike the BSP, the BJP has a strong pan-India presence. While the Dalits do remember the Congress positively, an increasing section is bitterly critical of them because of the Congress's lack of ideological clarity on key issues, and lack of sincere and principled engagement with the community itself. Seeing the Congress in governments also invites criticism about their inaction in providing the Dalits their appropriate share in Indian democracy.

If the BJP has managed to build its support among the Dalits today, it's in large part because of how unimaginatively the Congress has conducted itself, both as a party and as a government, in dealing with the aspirations of the Dalits. It is therefore easy for the BJP to highlight the Congress party's reluctance in taking bold decisions, and its lack of ideological and programmatic fervour in implementing its agenda. That is one of the reasons why the BJP aggressively projects Prime Minister Narendra Modi as resolute and intolerant towards inertia.

A Blueprint for Congress

Given their historical backwardness and vulnerabilities, the Dalit and marginal communities, especially in rural India, trust political parties easily. These communities welcome everyone who comes to them with a message of hope and resolves to address their aspirations. This is not to deny that there is an educated and mobile section within the Dalit community that is suspicious of political parties (a trait shared among all economically better-off sections in all social groups). However, despite these variables, what is seldom theorized about and discussed threadbare is how to talk to the various Dalit communities of India.

The major problem of the Congress, the foremost contender to the BJP, is that it is still talking with the Dalits in a rights-based language. There is no doubt that the Dalits want to secure their social and political rights. But they also want to hear a political language which gives them respect and dignity. The political diction that has evolved through this rights-based approach has a problem. On the one hand it assures the marginalized a share in the democratic benefits, but at the same time it patronizes the beneficiary. To rectify this, the Congress and its leaders (this is not limited to its top-most leadership) have to speak of and address the social, political and economic aspirations of the Dalits.

The Sangh routinely talks of, and evokes pride about, India's 5000-year-old history. If the Congress has to strengthen its position vis-à-vis the BJP, it must develop a counter-language loaded with the images of the past, present and future of Indian society,[13] while customizing it to address contemporary needs and aspirations.

Till Prime Minister Indira Gandhi, the Congress did not use the term 'Dalit' in a larger context in their political discourse. It was a term that was popular in academics, as well as in Left and Ambedkarite discourse. The Congress is now using the term freely in its political messaging. While this may create a connect among a small section of literate and urban Dalits, the larger Dalit population, especially in northern India, remains alienated. Their sense of alienation is sharpened because a section of youngsters and educated youth are actively resisting the use of this term as an umbrella identity. Kanshi Ram himself avoided using 'Dalit' and consciously adopted 'Bahujan' as an umbrella term for various caste identities.

His use of the term Bahujan was also strategically complemented with his attempts at methodically inculcating caste pride among more than a hundred Dalit castes. In doing so, he responded to the 'identity aspiration' of the marginalized social groups while coining a new catch-all term purely as a mobilizational tool. Therefore, an epistemological shift is needed in centrist politics in their interactions with the Dalit communities. The BJP uses the term 'vanchit' (deprived) and addresses the need for caste pride by recreating caste histories, appropriating Dalit icons and championing programmes to promote social interaction with the forward castes. RSS pracharaks are adept at navigating this transformation of Dalit to vanchit.[14] This is a well-thought-out strategy to provide the Dalits a dignified space in the grand Hindutva identity. Of course, how they would treat the Dalits once they have been co-opted is an entirely different matter, and evidence suggests they are reluctantly included.

To make space among the hearts and minds of the marginalized communities, the Congress should understand that political rhetoric alone will not help. Most communities are fatigued by electoral politics and are desperate to see social reconstruction through politics.

Mahatma Gandhi and the Congress were sincere and committed to the idea of 'social politics', i.e., political mobilization through social rejuvenation. Leaders from the freedom movement, including Mahatma Gandhi and B.R. Ambedkar, spearheaded social reform movements that were instrumental in strengthening the march for political freedom. The lines between social and electoral politics were often blurred. However, after India gained independence, electoral politics became central to democracy, and the parties engaged solely through this lens with the people.

The Congress must actively involve itself in social politics. This is especially pressing since the state alone cannot satisfy all aspirations, and the compulsions of electoral politics often curtails the ruling party's commitment to radical social transformation. The period in between elections is an opportune time for the Opposition to nurture and lend its support to social reform movements that reflect the progressive ethos of the Congress party and offers the Dalit community an alternative vision of progress. Agitational politics alone cannot be the answer.

Conclusion

As society is changing, the aspirations of the Dalits and other marginalized communities are also changing. Political parties have to change their conventional and outdated ways of understanding the Dalits and marginalized communities. They need to establish a dialogue and create a space for sustained interaction with all communities at all times, and not just on the eve of elections. Esoteric and rigid leftist and Ambedkarite conceptions about the Dalits need to be reconceptualized and overhauled. It needs to be acknowledged that even though the Dalits are economically underdeveloped and want to better their lives, they are equally seized of dignity as well as social acceptance (in which socio-cultural transformations are critical). Unless the Congress party and progressives engage with these imperatives positively and consistently, they are not doing justice to the Dalit community.

Today, political parties are struggling with the RSS–BJP's shadow, while the latter have moved far ahead. To counter the Sangh, these parties must reinvent their understanding of the Sangh, or lose the battle. Both the centrist and Dalit–Bahujan politics in India need to innovate a new language, and alter their agendas, actions and issues. They need to evolve a new understanding of the profound societal changes underway, particularly among the Dalit and Bahujan communities. There is a need to map, analyse and address the rising and altered aspirations of the Dalit middle classes and the non-dominant sub-castes (which also need to be politicized). The culture of objective self-criticism, which the Dalit–Bahujan movement lost due to its overconfidence in their understanding of the communities and their political and cultural attitudes, requires to be urgently revived. The main question that must be asked in this process of review is: How and why did Hindutva take root among the Dalit and marginalized communities? How the secular parties, Ambedkarites and progressive movements respond to this fundamental question will determine the future of Dalit–Bahujan politics, as well as of Indian democracy.

A Blueprint for a New Dalit Politics:
An Open Letter to the Dalits

Jignesh Mevani

Introduction: The Dream of a Better Future

When we think about what the post-colonial promise to the Dalits of India was, we immediately resort to the Constitution, which has allowed a humanist framework for making sense of our positions in the nation—where historically the Dalit community has been subjugated and othered by society. Where society has been evil to our community, the Constitution has given us an alternative dream for a better tomorrow. It strives to secure for all Indians, irrespective of caste, gender and religion, justice, liberty, equality and fraternity.

Despite all the historical injustices and moral horrors that the Dalit community has been subjected to, India's constitutional promise offers hope of myriad possibilities of a new world that Dr B.R. Ambedkar inscribed in our hearts. These possibilities have motivated many from the community to rise up and fight against the many social evils that persist to this day. It gives the community the forbearance to rise above the discrimination, the atrocities and the injustices, and keep working for a better future. It gives us the fortitude to confront Manuwad, which exploits us on the basis of both caste and class.

But there are many hurdles, both within the Dalit community and in Indian society and politics, that impede the realization of that future. These are conceptual, ideological and organizational hurdles. Without tackling them comprehensively, the Dalit community will never be truly emancipated or empowered.

Hurdles to Dalit Emancipation

The first conceptual hurdle hampering the progress of the Dalit community is that a section of the Dalit political class is viscerally against aligning with anyone outside the Dalit community. Given how the Dalit community has time and again been used and cheated, this reluctance is understandable. However, we live in unprecedented times. Old suspicions and fears prevent honest engagement and alliance-building. This is detrimental both to the larger cause (that is, the defence of our constitutional values) and to the Dalit community's socio-political empowerment.

One of the tragedies of conventional Dalit politics is its putative grammar, which has for long maintained a sense of sanctity for many of our political actors who are quick to caricature anyone from the Dalit community as a 'stooge' or a 'chamcha' whenever they deviate from an accepted set of positions or predetermined norms. Such internal divisions are not fruitful for critical political dialogue and merely allow the Manuwadi regime to continue its programme of divide and rule, and continue their systematic attacks on the Dalit community. This derails the growing alliances between progressive forces in the country, which is essential at this juncture in Indian political history. With the behemoth juggernaut that Hindutva has become today, it is also important to understand and address the bitter reality that the Dalits can and are being co-opted by fascist forces trying to camouflage their strategy of preventing Dalit–Muslim unity. They do this under the guise of annihilating caste, a goal which is furthest from their ideological and political agendas.

Secondly, the very premise of 'Dalit politics' is itself a roadblock to the annihilation of caste. Ambedkar had correctly recognized that caste is at the root of India's problems and that we must work to annihilate it *completely*. For too long, we, as a nation, nurtured the filth of caste and never felt morally outraged. Free markets, liberalized capital flows and even political empowerment have not been able to kill this monster of caste. This is partly because progressives don't acknowledge caste as a serious problem or a moral blemish that impedes progress. This caste-blindness is one of the biggest hurdles to annihilating caste. On the other hand, the problem with 'Dalit politics' is that it continues to carry the burden of an identity-association and has not been able to organize and mobilize a sizeable cross section of non-Dalits under a larger anti-caste coalition. This failure to look beyond identitarian associations is self-defeating. Collectively, caste blindness and identity politics perpetuate and prolong the evils of the caste system.

As a nation we should first admit to ourselves that we are a very casteist people. Until we acknowledge this moral rot, we won't be able to deal with it. Then, all movements—progressive, Dalit, communist, etc.—must come together to prepare a blueprint for the annihilation of caste, as envisaged by Ambedkar in his seminal treatise *Annihilation of Caste*. Phule, Periyar, Ambedkar and Marx delved deeply into how we can annihilate caste. Inter-caste marriages and radical cultural and political reforms are just a few among the plethora of strategies that can be deployed. We need to understand that caste is a multidimensional phenomenon, and every dimension must be addressed. One of the key elements to this would be destroying caste-based clusters that are evidently visible. How? Under various public housing schemes—like the Sardar Patel Awas Yojana, the Indira Gandhi Awas Yojana and the Ambedkar Awas Yojana—people from various castes should be allotted houses to live together in such colonies. These colonies should have well-maintained public facilities, like playgrounds, swimming pools, libraries, etc., so that children from all castes and religions can swim together, play together, read together in a library. Only then will there be brotherhood between them, only then will they exchange their cultures, fall in love and intermarry. Only then can we comprehensively expunge caste from our social consciousness.

Thirdly, India faces an unprecedented social and political crisis today. Going beyond Dalit politics of the past and present, there are many personalities, variables and dynamics that are reorienting Dalit politics and outlining a vision for one that transcends the traditional politics internalized in the popular psyche of the Dalit political actor.

Yet, anyone who practises or propounds such an eclectic progressive politics is harassed by the dreaded apparatus of the Big Brother-like state that India's government has morphed into. What is looming large over our lives is unadulterated fascism. An alliance of the worst evils of society—feudalism, casteism, communalism and fascism—is working non-stop to destroy the possibilities that our Constitution offered us. Many, like Anand Teltumbde, have faced the perils of daring to dream of a different and better India, of taking a stance that furthers India's constitutional values and does not respect conventional political boundaries.[1] Yet, he has inspired many like me to do the same. While we grieve for Anand, we must continuously rethink what the future of Dalit politics is to be like, and what paths we will take to achieve the dream that Ambedkar showed us.

A Futuristic Dalit Politics

The time has come to reinvent Dalit politics. This would require concerted efforts from within the Dalit community and the progressive movement as well. In the light of the *much* bigger threat we all face, it is critical that this is done urgently, for it is the very future of India that is at stake. Unless we do so, the few successes we have institutionalized in the past seventy years will undoubtedly be reversed, and India will become a communal, fascist and casteist society.

Firstly, it is crucial to shift the focus to anti-caste and pro-poor politics, and not just pigeonhole all struggles into 'Dalit politics'. In doing so, we can gainfully engage with material issues of labour rights and economic access, both of which are integral to the annihilation of caste. In terms of its political methodology, post-Ambedkar Dalit politics did not quite capture the nature of the struggle of the streets as much as they should have. While there have been some famous interventions of this nature many times since Independence, the dominating framework dictating our political methodology remained constitutionalism. Consequently, the Dalit movement in present-day India is locked in the dilemma of abstract versus concrete politics. As we make discursive shifts by attacking the politics of ideology, we forget how we are being beaten by concrete and material forces on the ground. In couching our politics in purely ideological terms, there is a tendency to overlook the very real developmental needs and aspirations of the poor, the Dalits, women and the adivasis. It is critical to synergize issues of lives and livelihoods with ideological questions, so as to ground value-based politics in real concrete politics.

Similarly, representation is of paramount importance for a future that is not hegemonized by the upper castes, and where the Dalits can make effective choices about their lives in the given structure. It is equally true that representation has many other psychological benefits when individuals see role models from their marginalized communities excel. This inspires them to continue their struggle against a society that wilfully denies them opportunities. However, such positive aspects of representation alone are not enough to ground a sustained political project at a time when Manuwadi forces have joined hands with the market.

Let us not forget that the BJP–RSS excel at token representation, while siding with big corporations occupying land, scuttling affordable public education and consistently undermining many serious material problems of the Dalits, the adivasis and the poor. The deliberate undermining of socialist goals of welfare, wealth redistribution and land rights as an inherent and necessary part of a radical Dalit politics is lamentable. While we see constant, admittedly justified and essential defence of the Constitution from Ambedkarite groups, when the right-wing tries to dismantle India's egalitarian premises by distorting the welfare state, there is hardly a murmur. There is scant recognition of the multiple ends that the Constitution has promised, of a vision to actualize those ends, from those who claim to be champions of the Dalit community. This amnesia includes the issue of land reforms, which is wholly imaginable if we go by the principles of the Preamble to the Indian Constitution.

This non-recognition and selective amnesia have been impediments to the emergence of radical movements in and through Dalit politics. There are, in fact, many radical Dalit, or rather anti-caste, movements which involve socialist ideals and material issues. These radical movements are being demonized but are absent from mainstream Dalit politics. The example of the Bhima Koregaon witch-hunt and arrests is a sufficient illustration. To caricature anti-caste, left-leaning forces as 'Naxals', when all they seek is to draw attention to material issues, is untenable.

Red Flags to Avoid for New Dalit Politics

The usual retort to any Dalit political activist as a 'communist stooge' who tries to forge a broad coalition of anti-caste and leftist forces has demotivated many dedicated activists from coming together. In the larger ambit of subaltern solidarity, such bitterness has disallowed synergy between caste and class analyses. This has affected both our political theory and practice. In the domain of political theory, we have only focused on questions of identity and recognition, which, no matter how relevant, do not contextualize these relations in the political economy of Hindutva neo-liberalism of today's India.

Secondly, some Dalit movements lack the zeal of communist struggles in India, disallowing Dalit politics to expand its horizons and capacities in the process. The problem is that Dalit identity politics has not seen the sanitation worker or agricultural labourer as 'the Dalit' or the 'woman'. The communist movements, on the other hand, address the exploitation that emanates from being a Dalit. But Dalit identity politics fails to recognize the intersectionality of these issues and hence does not align with other movements.

Thirdly, when the BJP–RSS have mounted an attack on the minorities and other marginalized sections of society while symbolically putting a Dalit representative in the presidency, one cannot help but question the axiomatic position that we have granted to the concept of representation in our own politics. Many Dalit politicians, on whom we placed our hopes for a progressive Dalit politics over the last few years, have unfortunately betrayed us by moving in the same direction as the Hindu nationalists or joined forces with them. It is therefore important to rethink Dalit politics in a new light and find new champions who can pursue a progressive politics.

Fourthly, this conservatism notwithstanding, there are newer orientations that are challenging the conventional anti-caste politics with a political enthusiasm that has managed to bring many others into our struggle. These are paradigms that have demonstrated not only a commitment to the Constitution and its aspirational legacy but also to the power of people's struggles and battles for justice fought on the streets.

Whether it is Prakash Ambedkar's Vanchit Bahujan Aghadi, which has managed to bring together numerous caste groups from the SC/ST and OBC sections along with Muslim groups in Maharashtra on a platform that effectively talks of the unity of the oppressed, or the newly formed Azad Samaj Party, the political wing of Chandrashekhar Azad's Bhim Army, that has reinvigorated Dalit assertion in parts of north India by showing what reclaiming the streets means. There is a movemental organicity that both these groups demonstrate, which brings forth a fresh political project for the masses, including and especially the Dalit community. However, as it seems clear from the articulations made by their leaders so far, both these groups, like many others, remain fixated on questions of identity and its assertion, and seem occupied in the fight against the ideologies of Manuwad, Brahmanwad and Hindutvawad.

These are extremely important struggles to be engaged in. But the limitations of a politics that never moves beyond the questions of identity is clear from the status of identity politics in other countries, where they get co-opted by neo-liberal forces which are so dear to our own Indian right wing as well. To save questions of identity from becoming merely a talking point for a neo-liberal culture, we must infuse it with class politics too. This is where figures like Dadasaheb Gaikwad and Anand Teltumbde come in, who challenge the binary of either anti-caste or anti-class politics.

These new political struggles highlight the possibilities of an anti-caste movement informed by questions of class and its ability to evolve a more inclusive political vocabulary. This was our hope during the struggle in the aftermath of the Una incident, when the Dalit community came together to rally along raising the slogan, '*Gaay ki poonch tum rakho, hamein hamari zameen do* (Keep the tail of your cow, give us our rightful share of land)!'[2]

Conclusion

In a political atmosphere where two strong forces, of neo-liberalism and Hindutva, have come together, the distrust among the Ambedkarites and the communists in India fuels the further stratification of the remaining political forces that are pro-people. While the electoral *mahagathbandhan* failed due to many compromises and mishaps, a social–democratic mahagathbandhan is essential, where not only leaders from Muslim politics, the Dalit community and OBC groups come together but also the many forces aligned to Left politics in India. The young activists in India recognize this, and therefore they are ready to make alliances across ideological lines.

There is a way in which one can walk the thin line of staying committed to radical politics essential for a structural transformative change in society while retaining the pragmatism essential for politics in precarious times. This ability is best exemplified by many young students and activists who have emerged in the last few years of Indian politics and have inspired many more to raise their voices. It is this kind of strategy that will enable us to have maximum impact on the forces that are dismantling our democracy today.

Additionally, Dalit politics must necessarily address questions of class, gender, sexuality, religious persecution, language as well as the role of the state in our lives. In an age when climate change is adversely impacting the entire world, Dalit politics should also be concerned about how the government seeks to respond to these challenges. Is it not necessary that people get enough water to drink and sustain themselves, regardless of whether or not they are Dalits? Such intersectionalities can only be understood truly by those who have nothing to lose. In India, is that position not occupied by a Dalit who has been the historical survivor of caste violence and a collateral damage for capitalist forces? As those who have lived through a rather long trajectory of alienation and humiliation, it is our responsibility to fight against all kinds of violence. A new Dalit politics must be fundamentally based on such a principle of intersectionality.

The contemporary political landscape is dominated by hollow ideological cries, including in the Dalit community. It is time to reimagine this comprehensively. For example, the Dalits can regain self-respect through access to land. The usual retort has been to dismiss such demands because the Dalits have toiled lands for centuries, and it is education and respect that are a stronger and more effective currency. However, Dalit politics can fight for both. Members of the Dalit community and other oppressed classes of our society are in need of both land and dignity.

This is also time to rethink the responsibilities of the state in the era of unbridled capitalism and demand a socialist programme that alleviates poverty for all. We should demand environmental protection on different fronts, because the marginalized suffer the most during a pandemic or an environmental catastrophe. We should raise our voices as forcefully for access to quality public health care as against every caste atrocity. And if practitioners of traditional Dalit politics believe that this marks a departure from the Ambedkarite spirit, it would be good for them to remember that a substantial population among the lower classes in the country belongs to the scheduled castes. They endure the biggest losses in the event of a natural calamity or pandemic.

When I imagine what I can do for my own constituency in the near future, I think of children being able to watch a new movie on the big screen without having to pay for it. I think of emerging political leaders who can use technology to reach out to people. I think of the budding scientists and innovators in my community. Where a worker lives a life of dignity and self-respect, and has the power to bargain and the right to good wages. A world where one does not need to 'crowdfund' their surgeries in private hospitals, because quality public health is available to all. A space where people can claim ownership over material resources without any fear. And where these can be shared among the people as a collective good. I think of them capturing all the spaces that have been denied to them so far. I think of everyone being able to dream without anxiety—whether they wish to see the Eiffel Tower in Paris with their spouse or visit the Van Gogh Museum in

Amsterdam. These are not merely random wishes; they underpin a society where your class and caste do not dictate the kind of dreams you can have and the kind of world you can be exposed to.

As a political leader, I do not have elaborate blueprints. Many great intellectuals before us have shown what a casteless and a classless society could look like. As conscientious Indians, we are free to choose those elements that would do the most justice to our current circumstances. Anti-caste politics that respects and recognizes the dreams of the people, even those dreams that transcend their current condition, so as to help actualize them is enough. Engaging in such politics will mean we have done enough.

New Phase in Dalit Politics:
Crisis or Regeneration?

Sudha Pai

An analysis of the Dalit movement in the country today reveals a paradox. On the one hand, Dalit parties are in electoral decline as sections of the Dalits have moved away to non-Dalit parties, impacting the unity and strength of the Dalit movement. On the other hand, Dalit assertion remains strong, as seen from the strident reaction to atrocities in recent years and emergence of organizations/movements led by new Dalit leaders, such as the Bhim Army in Uttar Pradesh (UP) by Chandrasekhar Azad or Ravan; the Una Dalit Aytachar Ladat Samiti (Una Dalit Atrocity Fight Committee) by Jignesh Mevani in Gujarat; and the Vanchit Bahujan Aaghadi (Coalition of Exploited Bahujans) by Prakash Ambedkar in Maharashtra. These organizations appeal to both the younger educated generation and the rural smaller Dalit groups who, disappointed with older Dalit parties, are moving away to non-Dalit parties. While these changes are manifest in parties such as the Republican Party of India in Maharashtra[1] and the Liberation Panthers in Tamil Nadu,[2] UP provides the best example of this phenomenon as it is the state where Dalit assertion over the last few decades has determined national politics.

The 1980s and 1990s witnessed the rise of political consciousness and strong movements among the Dalits in UP, leading to a dominance of lower-caste parties and identity politics that drove both electoral and mass politics in the Hindi heartland. National parties like the Bharatiya Janata Party (BJP) and the Indian National Congress (INC), traditionally viewed as Manuwadi (upper-caste) parties, went into decline, and the Bahujan Samaj Party (BSP), institutionalized as a party espousing social justice, self-respect and dignity, was able to capture state power. The 2000s, in contrast, have witnessed the collapse of the BSP and the revival and strengthening of the BJP. The BSP, which gained a majority in the 2007 assembly elections, failed to win even a single seat in the Lok Sabha election in 2014,[3] nineteen seats in the 2017 assembly elections[4] and ten seats in the 2019 Lok Sabha election,[5] though it managed to gain around 20 per cent of the votes each time. While there have been defections from the BSP since 2014, in January 2020, a large number of party workers in eastern UP joined the Samajwadi Party (SP). These developments have led commentators to point to the collapse of the BSP, arguing that Mayawati no longer commands the loyalty of Dalit voters.[6]

However, such analyses merely focus on the electoral fortunes of a significant Dalit party. This essay argues that in the 2000s, the Dalit movement in the country entered a new phase and acquired a more complex character. In contrast to the 1990s, it is experiencing internal fragmentation, which has created uncertainty and ambiguity over both ideology and action.[7] Two significant developments have been responsible for this. First, the waning of identity politics and a shift from the desire for social justice to aspiration impacted by the twin forces of globalization and cultural modernization, creating a divide between the better-off middle class and the poorer, marginalized section of the Dalits.[8] Second, the revival of the BJP under a new-generation leadership, and its

promise of economic development and cultural inclusion within
the saffron fold, has attracted the lower *jatis* (sub-castes) and created
an ideological divide between the Ambedkarite or pro-BSP and
Hindutvawadi or pro-BJP Dalits. The lack of cohesion within
the Dalit movement in Uttar Pradesh is also visible in the shifting
modes of political action: support to the BJP in the 2014 national
elections, but in more recent years, disillusionment, antagonism
and strident opposition to the BJP.[9]

In this situation, the earlier ideology and forms of mobilization
used by the older Dalit leaders no longer seem to be of appeal.
Having achieved a modicum of political empowerment, identity
and self-respect in the 1990s, the Dalits today are in search of a
political party/movement that can offer them economic betterment.
It is on these twin developments, of decline and regeneration, and
how they are shaping the future of Dalit politics in the country,
that this essay focuses.

New Ideas, Aspirations and Activism in the 1990s

In the 1990s, India witnessed the gradual emergence of a small, but
influential, young, educated and politically conscious Dalit middle
class. This new class reached a 'critical mass' precisely when the
Indian polity experienced globalization, moving towards a market-
oriented economy, and it represents a different strand in the Dalit
movement as it has evolved over the last two decades. While Dalit
movements and parties such as the BSP mobilized on issues of
socio-political empowerment, such as identity, dignity and self-
respect, the rising middle-class Dalit intellectuals have emphasized
the need for economic empowerment through a variety of new
means, representing the rise of middle-class activism among Dalits.[10]

These new aspirations are best exemplified in the 'Dalit
Agenda'[11] formulated at the Bhopal Conference in January 2002,[12]
which advocated new policies such as Supplier Diversity to create
Dalit entrepreneurs.[13] The authors of the Dalit Agenda argued

that under the traditional policies of affirmative action and state welfarism, the Dalits have remained mere recipients of welfare, have remained landless/asset-less, below the line of poverty, without a share in the capital in the economy and unable to improve their socio-economic status. Only a tiny elite section of the community or 'creamy layer' has been able to improve their educational attainments and economic status, as well as enter into high-paying jobs in the government, various professions, the media, arts and, increasingly, the private sector. Arguably, even the extension of reservation of jobs to the private sector would help only this small elite, which is why the Dalit Agenda argued for the need for the 'democratization' of control over 'capital' and a strong Dalit business/industrial class, which could participate equally in the national economy.[14]

The setting up of a Dalit Chamber of Commerce, too, has been the work of this new class. It is also visible in a spate of academic writings—an attempt to reinterpret Dalit history and politics by a new generation of Dalit scholars, examples being Suraj Yengde,[15] Chinnaiah Jangam[16] and Sambaiah Gundimeda.[17]

Simultaneously, the smaller and poorer Dalits, also aspiring for upward mobility, have moved away from traditional parties. There is considerable disillusionment over the failure of the BSP to put forward a socio-economic vision or agenda to address the specific problems of deprivation faced by the Dalits. After the capture of power by the BSP in UP, with a majority in the 2007 assembly election, the Dalits had expected not only self-respect but also improvement in their material situation. While there was some improvement in their socio-economic situation, it did not meet their enhanced expectations. Mayawati is no longer respected as before. Her shift from a Dalit-oriented to a *sarvajan* policy was viewed to have primarily helped the Jatavs (the dominant sub-caste among the Dalits) and the upper castes who had helped her gain power in 2007. Furthermore, the BSP, since the mid-1990s, because of its preoccupation with gaining state power, has not been a democratizing force as before, when it had moved downwards to mobilize the smaller, poorer Dalit groups, particularly in the backward regions in UP, who have recently entered the mainstream. Consequently, large sections today view it as a purely Jatav party.

The process of modernization often tends to proceed unevenly, benefiting some sections more than others, leading to conflict and competition for political power, economic benefits and social status among social groups both within and across different ethnic categories. Today, the poorer and marginalized Dalit sub-castes who are undergoing a process of cultural modernization influenced by the Hindutva ideology aspire to be part of the larger 'Hindu' identity. BJP–RSS leaders have worked silently among these groups, which began to enter the democratic arena, unearthing local histories and myths by which they could link them to Hindutva. For example, the attempt to link three Dalit communities in eastern UP, the Pasis, Musahars and Nishads, with the Ramayana.[18] In a recent study, Badri Narayan has comprehensively shown and provided rich insights into how the Sangh and its vast network of cultural and social outfits have been refashioning its modes of mobilization, thereby assimilating the Dalits, OBCs, tribals and other marginalized communities. The RSS has made the 'Hindutva meta-narrative' appeal to a large section of Indians, particularly the lower castes.[19] Hence, what we are witnessing in UP is 'politically induced cultural change', the process by which political elites select some aspects of a group's culture, attach new value and meaning to them, and use them as symbols to mobilize the group.[20]

It is this fragmentation within the Dalit community and the highly divisive strategies of mobilization used by the BJP that led to as much as 45 per cent, 38.9 per cent and 48 per cent of the non-Jatavs voting for the BJP, in the 2014, 2017[21] assembly and 2019[22] Lok Sabha elections respectively. This division helped the BJP obtain high seat and vote percentages at the Centre and in UP, while the BSP lost considerable Dalit support.

Following its victory in the 2014 elections, the BJP attempted to consolidate its support among the Dalits by spearheading numerous projects that they felt would appeal to the Dalits. Some of the most significant initiatives included the various attempts to appropriate Dalit icon B.R. Ambedkar: the foundation stone for an International Ambedkar Centre in Delhi; a memorial at the Indu Mills Compound; the Dr Ambedkar Memorial in London; and a committee to celebrate his 125th birth anniversary, among others. In addition to that, Ram Nath Kovind, a Dalit from Uttar Pradesh, was appointed as President in 2015.

However, a number of atrocities across the country, beginning in 2015, and the lack of remedial steps by the BJP antagonized the Dalits, leading to angry protests by a section of the Dalits, which has acquired an increasingly violent character that points to increasing disillusionment with the BJP. This has been exacerbated by an increasingly pervasive impression of the BJP–RSS's unwillingness to continue reservations (an emotive issue for the Dalits); the amendment made to the Constitution to provide for reservations for the economically weaker sections (EWS); the efforts to undermine pre- and post-matric scholarships for the Dalits; and the government's overall unwillingness to crack down on atrocities against the Dalits. The decision of the Central government to privatize public-sector undertakings is seen by Dalits as a decisive move before doing away with reservations in jobs.

Emergence of New Dalit Groups

While assertion at the grassroots level has been a constant feature in many parts of the country, parallel to the rise of Dalit parties, the emerging leaders and their organizations are significantly different. Young, educated and popular among the younger generation, they represent a new, aggressive Dalit politics, reflected in their immediate response to atrocities against the Dalits, as well as in the tremendous support they receive. Apart from articulating themselves differently and aggressively, they are much more creative in terms of political tactics.

For example, the Bhim Army, named after Ambedkar and formed by Chandrashekhar Azad and Vinay Ratan Singh in 2015, has over 20,000 followers in the Saharanpur region of UP. Its declared aim is 'direct action based on confrontation to preserve or restore the dignity of Dalits'.[23] In April 2017, the Bhim Army rally in Saharanpur, against the atrocities committed against the Dalits by the Thakurs, received tremendous support. At least 50,000 Dalits gathered at Jantar Mantar on 21 May 2017 in New Delhi.[24] Other incidents include clashes over a signboard, 'the Great Chamar', put up in his village by Azad; action against the removal of a Dalit groom from his horse by Thakurs; agitation in February 2020 against the demolition of a temple dedicated to Sant Ravidas in Tughlaqabad, Delhi—all of which received huge support.[25] The UP government attempted to rein in Chandrashekhar Azad, and he was detained under the National Security Act till September 2019, despite the grant of bail by courts much earlier.

Similarly, the suicide of Rohith Vemula sparked protests by Dalit student organizations, while Jignesh Mevani has led protests against the Una incident in Gujarat, where seven Dalits were attacked by cow vigilantes in July 2016,[26] and the violent attacks on Dalits at Bhima Koregaon. The protests in Una led to the formation of the Una Dalit Atyachar Ladat Samiti, which has been fairly active in raising Dalit issues since then. Similarly, the Elgar Parishad rally in Bhima Koregaon was attended by Mevani, Azad, Vinay Ratan Singh, Prakash Ambedkar and other activists.[27] Mevani also led a Dalit Asmita Yatra from Ahmedabad to Una, which culminated on 15 August 2016 and was attended by some 20,000 Dalits who pledged to give up their traditional job of removing cow carcasses. There have been more recent incidents, as in Hathras in September 2020, where it was alleged that the state apparatus attempted to conceal the rape and subsequent murder of a Dalit girl, which created considerable anger.[28]

But the most important protest was in March 2018, against the apparent reluctance and delay by the government in filing a review petition in the Supreme Court against its 20 March order that called for changes in the SC/ST (PoA) Act, 1989.[29] While India has witnessed agitations by the Dalits in the past, the sheer scale of this protest—which spread across several states, and ultimately left eleven persons dead, many injured, public property damaged—was unprecedented, and pointed to disillusionment and rising anger against the BJP. These assaults fuelled a new, all-India Dalit consciousness and movements in support of leaders such as Mevani, Azad and Prakash Ambedkar.[30]

The new organizations are also quasi-political forces that go beyond traditional Dalit parties in their attempt to address Dalit needs and aspirations. The Bhim Army runs over 350 free schools for Bahujan children in Saharanpur, Meerut, Shamli and Muzaffarnagar, as Azad believes that education will take then Dalits forward. Similarly, Mevani, in his assembly constituency of Vadgam in Gujarat, has worked as a social activist and lawyer, and attempted to organize a 'socio-cultural movement'.[31]

Interestingly, both Mevani and Azad have kept their organizations independent of Dalit and non-Dalit parties. Mevani won the reserved Vadgam assembly seat as an independent, defeating the BJP candidate by 23,000 votes with the support of the Congress and the Aam Aadmi Party. While Azad had initially tried to move close to the BSP, criticism by Mayawati, who viewed him as a rival, led him to move away. He also pointed out that the BSP had voted for EWS reservation, Article 370 and the Citizenship Amendment Act (CAA) in Parliament, thereby 'murdering' the Constitution and weakening the Bahujan movement. Azad had also announced at the time that his organization would not join hands with or support the Congress party in the 2019 national elections.

Most importantly, a feature of this new leadership, not evident in the narrower canvas of traditional Dalit parties, is that while focusing on Dalit needs and desires, it has linked them to larger issues of national significance and provided support to widespread protests by citizens of all communities, against the CAA and NRC (National Register of Citizens), and in upholding the secular fabric of the state. This is seen in Azad's reading of the Preamble to the Constitution at the Jama Masjid in Delhi, and his support for the protests at Shaheen Bagh and elsewhere. Both Mevani and Azad have taken an inclusive stand on the citizenship issue and endorsed the idea of a plural society, in contrast to the attempt by the BJP to polarize the Dalits and Muslims, and pit them against each other.

In December 2019, Azad announced that he would form a new political party, an alternative for the Bahujan community, and on 15 March 2020 he formed the Azad Samaj party.[32] Based on the values and ideas of Ambedkar, the party aims to accomplish the political goals of the BSP leader Kanshi Ram, invoking his ideological proposition, *bahujan hitaya, bahujan sukhaya* (for the welfare of many, for the happiness of many). Unlike Kanshi Ram, who dispensed with his grassroots organization, the BAMCEF, in favour of the BSP, Azad plans to retain the Bhim Army and run it as a parallel outfit. The organization has units in Delhi and many other states, including Kerala, Tamil Nadu and Odisha; Azad has visited most of them and met local Dalit leaders. Party activists point out that many spontaneous Dalit organizations have emerged across the country, and the Bhim Army hopes to bring them on to a single platform. They claim to have received a positive response from some states, and there is enthusiasm and hope that if determined efforts are made, a strong party can emerge.[33]

New Dalit Movement: Possibilities and Limitations

The 2000s witnessed a fundamental change in the Dalit movement and its fight against upper-caste domination. Older movements/parties are facing a predicament; the ideology of self-respect and empowerment, though still important, can no longer by itself hold much social/electoral appeal, as material concerns are becoming increasingly important. The larger social, political and economic arena, within which Dalit politics operated earlier, has significantly altered. But Dalit assertion against upper-caste oppression and atrocities remains strong and has thrown up new leaders and organizations. The Dalits, particularly the younger generation, see in leaders such as Azad a new force to spearhead the Dalit movement and fill the space left vacant by Mayawati's diminishing popularity.

The emergence of the Bhim Army under the leadership of Azad does signify a new, aggressive phase in Dalit politics. The party has provided support to Dalits facing increasing atrocities, and, once established, it moved beyond Dalit issues and has entered national politics, upholding the Indian Constitution and the values of secularism, equality and universal citizenship for all sections of society. While initially, Azad's focus was on dealing with atrocities, fighting injustice and providing schools for Dalit children, in recent months he has shown interest in electoral politics. If his Azad Samaj Party joins or supports the SP–RLD coalition formed by Akhilesh Yadav, this would strengthen the alliance against the BJP and affect the fortunes of the BSP in western UP.[34] In the run-up to the 2022 UP elections, Azad had announced that he would fight the election against Chief Minister Yogi Adityanath from any seat the latter selects. 'I have to stop the BJP . . . I am strong and I can take on Yogi Adityanath.'[35]

Some commentators have argued that the transformation of the Bhim Army from a local resistance group against caste discrimination in UP to a political party, signals the reinvigoration of the Dalit movement.[36] On the other hand, scholars such as Suryakant Waghmore argue that the Bhim Army has to decide whether to take the electoral leap or continue as social radicals. He feels that Azad has a formidable 'opponent' in Mayawati. Political analysts and adversaries keep writing Mayawati off, but the BSP remains a national entity. She has always tamed competition from within the Ambedkarite universe, and kept her party a coherent and dominant force in politics. There are today, Waghmore feels, 'competing armies of Bhim', and it remains to be seen which will take the movement forward.[37]

Does the Azad Samaj Party, under the leadership of Azad, have the potential to emerge as a strong, pan-Indian Dalit party? The difficulty is that the Dalit movement, almost everywhere in India, has shifted from 'successful social mobilization to political institutionalization' in the form of parties.[38] While this transition is made to capture power and obtain justice, party politics also deprives social movements of their radicalism, as success in electoral politics demands that you accommodate competing castes/communities and ideologies. There are benefits that ensue from this shift, but institutionalized actors may lose the relative autonomy to criticize existing politics and articulate alternatives, and they seldom return to the politics of protest. Attempts in the recent past to transform successful Dalit organizations into political parties have had only partial electoral success, that too when they could join pre-poll alliances. The Dalit Panthers in Maharashtra in the 1970s, and the Dalit Panther Iyakkam (DPI) and the Puthiya Tamilagam (PT) in Tamil Nadu in the 1990s, and their coalitions, to survive, with the Dravidian parties, are good examples of this predicament of Dalit politics, which often leads to an impasse.[39] Yet, at the same time, the increasing disillusionment of Dalits with the BSP has opened up the political space for Azad and other Dalit leaders, creating the desire to compete for power.

Equally important, can the new Dalit organizations build a new movement/party given the tough challenges they face in the current political environment? Many Dalits across the country today feel that the actions of the BJP, since it attained power, have been anti-Dalit. All disadvantaged groups, including the Dalits, are facing the onslaught of a right-wing, Hindu majoritarian party supported by a conservative upper-caste society and a centralized, authoritarian government. In this situation, for the new Dalit leaders to fight atrocities, build a new movement that unites all sections of the Dalits, fulfil their aspirations and tackle the divisive politics of the BJP, will be a herculean task.

The Bhim Army has built a space for itself on the ground in UP fighting atrocities and taking up unjust national issues. But entry into electoral politics even within UP, given the forces ranged against it, will be very difficult. At best, it represents a strong social force at the grassroots level against upper-caste domination and oppression, and the failure of the state to protect the lives and properties of the Dalits. Does the Bhim Army, with its limited reach, represent both the crisis affecting the Dalits as well as a hope of regeneration which has yet to take shape? Or, is the Dalit movement moving towards a greater crisis with implications for India's democracy?

Dalit Cinema in India

Pa. Ranjith

I would like to begin this essay by referring to a tale that unfolded in one of India's most picturesque states, Kerala, also known as God's own country. This is the story of P.K. Rosy. Born in 1903 and the child of Nandan Kodil Paulose and Kunji from the Pulaya community, who had converted to Christianity, she lost her father when very young. She had to work for a living from early on in the fields. Later she joined a theatre company in Trivandrum, at a time when women who were part of theatre groups were considered immoral and termed prostitutes. But since she liked the theatre and needed to make a living, she continued to act.[1]

That was the beginning of the silent film era in India. J.C. Daniel, considered a pioneer in Malayalam cinema, wanted to feature Rosy in a film that he was making, *Vigathakumaran*. In effect, Rosy was the first Malayalam actor to make it to the world of cinema and the first Dalit woman actor in all of India.

From the day he signed a contract with Rosy, Daniel faced the wrath of the dominant castes, which only grew as the film was made. They objected to the fact that he had asked an untouchable Pulaya woman to act in his film. But Daniel was determined to continue with his venture and went on to complete the film. Once

127

done, he looked for ways to screen it. Dominant-caste persons, who were already angry with him for having asked a Pulaya woman to play the role of a Nair woman, opposed his attempts at screening the film and ensured that no theatre was made available to him. And when, finally, he did get a place to screen, people in the film world and those who were socially powerful refused to go to the theatre to watch the film.

Daniel continued to work at getting an audience for his film and finally, *Vigathakumaran* was screened at Capitol Theatre. But there was another problem: Daniel was told that he ought not to invite Rosy for the screening. However, Rosy did arrive at the theatre, whereupon men from the dominant castes prevented her from entering the premises. She ought to stay away till they finished watching the film, they insisted. So Rosy was made to wait outside the theatre while the film was screened inside. Since it was a silent film, a man sat on stage and described the scenes as the film unfolded.

One scene proved fateful: Rosy as the Nair girl walks down a road, with flowers in her hair. The hero of the film comes by on a cycle, accosts her and, drawing close, takes in the scent of the flowers. As soon as they witnessed this scene, the audience, including those who were part of the world of cinema and social bigwigs, got incensed. Annoyed as they were that a Pulaya woman was playing a Nair character, they could not bear the sight of her being romanced by a man from a 'higher' caste and the fact that he was intimately sniffing the fragrance of her flowers. Daniel was beaten up badly and the theatre destroyed. Daniel fled to save his life. Meanwhile, the mob attacked and burnt his house.

Rosy somehow got away from the mob with the help of a lorry driver. It is said that she left Trivandrum and went with the driver to Nagercoil and sought refuge there. Subsequently, she appears to have married the driver, Kesavan Pillay, and had a child by him. Till the very end, she kept her identity as an actor hidden. It is evident that whatever happened to Rosy was on account of her being born into the untouchable Pulaya caste, which was considered barely human. In short, she was an *avarna*, and therefore placed outside the caste order and kept away from it.

There have been educated and talented Dalits in Indian cinema since Rosy's time, just as there are many today. It is possible, too, that many have been in situations where they could have faced the sort of horror that Rosy was subjected to. It is also likely that aware as they are of the fact that from their moment of birth they are considered untouchable, they felt fearful at the prospect of social boycott. In any event, many of them did not come out as Dalits. And such is the case even now: Dalits in cinema continue to pass as people from the 'socially respectable' upper castes.

Rosy's story and the fact that Dalits continue to be invisible in cinema are the starting points of this essay.

* * *

Caste Hindus consider the varna–caste order to be designed by God and accept it as such, and lead lives in accordance with appropriate rituals and customs. When they came to films, they made content in keeping with the place designated to them in the social order. While they were able to address and analyse concerns to do with religion, colour, sex and class, they were not able to—indeed, they refused to address—matters to do with caste and caste-based exploitation. To do so would mean that they admitted to their own complicity in the caste system.

On the other hand, since film-makers wished their films to be viewed widely, theatres for screening were thrown open to all castes. In many instances this led to protests and violence (as we saw in the 1990s in Tsundur in Andhra Pradesh). Film-viewing spaces remained relatively open in places where it was considered polluting to be touched by a Dalit and Dalits were forbidden from accessing common village wells, tanks, temples and not allowed to enter upper-caste neighbourhoods. The commercial success of cinema was responsible for this development.

From its earliest days and until now, cinema in India has reconstructed itself in keeping with changes in the world of film-making, whether this had to do with the use of technology, storytelling, modes of picturization or acting. And today, Indian films vie for honours with films from other countries at the global level. Indian film-makers and artists have earned worldwide recognition and garnered their share of awards. The question, though, is this: What is the nature of reality that Indian cinema typically features? What impression is this cinema likely to make on an audience that is not directly familiar with Indian realities?

If the audience enjoys standard Indian commercial cinema, they are likely to go away with the impression that India is home to an ancient culture, dominated by exotic customs, philosophizing and a veneration of the family. Or if they are to watch the more recent crop of films, such as *Slumdog Millionaire, Life of Pi* and *The Lunchbox*, they are likely to associate India with sad poverty on the one hand and, on the other, with good-hearted and progressive Indians who are looking to change things in India.

Sadly, Indian film-makers have not managed to convey that only a small percentage of people live this life of exotic happiness, while the rest are poor and subject to caste-based exploitation under the aegis of modern capitalism. Ironically, neither has the Indian audience been given the opportunity to grasp this reality through cinema. In this context, one could say that some Bengali film-makers have attempted to produce a different kind of cinema. Satyajit Ray's neo-realist films, especially the series that he began with *Pather Panchali*, featured poverty in all its human richness and remain the measure of realistic cinema in India. But the characters in these films are from the Brahmin caste, that is, they are not habitually part of the working class and castes. Mrinal Sen and Ritwik Ghatak approached caste, poverty and gender narratives from a Marxist perspective, as is evident from their films, and Sen's *Oka Oori Katha* featured Dalit life-worlds.

In Tamil Nadu, right from the 1930s, the audience has relished a mix of films: puranic stories, tales of kings and queens, scripts to do with the freedom struggle and narratives that foregrounded Gandhi's 'Harijan seva', and later on, films that featured larger-than-life heroes, family plots and adventure stories. In the 1950s, when the Dravidian movement was turning politically popular, films that expressed the basics of the Dravidian ideology—that is, a world view critical of faith, superstitions and caste—were produced. Those who made these films realized that at a time when the Dravida Munnetra Kazhagam (DMK) was gaining ground, chances were that their films would be commercially successful. Many a film from this genre went on to feature the DMK's flag, photographs of its leaders, as well as slogans against poverty, caste and obscurantism—and they found a welcoming audience.

These films did have Dalit characters, but the films were not about them, and even when it appeared that they were, the identities of the Dalit characters were not visually foregrounded, and very subtly, all talk of caste was avoided. A good example of such a film is *Madurai Veeran*, which had M.G. Ramachandran (MGR), who went on to become chief minister of Tamil Nadu, in the lead. He plays the protagonist, who is the son of a cobbler and does very many heroic things, in spite of his 'low' birth: he marries a princess and helps another royal rid his land of thieves. Nevertheless, he is punished because the courtesan at the king's court falls in love with him. His hands and feet are cut off. However, we realize the unfairness of this punishment—we are told that he is not a cobbler but a prince who was abandoned as a baby in the forest. Finally, both wife and courtesan join him in heaven.

Such stories are legion in Indian cinema: when love is transgressive, of caste, religion and class, or someone succeeds at something, in spite of being limited by these structures, such transgression is 'normalized'. Even though it appears that the hero has crossed acceptable social limits, it's not really so, because he is actually from the upper classes, and if he has fallen in love with a woman from the upper class, or if he has come to inherit property, it is all because of his original status. Thus, social inequality is justified, and this is true of many films even today.

MGR's films featured many characters from society's margins. His films were essentially about the poor, whatever castes they were from, and he was the protagonist who fought for them. While he did not ever portray a character who took up the fight against caste, his films were peppered with words and phrases that opposed caste, and he took on roles such as that of a rickshaw-puller, which went down well with his audience. The latter could not but think that here was a man who ate like them, married girls from families such as theirs, spoke up for them, talked like them and was intimately familiar with them.

Here, we need to keep in mind the following: in the early days, Tamil cinema, as indeed Indian cinema, was dominated by the Brahmins, and the non-Brahmins—men and women from communities traditionally associated with music, dance and public performance, and those who migrated to cinema from the stage—were usually from the so-called backward castes. But the films made during this period featured mostly upper-class and upper-caste lives. In this context, MGR's films were somewhat different.

This period, the 1960s, also saw the emergence of the typical family film, which relied on the single charismatic hero. Love and familial relations were the favoured subjects, while poverty remained a major hurdle to happiness. The films featured contradictions between the rich and the poor, but the stories that unfolded on the screen were of Brahmin, Vellala, Chettiar and Mudaliar households. Characters were referred to by their caste names, almost as if it was natural to do so, and they were shown speaking, eating and dressing in the way that matched their caste status. This was as true of negative characters as it was of the heroes and heroines.

Sometimes, the villain's henchmen would be shown to be Dalits or given names associated with the latter, such as 'Veerappa' or 'Kabali'. Typically, such characters, especially in movies with an urban setting, would sport a lungi, a *banian* and a kerchief knotted around their necks. Elaborately mustachioed, they would speak in what was recognized as 'Madras Tamil' (on account of it being spoken by the city's Dalit working class). Additionally, they were shown to be wayward. Sometimes, it was not clear whether such characters were merely backward or Dalits—in any case, both classes of people were of the same low status for the upper-caste producers and directors.

The form and content of Tamil cinema began to change from the late 1970s. From then onwards, regional dialects and the village folk that spoke them, more specifically those who were from dominant castes in rural Tamil Nadu, featured in films, which now began to pay heed to their narratives. This cinema made it clear that its protagonists were distinctive, that they were as good as heroes and heroines from the upper castes, and definitely different from and socially above the Dalits. Further, rituals, customs, specific to these castes, the inherent 'courage' of the men, their capacity for love—these found their way into cinema and helped replace older representations with newer and more self-conscious ones. Given the worlds these films portrayed and the social realities they brought to the screen, they proved immensely popular. Being commercially successful, they energized the field and soon, a number of writers, actors, directors and producers from the so-called backward castes thronged the industry.

This moment in the history of Tamil cinema is best identified with director Bharathiraja's films. He came into the field in the late 1970s—his first film was released in 1977. His early films, *16 Vayathinilae* (When Sixteen Years of Age), *Alaigal Oyvathillai* (Waves Don't Cease to Be) and *Vedam Puthithu* (A New Veda), all made within the decade, provided an unusual gloss on matters to do with caste and religion, and brought a new perspective to familiar film themes. At the same time, he also made films that accentuated a particular caste identity, evident in his *Mann Vaasanai* (Smell of Earth) and *Muthal Mariyadai* (First Respect). Drawing on this kind of cinema, several other films, which foregrounded the caste identities of locally dominant non-Brahmin groups, came to be made.

Starting from the late 1980s, there was another noticeable change: films featuring love stories that addressed caste contradictions began to be made in noticeable numbers. These films are best analysed separately (Stalin Rajangam has, in fact, written widely on this theme in Tamil). The point is, once caste identities were made visible in films, it was to be expected that films that addressed caste-based realities would be made. But on the contrary, very few films featured Dalits in a respectful way.

The year 1991 marked the centenary of Ambedkar's birth. Extensive debates began in the fields of art, literature and politics. As a result, the phrase 'Dalit politics' acquired salience and became the subject of intense critical attention. Dalit life-worlds and the political contexts that shaped them became favoured literary subjects. In Tamil Nadu, Raj Gauthaman, Bama, P. Sivakami and many others came to write creative as well as critical literature. This was also when we came to know of Dalit writers from elsewhere: Daya Pawar, Arjun Dangle, Sharankumar Limbale from Maharashtra; G. Kalyana Rao, Arvind Malagatti, Siddalingaiah and Devanur Mahadeva from Karnataka. The transformations we witnessed in the literary world, and the very distinctive Dalit texts that we got to read, led some of us to bring forth critiques of cinema and raise questions about its content.

* * *

Why were Dalit life-worlds not featured in cinema? And when Dalits were shown on screen, why were they shown in stereotypical ways, as lowly and below contempt? Do Dalits not have a culture and cultural values of their own? Have they achieved nothing in art, literature and politics? Why are Dalits, who have been a resistant group since the times of the Buddha, always shown as abject and unable to oppose authority? Why must they always be viewed as dirty, immoral, capable only of wrongdoing and violence?

In raising these questions and trying to find answers, I essayed my own path into cinema and came to make films that were mainstream and commercial, but which featured Dalits as protagonists and narrated their stories. The films I wrote and directed—*Attakathi* (Paper Knife), *Madras*, *Kabali* and *Kaala*—and the ones I produced—Mari Selvaraj's *Pariyerum Perumal* (The God Who Rode a Horse) and Athiyan's *Irandam Ulagaporin Kadaisi Vedigundu* (The Last Bomb of World War II), might be viewed as examples of 'Dalit cinema'. There have been others, too, who followed the path we walked, and so you have films that foreground what might be called Dalit themes: Vetrimaran's *Asuran* and Susindran's *Maaveeran Kittu* (Kittu the Warrior).

It was around this time that Nagraj Manjule made *Fandry* and *Sairat* in Marathi. We have had other films that are expressions of Dalit cinema: the Malayalam film *Kammatti Paadam* and the Telugu film *Palasa 1978* are notable in this regard. Dalit cinema is yet to come into its own in Hindi, but you do have the instance of Neeraj Ghaywan's *Masaan*. In spite of these developments, and in spite of the commercial success of Dalit cinema, it is still not considered 'normal' to feature Dalits as worthy characters or Dalit narratives as valid as any other. It is as if Indian cinema is not interested in such narratives, or perhaps it does not wish to endorse or support such films.

The reasons are two-fold: one, the habitual disgust that Indian society reserves for the Dalits; and the other, the more mundane one, being the claim, in spite of all the evidence to the contrary, that Dalit cinema is unlikely to be a success at the box office.

* * *

Ritual and culture, Hinduism and its Manudharmashastra: these are the means through which hatred towards the Dalits continues to be expressed by caste Hindus. It is so ingrained that even in the time of the COVID-19 pandemic, which made us all equally vulnerable, we were witness to expressions of this hatred. Many instances might be cited, but I shall restrict myself to one: in Uttar Pradesh, a Dalit was shot dead by a caste Hindu for having entered a Hindu temple.[2] Even in a time of common crisis, we are not able to rise above the habitual feeling of hatred and revulsion that many caste Hindus express with regard to the Dalits. It is not that our social contexts have remained static. Indeed, as a society we have changed and grown, and become modern, so to speak. But our modernity has been restricted to rendering our external worlds modern. The feeling of caste hatred that has taken possession of our minds remains unaffected, and we have ensured that we stay that way. Even if one is poor, a citizen equal to other citizens, a creature of the digital age, one still feels anchored, finds himself rooted only in the place that has been accorded him in the caste order, and in keeping with the norms outlined in the Manusmriti. He holds on to that place, and in view of his faith, whose sanctity he wishes to protect, and in keeping with what he has been told, by way of cultural knowledge and across generations, he marks the untouchable person as such, isolates her and makes her the subject of his hatred. He secures legitimacy for his actions in the logic of the social order to which he belongs.

India's village structure is itself symbolic of this hatred. All those who are part of the varna system, whether Brahmins, Kshatriyas, Vaishyas or Shudras (and all castes associated with each of these varnas), live in the village, in the *oor*, as it is known in Tamil. The avarnas, those who are outside of the varna structure and who do not accept its logic, live outside the village. From the Brahmins to the Shudras, they follow caste-specific rituals and customs, and none will receive a bride or groom from the other. They are all bound by the caste order. It not only unites them, but they are unified in their desire to protect it.

Thus united and willing to close all differences, as well as accept, implicitly, the logic of high and low, all castes stand opposed to the Dalits. It is as if, like the rituals and customs that have been handed down over the ages, this hatred, too, has been inherited. Today, this hatred has crossed village boundaries, and untouchability has travelled as well. Both are present among us—they shadow the modern lives of caste Hindus and are reflected in all that they do.

As far as cinema is concerned, how does this hatred manifest itself? On the one hand, we see it in the way cinema refuses to 'speak of' Dalit lives and has shown itself determined to not heed Dalit assertion. On the other hand, we see it in the tendency to conclude—at least in Tamil cinema—that, with Shudra narratives having found their way on to the screen, all that needed to happen by way of social change has already taken place, and that no further changes are necessary or required. Also, there appears to be a consensus that the Shudra life-worlds depicted so far in cinema— which, as I have indicated, are really portrayals of the dominant rural castes—are all there is to the Dalit life-worlds as such and there is nothing else to feature on screen.

Let me explain what I mean here with an example. In recent past, there has been a spate of films featuring names of particular castes as their titles; and such films also have characters whose castes names are casually referenced throughout the film in question, as if this was the most natural thing in the world. In this context, one needs to raise the question: Will these producers support a film that has a Dalit caste name or a name with a Dalit caste suffix as its title? Tamil films reference the Iyers, Mudaliars, Chettiars, Thevars and Gounders; Telugu films routinely feature the Reddys and Naidus; Kannada films, the Gowdas; Kerala has its Nairs and Nambudris; in Hindi cinema, we have the Thakurs, the Rajputs . . . Will these film-makers, who do not hesitate in using caste names, be so bold as to present films that bear the names of Dalit castes: Paraiayar, Pallar,

Arunthathiyar, Pulayar, Mala, Madiga, Mahar, Mang, Chambhar? Indeed, will they come forward to make films that feature avarna caste names? What stops them from doing so? If they can flaunt the caste names of communities that are included within the varna order, they ought to be comfortable affixing Dalit caste names to their films. If you accept caste in one instance, what stops you from doing so in another?

Cinema in India has come to accept the caste order that implicates all communities within the varna system, but it is precisely because of this that it separates out the avarnas. This is, of course, a form of untouchability. The castes within the varna order are eager and enthusiastic to consort with each other and think through their differences. But when it comes to the Dalit representative claims in respect of the social order, all conversation ceases. Indian cinema has been open to technological and other changes, as we have noted, but now that the Dalits have come forward to present their own life narratives, not only do they face criticism, but there is a concerted attempt to prevent such efforts from being taken forward in a dynamic manner. All such efforts are being thwarted. In the context of politics, representatives of all non-Brahmin castes, including Dalits, have forged political alliances of one kind or another in Tamil Nadu, but when it comes to the realm of culture, the Dalits find themselves alone, even as the other castes identify themselves with Brahminical world views and customs.

Now let me come to the second reason as to why Dalit cinema narratives have not found traction widely: the claim that they are not commercially viable and therefore no one wishes to risk making such films. With respect to commerce, let us ask a few questions: Where is the market in most villages? Who are the traders and merchants in our villages? We know for a fact that in our villages, markets are found in the village quarter mostly and not where the Dalits live. Initially, only people from the upper castes were traders, and they alone had the right to sell. Gradually, as needs grew and a market for diverse goods followed, the opportunities for trade widened, and traders from the so-called backward castes were also encouraged to set up shops. But no such facility was given to the Dalits. In any case, how might a Dalit expect to open a shop next to the shop of a caste Hindu and in the village? Even if he does, who would be his customers? Would caste Hindus patronize his shop? For all castes, their caste identities and networks serve as capital, whereas for the Dalits, their caste identity, as Ambedkar noted, could only be a cruel tragedy.

True, our villages are not so insular any more and many have been transformed into small towns. Our markets are flooded with goods of every kind, including fancy electronics, and globalization has connected disparate parts of our economy together. On account of these changes, it has been possible for Dalits to set up commercially viable establishments. But it is a moot question whether such Dalits who have successfully done so are able to function, wearing their identities openly. It is more likely that they do not call attention to their caste. In any case, it is not easy for Dalits to avoid being recognized as such. For ours is a society where, on first acquaintance, it is habitual for people to start probing into one's caste background. This remains the case, whether one wants to open a shop, acquire land, undertake a new trade or buy/rent a house. A separate book needs to be written about the desperation and heartache that are caused by having to hide one's identity.

In such a context, commercial success is contingent on one's caste status, and in a society where commerce is underwritten by caste, it is no wonder that films which feature Dalit lives or even credible Dalit characters are not viewed as commercially viable. The stated fear is that if such cinema was to be produced, the producer, director and all else would become the targets of social hatred. As a result, few people come forward to narrate Dalit stories, and it has not proved easy for Dalits to portray their lives either, openly and without fear, as it is for those from the Brahmin and other dominant communities. Even when they did, or tried to do so, they did not find it easy to get producers. And even when someone managed to convince a producer that 'look, this is really not about Dalits', their films would often get stalled at the distribution stage: for one has to screen the film for distributors, and if they feel that it is 'Dalit' in content, they refuse to distribute it.

It is possible to look for screening options, independently, but for those who attempted to work this choice, it was not easy to find theatres that would screen such films. Basically, distributors and theatre owners are from the upper castes, and they are not interested in Dalit themes. So even on the rare occasion when, in the past, such themes were featured in films, the film-makers had to concede ground and face defeat.

* * *

When I came to cinema, things had somewhat changed. This was largely due to the political changes brought in by Dalit assertion, and also because the films we made were true and resonant in a way that could not be refuted. So, we had an audience, comprising critical-minded Dalit youth and those from non-Dalit communities who were committed to an anti-caste world view. The problem was that producers and distributors did not think that this emergent new audience could guarantee commercial success.

I would like to narrate here an incident that unfolded when I was filming my first venture, *Attakathi*. This was a film about teenage love. On the surface, it appears a comedy, but its background, that is the social context it features, has to do with Dalit lives and realities, and I had written the script in that manner. When I was looking to interest a producer in my story, I met one who was taken with it, and he agreed to support the film. We signed a contract and started filming with a totally new cast and technicians. For a while, things went smoothly, until the day when the crew was getting ready to shoot the protagonist's 'entry' scene. The art director Ramalingam had got the hero's home ready and in place.

Just then a person from the producer's office came and told us that the filming had to stop. When we asked why, he said, 'You've got a photograph of Ambedkar on a wall in the hero's house. If you are to retain that picture, the producer is sure to incur a loss. For the audience in Madurai will not countenance seeing Ambedkar thus. And the producer feels that if we do not anticipate the audience's reaction and go ahead, chances are the audience will vandalize the screening theatre. So either you remove the photograph and continue filming or you stop filming.'

I was very upset and worried. My technicians exhorted me to give up on this shot and continue. I closed my eyes, begged pardon from Babasaheb and took off his photograph, and continued shooting the film. Since the on-location shoot was in villages where Dalits lived in large numbers, we finally did have Ambedkar in our footage—he was on every village wall, and there were umpteen statues everywhere. I also managed to fit in a scene which referenced beef-eating. In any case, once the film was done, the distributors were convinced that it would succeed commercially, its politics notwithstanding. So they agreed to distribute the film, and it did go on to do well, leaving both the producer and distributor with a measure of profit.

Riding on the commercial success of *Attakathi*, I went on to make *Kabali* and *Kaala*. The enthusiasm with which these films were received led me to production, and that was how I came to make *Pariyerum Perumal* and *Irandam Ulagaporin Kadaisi Gundu*. I was successful in both ventures and have demonstrated that Dalit life-worlds could be brought into mainstream cinema. I am not alone in this. Since the second decade of the twenty-first century, we have seen many such efforts across India. As I noted earlier, these efforts are more visible in south India than elsewhere (the Hindi film *Masaan* being an exception for the north).

Article 15, which came out in 2019, was viewed as a film featuring a Dalit theme, was commercially successful and also won critical attention. While the film was about the Dalits, it portrayed them in an usual manner—they are shown as not possessing the wherewithal to take on authority and power, and, as in earlier films, it is an upper-caste hero who is their saviour and who fights for them.

This film led to a great deal of discussion with regard to characterization and storytelling, and raised issues having to do with the politics of Dalit representation, which is something to be welcomed. In south India, it is evident that there is a generation of Dalit film-makers who do not see the need to hide their identities and who openly declare who they are and tell their stories boldly. In Tamil Nadu, these film-makers have forced a dialogue on the subject. That time has passed when it was thought that showing an Ambedkar picture in the hero's house might be the film's ruin. In films made by directors whose social concerns are not in doubt, we find Ambedkar, his face uncovered and glittering.

At the same time, there are other issues that have cropped up. It has been claimed that in the name of narrating Dalit stories, attempts are being made to disturb public peace, and that to thus foreground Dalit lives is equally a form of casteism. In fact, a production company announced it would have nothing to do with such films and those who have scripts that have to do with these themes ought not to approach them! I also know that young assistant directors who worked with me and who wish to make their own films have found it hard to interest producers in their stories and fear that they are being ignored due to their being associated with me.

The important thing to keep in mind is this: we need Dalit cinema. For centuries the Dalits have been denied their humanity, treated worse than animals, and we need to show the world Hindu society's real face and point to how it is essentially the face of a casteist social order. For this, we need to create visual texts that depict Dalit lives and show worlds that pertain to Dalit realities. Further, in order to go against the grain of common belief that the Dalits do not have a culture, that in a literary and artistic sense, they possess very little intelligence, that they are barbaric, without morals, incapable of raising their voice to assert their rights, that they are not beautiful, are abject, violent and polluted from a religious point of view—to go against this mindset, we need Dalit cinema. We need to challenge existing narratives and put new ones in place.

For, to represent Dalit life-worlds, to take forward Dalit politics, is to embrace the path of liberation. Today, the Dalits stand poised, all set to do this, and they need to do this. As Babasaheb Ambedkar reminded us, 'Ours is a battle not for wealth, nor for power, ours is a battle for freedom; for the reclamation of human personality'— one that has been maimed for centuries by Hindu society.

Education and Dalit Liberation

R.S. Praveen Kumar

'I am Guntikadi Rani, alumna of Telangana Social Welfare Residential Degree College at Mahabubnagar. My father is a mason and mother is a daily wage labourer. A career in information technology is my childhood dream, and I saw Engineering Common Entrance Test as my ticket into the world of technology. However, my financial background stopped me from pursuing BTech and I had to settle for BSc. in maths and physical sciences. Little did I know that this would be a turning point in my life. When the TSWREI society announced the data science training programme, I jumped at the opportunity and gave my best to secure a spot in the camp. Our trainers at the camp helped us acquire the essential skills of a data scientist and helped me take my first step into Cognizant, where I worked for the client Google as a data analyst. Thanks to the SWAERO Commandments, I landed in Twitter with a very decent pay package. I am an aspiring entrepreneur and I wish to inspire young women from my community to come out of the fears that were fed to them by society and work to make their dreams come true.'

These heartwarming words, of a former student of the Social Welfare Residential School in Telangana, spoken on 28 March 2021 at a students' meet in Kollapur, in the Nagarkurnool district of Telangana, may sound alien to the majority of Dalits and adivasis in India! It might be a common trajectory taken by students in the elite private schools of urban India, where caste and class privilege intersect, giving privileged children opportunities and resources to realize their dreams. Even if poor children work hard and cross barriers to reach the institutions, caste stigma and its accompanied burdens strangle their dreams. Rohith Vemula, who dreamt of becoming a space explorer and science fiction writer like Carl Sagan, was suffocated to death by circumstances beyond his control at the University of Hyderabad. The stolen dreams of scholars like Rohith are recreated at the Telangana Social Welfare Residential Schools through the perseverance of students like Guntikadi Rani.

The New Education Policy 2020, while acknowledging the needs of the 'socio-economically disadvantaged groups' (SEDGs), does not specifically delve into the interventions that address structural barriers faced by students due to caste discrimination. Caste remains a key determinant of access to educational opportunities and has a profound impact on the overall academic experience of individual students. And Dalit students continue to face discrimination in the schooling system.

While several programmes have been implemented to increase enrolment and improve the educational outcomes of Dalit students, the Telangana Social Welfare Residential Schools is a model that seeks to address the intergenerational disadvantages and the institutional discrimination faced by Dalit students. From their inception, the residential schools were committed to creating a conducive environment for first-generation learners. While academic excellence is central, the schools endeavour to nurture a generation of confident young Dalits ready to take on emerging opportunities in a globalized world. In a deeply hierarchical society, information asymmetry and the absence of social networks are major impediments to navigating opportunities. The schools aim to instil a sense of pride in students and challenge the predominant narrative of powerlessness.

Through the examples of Malavath Poorna, the youngest-ever female to scale Mount Everest, and Anand Kumar, perhaps the first Dalit boy to scale the same peak, and through the teaching of programming languages like Python, the Telangana Social Welfare Schools are charting a radically different path in educating the next generation of marginalized children in India. This essay outlines the critical role of residential education in the pursuit of social justice and takes a closer look at the experiment of Telangana, the challenges ahead and the 'quantum leap strategy' to realize the grand dream for the emancipation of the marginalized people through quality education by 2050.

Birth of the Residential Education Model

Following the boarding model of education, the Government of Andhra Pradesh started residential schools in 1971 for the benefit of talented children from all communities in rural areas. Children educated in these institutions gained admission in prestigious medical and engineering colleges, and entered Indian civil services. Many went on to become accomplished scientists, doctors and professors in the humanities around the world. The Government of Andhra Pradesh organized a State Harijan Conference in 1976. One of the important resolutions of the conference was to extend the coverage of special residential schools to the scheduled castes and scheduled tribes. S.R. Sankaran, senior IAS officer and the then secretary of the social welfare department, took the initiative to establish Social Welfare Residential Schools across the state in 1984. Admission in these schools was based on a competitive entrance examination. After the bifurcation of Andhra Pradesh, the newly formed Telangana government continued to support the residential model of education under 'Mission KG to PG' (Kindergarten to Postgraduation) by rapidly expanding its scope from schools to colleges.

The residential schools are a home away from home. Every school complex has an academic block, dormitory, kitchen, dining hall, residential quarters for staff members and a playground. The minimum land that is required to construct a government residential school is 7–10 acres, depending on the terrain. Each school accommodates approximately 640 students from fifth to twelfth grades. The classrooms are designed to accommodate not more than forty students, and there is at least one teacher for every twenty-two students. In addition to the residential schools, the government has established thirty residential degree colleges for SC women.

The residential schools are governed by a society, which is registered under the Societies Act. The head of the institution is a secretary, guided by a board of governors appointed by the government. The main motto of the schools is to inculcate self-discipline and confidence, and encourage students to aspire for big goals in life.

Turning Teachers into Transformers

Over 10,000 teachers are part of the Telangana Social Welfare Residential Schools and are the foundation of the residential schools. They are instrumental in identifying and nurturing talent. These teachers are selected through a rigorous examination process in three stages by an independent recruitment board. They are tested for proficiency in the English language, subject knowledge, pedagogical approach and social sensitivity. After selection they undergo rigorous training that includes the participation of students and parents, to sensitize the teachers about the real experiences and the neglect the former had endured.

The training consists of interactive methods and teaching through lived experiences. As part of the training process, teachers are sent for an intensive immersion exercise and visits to the homes of the students for a couple of days. On their return, they share their experiences at the training academy. On completion of the training they are assigned a mentor in their respective district for two years as trainees. This equips teachers to handle complex situations to help the students from the most marginalized backgrounds with innumerable challenges.

Teachers play an important role in this mission of emancipatory education. Each teacher is assigned a role as guardian for a group of forty students, and takes care of their emotional and academic needs. Most teachers live on campus along with their families, and they become part of the educational experience of residential school campuses. The students are supported by a command centre, which monitors the health of every student throughout the year, even during vacations.

Self-Organized Learning is the Key

The main mission of residential schools is to prepare self-confident aspiring students to be role models in society. They are also taught to take responsibility and become leaders in various aspects of life. For instance, the student council members elected by the student body share the responsibility of the smooth functioning of the school and act as a support to the principal. As a collective body, they take care of the upkeep of the school premises, actively engage in building social communication skills and facilitate a culture of educational enrichment. They run multiple clubs independently and in the classroom act as teaching assistants to supplement the efforts of the teachers.

Academic schedules are implemented through 'unique quartets', a system that is organized in such a way that every group of four students is as heterogeneous as possible in terms of their overall performance. These quartets are platforms for self- and collaborative learning. The teaching assistants are exceptional students. They deliver lectures on live television that reach the entire state. Some of them work as Green Gurus (Student Teachers) in schools to facilitate teaching. Every school has fitted mirrors at different corners for students to talk to their own images as a form of 'reflective learning' that helps them to improve their language and communication skills. In addition to classroom teaching, students are given opportunities to go on field trips and camps under the banner of Summer Samurai. Summer camps provide incredible opportunities for students to interact with university students and knowledge partners. Skills ranging from horse-riding and coding to making drones are taught at these camps. But underneath this bubbling enthusiasm there is a serious churning of 'who we are' and 'what we must be'. We will examine this now.

SWAERO: Birth of a New Bond

The Social Welfare Residential Schools in Telangana assiduously promoted a collective sense of new identity among all stakeholders and pride in its larger purpose. On 22 October 2013, coinciding with the birthday of S.R. Sankaran, around 100 alumni of the state welfare hostels and residential schools launched the SWAEROES Network. The SWAEROES ('SW' stands for 'State Welfare', which invokes institutional association, and 'AERO' symbolizes air and the sky, towards which their life aspirations must be aimed at always) is an aspirational identity—a way to discard all the imposed humiliating identities like Dalit, *achhut*, *pichchde*, Harijan, etc. The aim of the SWAEROES network is to promote excellence in every field pursued by students, build community and school networks to fight the social evils plaguing the marginalized communities, and lend a helping hand to those who are less fortunate. As an antidote to the traumatized and stigmatized experiences in their lives, students recite the following ten SWAERO commandments every day in the school assembly:

1. *I am not inferior to anyone*
2. *I shall be the leader wherever I am*
3. *I shall do what I love and be different*
4. *I shall always think big and aim high*

5. *I shall be honest, hard-working and punctual*
6. *I shall never blame others for my failures*
7. *I shall neither beg nor cheat*
8. *I shall repay what I borrow*
9. *I shall never fear the unknown*
10. *I shall never give up*

They are encouraged to practise the commandments in life to overcome any challenges. The SWAEROES network has grown into a 30,000-strong community of alumni in Telangana and Andhra Pradesh. But the proactive role played by the parents' wing of the SWAEROES network merits a closer look.

Parents as Stakeholders of the Institution

The Telangana residential schools model is all about community participation in educational institutions. With their loved ones away from home for almost 245 days in a year, the trust of parents in running the institution is very critical. But despite the fact that they are away from the children, the parents make their presence felt in every aspect of school life. They campaign for admissions and participate in the smooth conduct of entrance examinations. Moreover, as stakeholders, they help the principal maintain the school properly and engage with the students who are at risk. They regularly attend parent–teacher meetings, share their experiences of all training programmes, and facilitate community-immersion programmes during the induction of new teachers. Most importantly, they identify and felicitate committed teachers after the end of the academic year. The annual feedback by the parents becomes an important part of the school-inspection process. The department of alumni relations and outreach trains parents regularly on how to be a supportive parent and a progressive influencer in the community.

Since most students are first-generation educated, they are encouraged to share their experiences with parents, especially about their learning and aspirations. The Summer Samurai projects are designed to help them apply what they learnt in school to solve real-life problems. Parents and community members get impressed when their children speak impeccable English and apply their skills. The experiences and success stories of students in competitive exams, sports and other aspects of academic and professional fields are widely circulated on social media and disseminated in all villages. The success of students is celebrated, and they are felicitated along with their parents at a grand function in the district and state headquarters every year. In this way, a marginalized community has been looking at education with a new hope.

Non-Stop Success Stories

It is impossible to capture the imagination of the community without a string of visible and tangible achievements. Every year, the Telangana Social Welfare Residential Schools Society launches adventurous expeditions with students, and it has produced Poorna, the world's youngest woman to have scaled Mount Everest, as well as Anand Kumar, India's first Dalit male mountaineer. Both placed photos of B.R. Ambedkar on the summit.

Even in terms of academic achievements, the schools excel in every exam. The average pass percentages are always 15 per cent above the state average, and those of the women's degree colleges are 40 per cent above the state averages in each semester. Most importantly, a large number of students secure admissions to prestigious public and private universities like the IITs, NITs, IISERs, University of Delhi and various medical and dental colleges. Many of them secured admission to prestigious private universities like Azim Premji University, Ashoka University and Krea University, and secured scholarships funded by corporate philanthropic foundations. Every year, more than 100 students visit foreign countries on exchange programmes funded by the state government. Students returning home with achievements are treated with respect and awe. Such stories get circulated through multiple mediums, from street murals to social media posts. These positive stories stimulate young brains and become subject matter of conversations among communities. The legacy of oppression and discrimination that looms large over the Dalit community is undone by sharing the successes of Dalit children at the community level.

Limitations of the Residential Education Model

The Telangana Social Welfare Residential School model demonstrates that quality education can be guaranteed to Dalit children, if the central and state governments are serious about it. The cost of running such residential schools may be higher when compared to normal day schools. Residential schools in each state may not cover more than one-fourth of Dalit students due to budgetary constraints. Even so, there is a strong case for replicating the Telangana model across the country. Given that residential education has limited but deeper impact, there is an urgent need to secure quality education for the remaining three-fourth of the generation of Dalit students as well. In the following sections, we will examine the strategies to realize this goal.

Leap or Be Lost

The world over, the wealth gap between the rich and poor is widening. Rapid technological innovations, coupled with right-wing populism, are likely to exacerbate this disparity. In this context, it is important to assess the progress made and the road ahead for the Dalits in India. Seventy-five per cent of Dalits still live in rural areas, and the rate of literacy continues to be lower than the national average. The average household size is 5.7, while 43 per cent of the SC population still work as farm and non-farm labourers. Sixty-five per cent of SCs are landless and only less than 3 per cent have land holdings of more than 5 acres even after 70 years of independence.[1] The lack of assets perpetuates a cycle of economic precarity. The Dalits lag behind in all the social indicators.[2] Dalit women reportedly die fourteen years younger compared to the upper castes. These inherited socio-economic handicaps are impediments to socio-economic mobility.

The only way out for Dalits is to adopt the 'Quantum Leap Doctrine'. This demands firm determination to rise above fear and march into unchartered terrain. Such a shift requires unwavering commitment from both the Dalit community and their elected policymakers. The doctrine intends to discard age-old thinking and to equip the Dalits with new thinking and an educational engine. The intention is not to hand machines to manual scavengers so that they can clean the gutters more efficiently and lead the Clean India Mission from the front! On the contrary, this doctrine lays the designs to transform *all* the children of manual scavengers into suave white-collar workers who can confidently fit in the matrix of Industrial Revolution 4.0. Many experts might immediately retort that this is a distant dream. But this is the only way to effect a mass transformation that has eluded the Dalit community for centuries.

Quantum Leap

Overcoming Social Conditioning

What really holds the Dalits back? Caste discrimination and its associated inflexible structural barriers, including the identity that is imposed on them. For generations, the Dalits accepted these inhuman violations for fear of social exclusion. Now, it is time that they destroy this fear decisively. It is the fear of the divine curse, the fear of walking on the main road, the fear of sitting on high ground, the fear of leading people, the fear of losing their livelihood, the fear of authority, the fear of someone who speaks English, the fear of going abroad, the fear of the one in uniform, the fear of failures, the fear of questioning—the list is endless. All these fears are not innate but have been drilled into their minds for centuries. They can only be undone through conversations. The seeds for this turnaround must be sown at home and in educational institutions. This calls for cultivating stimulating conversations at home, facilitating community activities and inviting inspiring figures to speak to the children.

Early Childhood Care and the first 1000 days

Due to discrimination, poverty and migration, Dalit children drop out of schools and get into work early on. The first 1000 days of childhood are crucial for a child's growth and neurodevelopment.[3] This is dependent on the nutritional status of the mother and the child. Dalit children lack access to sufficient nutrition in their formative years and are denied exposure to the outside world, unlike their savarna counterparts. Consequently, healthy development of Dalit children is compromised in their formative years. State governments must come forward to strengthen the Integrated Child Development Scheme (ICDS) in Dalit localities to ensure that children get access to nutritious food and their preschool education is joyful. The local community should play a central role in managing these initiatives.

Family as First Mentors

Generally, children spend 6–7.5 hours each day in school for over 220 days in an academic year. Outside school hours, they spend time with family or friends in the neighbourhood. Parents play a critical role in shaping the future of the younger generations much before the latter enter colleges and universities. The probability of a child's success is determined by the health and educational status of the parents. Unfortunately, the Dalit rural households are forced to rely on children for labour. This is particularly acute in the case of the girl child.

In view of this, it is imperative that the parents of Dalit children are oriented and motivated to encourage their children to move from schools to colleges, from colleges to universities. Community centres need to be established to organize regular orientation sessions for parents to recognize the value of education in the lives of the Dalits and realize the opportunities for economic empowerment. Educated parents should act as tutors and mentors to their children. Dalit homes should have small libraries, playing equipment, small blackboards, daily timetable and an annual calendar, wherein all family members can discuss and create knowledge in their own way. And every child must be able to share the knowledge with his/her parents as well. This one single measure not only boosts the self-esteem of the child when he/she goes to school but also acts as a powerful supplement to classroom learning.

Community Mentorship

Educated Dalit youth can play an important role in guiding and inspiring Dalit children. Unemployed Dalit graduates can be trained for community service. Community association networks can mobilize funds and hire such youth for community-development activities. These educated young community workers can offer remedial classes to school students and also provide career counselling. They can also assist with community-level data collection.

Community Elders as Agents of Change

There are many retired teachers, lecturers, officers and engineers from the Dalit community. They could utilize their experience and resources towards the welfare of the children and youth, and share their stories with the younger generations. They can start scholarships or bursaries, in the names of their parents or loved ones or in their own names, for the most talented students.

Reordering Priorities

The Dalit middle class is obsessed with erecting the statues of Ambedkar. Historically, Ambedkar statues remained a symbol of Dalit assertion and self-respect. Such statutes provide a much-needed sense of belonging and identity, but in reality do not result in any substantial material and intellectual progress. The Dalits should move beyond this symbolism and focus on issues of economic empowerment and social mobility. This calls for a forward-looking socio-economic agenda with coherent demands for economic progress. Economic precariousness, especially in rural areas, forces Dalit children to drop out. Economic security, particularly asset ownership, can offer a safety net, particularly during periods of uncertainty.

Nurturing Future Talent

As we live in a world dominated by technology, the only way forward for the Dalits is to catch up and run with it. Artificial intelligence and machine learning have become the buzzwords of the twenty-first century. With the advent of robotics, people have already started talking about the post-work world and universal basic income. The foremost thing every family must do for their survival is to teach their children the skill of computational thinking and coding. Robots must be the new toys in our homes. Solving puzzles must be our favourite pastime. Having been excluded in all earlier revolutions, the Dalits cannot afford to miss the bus of this big data revolution and remain in the margins. They must leap from security guard positions to that of cybersecurity experts and from being autorickshaw drivers become programmers of drones and driverless vehicles.

Besides the immense economic benefits, such next generational technological skills can bring the Dalits together, with the help of the social media, and make them part of a wider global network.

Fight Against Regressive Social Customs

Alcoholism, dowry and child marriages are some of the practices that particularly affect the lives of the poor Dalits. The community must dedicate itself to ending these practices. Community-driven social change is much deeper and longer-lasting than the efforts of the governments. But historically, across the world, it was the community and its leadership that prepared the ground for social mobility and made governments pay heed to their needs and aspirations. The advantage of self-reliance and liberation doctrine is that it can prepare communities to withstand the volatilities and uncertainties in politics that guide policy decisions. Community-led social change can also help historically marginalized groups reclaim their sense of moral agency, which has been denied to them for generations.

Vision for Policymakers

Any policy initiative to uplift the Dalits from poverty and stigmatized existence must have two dimensions. One is the commitment and participation of the community that takes responsibility for its emancipation. Second, the government should design and implement policies that take stakeholders' aspirations into consideration without being tokenistic. For instance, the recent initiative of the Government of Andhra Pradesh to introduce English as the medium of instruction in all government schools stands out not only as a bold but also a socially progressive policy intervention that has taken the aspirations of the Dalit and other marginalized sections into consideration. Similarly, the creation of residential degree colleges, with English as the medium of instruction, for

Dalit women under the SC Sub-Plan Act in Telangana also falls into this visionary category. Such bold moves are possible only when the policymakers unshackle from their antiquated thinking and boldly enter uncharted territories.

Establish Residential Schools for Every SC Block

The Dalits would have made their presence strongly felt in every field by now had there been concerted efforts to educate them with dedication. There is an urgent need for fresh thinking here to prevent further loss of learning and arrest subsequent rise of inequality. As an antidote, the experiment of residential education in English medium must be tried in every block in this country, with the cooperation of the states and union territories. This will create a talented generation among the poor. The efficacy of this experiment has already been proven in quite a few states and at the national level as well, through the Navodaya Vidyalayas and the Eklavya Model Residential Schools. Similarly, the governments must also start a large number of hostels in the public–private partnership mode in all major urban centres.

Start a Leadership Institute for Marginalized

The leadership potential of the Dalits is robbed from their childhood itself. Dalit children are exposed to trauma, uncertainty and perpetual dependence at every stage of their life in the formative stages. They acquire the skill to lead only when they come across well-meaning mentors and programmes in the schools. Most of the leaders among Dalits are shaped by the survival discourse after they become adults. This should not be the case anymore. The students or youth who have the leadership qualities must be groomed from adolescence itself and their progress must be carefully tracked. They should be sent to all the emerging fields which give them access to authority, protection, and status. Later, when they finish their higher education, they must be sent to various government departments, private corporations and ministries to work as interns. They must also have exposure to the work of NGOs and politics so that they get a sense of what happens on the other side of the table.

A National Museum of Dalit History and Culture

History is the harbinger of things to come. Ambedkar once said, 'Those who forget history cannot make history.' Like every ethnic community in this world, the Dalits, too, have a rich tradition and culture. Unfortunately, most of it is preserved and passed on as oral tradition in the communities. This aspect of Dalit life was never given importance. It is important for all citizens of this country to learn about the history of a quarter of the Indian population and their contribution to national history and culture. It is particularly important for the future generations of the Dalits to celebrate their history and draw inspiration from their ancestors. Museums not only offer interested visitors a comprehensive view of what happened over the last 2000 years, especially how castes have emerged, the roots of discrimination, efforts of various reformers and movements to end injustice, etc.

Conclusion

The key to liberation, happiness and resurgence of the oppressed lies in education. Quality education gives language; it becomes a ladder for people to enter a new world of opportunities and empowers them with a much-needed voice. Above all, it shapes leaders and thinkers who can change the course of history. Liberal education produced an Ambedkar who was not just a leader for the scheduled castes but for the entire country. As a potent transformative force, quality education must top the list of priorities of all those who want to see the end to discrimination decisively on the basis of caste, creed, colour and gender in this country.

The community, the elected representatives and the executive must share this vision and burden equally. For a change, the groundwork for such a revolution must be laid by the communities themselves, not the state. Governments must accelerate this transmutation by making pathbreaking interventions, for instance starting residential schools for Dalits in every block in this country. Before the much-awaited demographic window of opportunity closes in the next twenty-five years, India must do everything to produce prodigies like Poorna and Anand (the SWAERO mountaineers) in *every* Dalit household to stand as a beacon of hope for the rest of the world.

Annihilating Entrepreneurship Casteism

Priyank Kharge and Neeraj Shetye

Having understood the role of modernity in shaping the future of the Dalits and adivasis, B.R. Ambedkar became a strong proponent of industrialization, suggesting that it was the soundest remedy for the many economic and social problems of India. He believed that modern industry could break down the caste system by inducing professional mobility and economic freedom among those who had been denied this freedom for long. That was why his politics focused on the economic possibilities that could facilitate social mobility.

In Ambedkar's mind, economic inequality was a key determinant of caste discrimination and was insidiously used by vested interests to deliberately suppress the Dalits, adivasis and OBCs. The dismantling of this system of economic exploitation would be a direct threat to casteism and would go a long way in the annihilation of caste. That is why it is critical for India to evolve ways to empower the Dalits and adivasis in their economic aspirations. Only then can they achieve what Jawaharlal Nehru called 'fullness of life', and only then can India productively utilize its entire workforce for nation-building.

Rising Aspirations: The Entrepreneurship Revolution

The 1991 economic reforms dramatically altered India's aspirations. It unleashed the animal spirits in the economy and enabled millions of Indians to be entrepreneurial. Motivated by the consumerist spirit that liberalization unleashed, there was suddenly a fresh wind that blew across India. Everyone could do well if they worked hard, and no one would be excluded. The total middle-class population grew 9 per cent from 1993–94 to 2004–05, according to a nationally representative household survey conducted by the National Sample Survey (NSS). The population share of the middle class increased from about 29 per cent in 1993–94 to 38 per cent in 2004–05, as seen in the NSS report.[1] In the next eight years, the middle class doubled, from 300 million to 600 million.[2] This was an especially potent sign for the Dalits and adivasis because, unlike in structured opportunities, they could enhance their socio-economic status by themselves. This realization consequently enhanced the needs and aspirations of the Dalits manifold.

Even though the 1991 reforms allowed a break—to a considerable degree—in the monopoly of the dominant class over business and capital in India, only a minuscule section of the Dalits benefited from liberalization, privatization and globalization.[3] Dalit entrepreneurs have managed to do well only in traditional sectors and have a negligible presence in knowledge-based modern industries. Even the much-touted 'Dalit capitalism' has failed to create a wide base of Dalit businesspersons who have been able to make it to the top ten (or even 100) list of Indian businesses (in terms of capital and market capitalization). Nor have they been able to empower the community through positive interventions.

It was once argued that caste is losing its grip over the Dalits because India is industrializing, urbanizing and modernizing, and that Dalit capitalism will accelerate that process and will accord a human face to Indian capitalism.[4] Thirty years after liberalization, this understanding has been found to be stunted. Not only have the upper castes seen much more upward social mobility (in comparison to the Dalits, adivasis and OBCs), but they have also managed to transition to more modern industries, leaving the lower-end ones for the Dalits and adivasis. Additionally, the few 'Dalit capitalists' who have done well are islands amid a vast sea of poverty and backwardness.

It has been empirically observed that market reforms alone will not help the marginalized sections economically, because 'the notion of the market as an equalizer is a myth; instead of ignoring caste and treating individuals as pure economic agents, market relations are based on the exploitation of caste inequalities'.[5] The solution therefore lies elsewhere.

While there has been a spurt of entrepreneurship among the Dalits (especially in comparison to the 1980s), it is still negligible. The fourth All India Census of Micro, Small and Medium Enterprises (MSMEs)[6] shows that out of 93,09,486 MSMEs in India, the number of enterprises owned by Dalits is a meagre 17.02 per cent. A vast majority of this 17.02 per cent (i.e.,10,93,280) are micro enterprises. The number of small and medium enterprises owned by Dalits is 4,06,400 and 87,000 respectively. The representation of Dalit entrepreneurs in urban areas is even less, 14.18 per cent, but in rural areas, it is 20.36 per cent. As per the Economic Survey of Private Enterprises for 2013, the share of enterprises owned by Dalits was merely 10 per cent, which is very low considering their proportion in the population, which is 16 per cent.[7] Since market forces are prone to arranging the political order based on existing social hierarchies, governmental intervention becomes essential to direct the inegalitarian political economy toward progressive goals.

Therefore, the question facing India is this: How can we encourage a community which has been on the margins for centuries to start their own enterprises? What are the possible challenges we will face in this endeavour? This is an attempt to address this question while presenting a new alternative paradigm to boost entrepreneurship among the Dalits and adivasis.

Barriers That Dalit and Adivasi Entrepreneurs Face

While Ambedkar believed that industrialization would be a beneficial step, he was always sceptical about capitalism since it was blind to the issue of addressing inequalities, especially those which had existed for centuries. Entrepreneurship among the marginalized groups in India has to be, therefore, studied and addressed sensitively, keeping in mind the multifaceted aspects of casteism.

The economic injustices/discriminations that Dalit and adivasi businesses face, in terms of market access and profit-making, must also be contextualized through the lens of caste. There is limited research in this field due to the lack of structured data, but many studies have conclusively established the effect of discrimination on enterprises started by lower-caste groups, particularly those from SC and ST communities.[8] S.S. Jodhka has produced empirical data about the caste composition of Dalit entrepreneurship in north-west India. For example, a study found that that most businessmen from the Chamar and Valmiki castes 'affect(ed) their business directly or indirectly. They are considered "odd ones" in the social universe of business.'[9] Entrepreneurs from these communities routinely face discrimination in market access in the form of dearth of investment and limited market access, which results in poor economic outcomes.

In a study of ninety entrepreneurs in thirteen districts, it was found that SC/ST entrepreneurs faced significant problems in renting or buying strategically important physical spaces for their businesses because of their caste. This affected their potential to earn profits as they were forced to limit their businesses in their own neighbourhoods.[10] This not only stifles their growth but also hurts India's economy.

Marginalized groups that enter the field of self-employment also face discrimination in the form of consumer and credit-market discrimination. When an individual from a group which is discriminated against in the labour market starts a venture, they receive credit at less favourable terms, since the lenders know that the opportunity cost of entering self-employment for this individual is low; and hence, they are expected to take greater risks.[11] For example, only 11 per cent of the total loans under the Pradhan Mantri Mudra Yojana went to Dalits, and 4 per cent to adivasis. Reflective of pervasive casteism, the average loan size to Dalits and adivasis was a mere Rs 45,203, in stark contrast to Rs 10 lakh given to upper castes (who, incidentally, cornered 88.7 per cent of the loans granted).[12]

Entrepreneurship means independent resources, risk-taking and influential connections in the industry. It is challenging in itself. However, the risks become gargantuan when coupled with caste-based discrimination. The additional barriers to success that are laid in the path of the Dalits and adivasis can be crippling, and it is because of this that a targeted approach is required to combat entrepreneurship casteism.

Tackling Entrepreneurship Casteism: Centrality of the State

The argument that 'economic reforms [have] unleashed Adam Smith to chase Manu away from this planet'[13] is not only short-sighted but also fallacious. Given the insidious nature of casteism, and the fact that Dalit entrepreneurs have managed to carve out a niche mostly in micro industries, the state has to play a central role in providing resources and creating a platform where Dalit- and adivasi-led enterprises can be created and sustained. Article 15 of the Constitution promises equal rights to all citizens irrespective of caste, religion, race, sex or place of birth, and Article 17 abolished untouchability. So the state must guarantee assistance at all levels (Union, state and district/panchayat) to caste groups which have been marginalized historically under an oppressive hegemonic structure.

Motivated by the constitutional principle of deepening economic justice, the Department of Social Welfare, Government of Karnataka (DSW–GoK) in 2016–17 spearheaded a number of radical policies to boost entrepreneurship while addressing key concerns that Dalits and adivasis face. To this end, the department devised some policy initiatives with a view to encouraging the culture of entrepreneurship among the youth from the SC and ST communities. The policies were aimed at ensuring that educated youth from marginalized communities are able to lead and own enterprises rather than working for them. One of the key innovations here was targeted subsidies for enterprises (as against subsidizing every aspect of establishing an enterprise). Some of the successful initiatives of the DSW–GoK are detailed below.

The rise and growth of private cab aggregators, like Ola and Uber, is a prime example of the use of technology in employment generation. It allowed many individuals from towns and cities across the nation to register with an organization and earn their livelihoods. Many drivers would rent a vehicle from an agency to drive for the day by registering on these cab platforms. A sizeable portion of the income earned would be utilized in paying the monthly rent on the vehicles. If the nature of this transaction is beyond the purview of a registered entity, it puts the individual at risk. Accordingly, the DSW–GoK spearheaded the Airavatha scheme, which was launched to address this specific problem. It allowed drivers from the SC/ST/OBC groups to apply for a state assistance of Rs 5 lakh to buy a vehicle instead of renting it. Ownership of the vehicle provided stability to the individuals and gave them more disposable income.

A key aspect of Airavatha was linking the beneficiary to a taxi aggregator and ensuring that the government could track the beneficiaries' performance as well. By the end of the 2018–19 financial year, 4500 cabs were approved, which improved the standard of living among the SC/ST.[14] This scheme generated great interest among the younger generations struggling to find livelihood opportunities. It received a tremendous response and saw 12,000 applicants in just two weeks after its launch.

Entrepreneurship is also contingent on certain skills which are essential in managing and growing an enterprise. It includes the ability to pitch ideas, raise funds, run operations, as well as recruit and manage a team. The state can use its influence to mobilize resources and create effective programmes. That is why the Samruddhi (Prosperity) scheme, started by the DSW–GoK, is focused on providing opportunities for the economically weaker sections to enable them to become retailers or franchisees of established retailers. It is a scheme not only for the marginalized communities but also for retailers looking for newer markets in smaller towns and rural areas.

The beneficiaries of Samruddhi are eligible for seed capital of Rs 10 lakh to set up shop and undergo extensive training and certification programmes arranged by the retailer before they start operating their businesses. The beneficiaries, accordingly, become owners of an enterprise in their own locales. It allows them to generate employment in their communities, as they hire locally. To big businesses looking to expand, this franchise model offers easy access to newer markets at almost no cost. It is an efficient model, beneficial to all the stakeholders. The Samruddhi scheme can create 25,000 entrepreneurs in a period of two years and ensure the creation of more jobs at the ratio of 1:2. This kind of skill training can thus be a driving force for communities to gain economically.

The advancement of technology is an enabler of global economic advancement. While industrialization automated the manufacturing sector, technological development has revolutionised the service sector. The rise of Silicon Valley in the United States is a testament to the growth of start-up culture. Indians have utilized the opportunities by emigrating to these hubs in search of better livelihood. But the Indians who have been successful in these spaces are predominantly from the upper-caste, upper-class backgrounds. The marginalized groups, especially from SC and ST communities, have been kept out. The lack of capital, connections and financial aid options are some of the reasons for this exclusion. Similarly, it's because of the lack of these critical resources in India that the youths from the SC and ST communities are reluctant to participate in entrepreneurial ventures. The DSW–GoK's Unnati (Progress) scheme is the first of its kind initiative that looked towards encouraging knowledge-based entrepreneurial initiatives, with the government providing seed money of up to Rs 50 lakh to entrepreneurs from the SC or ST communities who are pursuing technology breakthroughs in their start-up ventures.

The programme provides end-to-end solution to start-ups and helps with all their requirements. From identifying innovations, mentoring, validating the idea, providing seed capital and eventually giving entrepreneurs market access, Unnati tries to provide a holistic helping hand. The uniqueness of Unnati is that it will also fund social innovations and inventions that can potentially impact marginalized communities positively. With an allocation of over Rs 25 crore, this policy is expected to immensely help enterprises started by entrepreneurs from the SC and ST communities.

The policies outlined so far have promoted entrepreneurship among people who are already willing to be entrepreneurs. However, it is important that marginalized sections are exposed to successful enterprises and mentored in how to be enterprising. The state is responsible to provide quality education to all its citizens. By extending this vision, the DSW–GoK introduced the Prabuddha (Enlightened) initiative. The objective behind this policy was to assist aspirants from the SC and ST communities to pursue quality higher education abroad. The scheme reserved as much as 33 per cent of its funds for women.

Prabuddha strove to ensure that India got more employable graduates from the oppressed communities by helping them specialize in professional courses, such as engineering, natural sciences, agriculture, medicine, humanities, fine arts and social sciences, at reputed foreign universities. Global exposure to cosmopolitan cultures, demographics and lifestyles would aid individuals in enhancing their capabilities and perspectives. Since India's economic future is moving towards a globalized, competitive system, we should make sure that everyone, irrespective of their identity, is able to participate and contribute in the nation's growth. The policy also enforces stringent regulations and it's ensured that the applicant has cleared all mandatory qualification examinations, like the GRE, GMAT, TOEFL and IELTS.

Conclusion: Constructing a Free Social Order

As the world's largest democracy, India's growth story is rooted in its constitutional principles of equality, liberty, fraternity and justice. The Constitution guarantees these to *all* citizens, irrespective of their identity. It is morally incumbent on every government to ensure that they are properly invested in these values and take appropriate measures to secure them for all. India's social justice paradigm is still wanting in terms of equal opportunity in education and employment. This needs to be complemented with radically disruptive innovations through a renewed approach relevant to the twenty-first century.

That is why we must collectively reflect on entrepreneurship as a means to transform the socio-economic status of the Dalits, adivasis and OBCs in India. It not only enables them to become independent and self-sufficient but can also help them overcome social and economic vulnerabilities. Given this, each of the innovative scheme outlined earlier can and *must be* implemented across India. Needless to say, the schemes ought to be appropriately customized to effectively tackle the unique circumstances of each state.

While economic empowerment is itself not a silver bullet to rid India of casteism, it provides a strategy for historically marginalized communities to pull themselves up and bypass the numerous glass ceilings they face. It must be emphasized that entrepreneurship must perforce be complemented by social, cultural and political reforms, so that the Dalits, adivasis and OBCs can achieve fullness of life as well as dignity.

Redesigning the Dalit Development Paradigm

Budithi Rajsekhar

Introduction

The story of Indian civilization would be incomplete without acknowledging the monumental contribution of the Dalits in every field. However, our collective memory has deliberately forgotten it, and in many instances, their contribution has been appropriated by the dominant castes. The symbols of prosperity we see around us were built on the backs of their labour. By relegating the Dalits to an insignificant place in our history, we not only rob them of dignity but also of their rightful share in our prosperity. The cumulative impact of this unjust scheme of things has denied generations of Dalits a fair shot at life.

It is especially shocking that India, which dreams of being a global superpower, deliberately denies millions of its citizens basic human dignities and opportunities. The bitter truth is that even though Dalit lives are better than what they were in 1947, when India gained independence, there are staggering differences between the Dalits and the rest of society. In terms of per capita employment, income, poverty, access to education, health care and other essential services, the Dalits are disproportionately disadvantaged. Because of casteism, the Dalits live in a different India—unjust, illiberal and unequal.

If India really wants to become a global leader, it needs to ensure that every Dalit has equal opportunities for a better life. Doing that means revisiting the current development paradigm and implementing a revolutionary leap-of-faith plan.

In the United States, the stark cruelty of George Floyd's death and, in the videos of the incident, the nonchalance on the face of the policeman convicted of his murder, Derek Chauvin, brought back the dark memories of slavery. In India, not long ago, the suicide note of a young aspiring Dalit research scholar captivated the attention of the nation and drew attention to the perilous nature of the lives of the Dalits. But unlike the #BlackLivesMatter protests in the US, this country has not seen any #DalitLivesMatter protests in the seven decades since Independence, despite the routine acts of gruesome violence committed against them. The humiliation heaped on the Dalits would have shaken the collective conscience in any other society.

It is time to shed this indifference and insensitivity, and to work towards building a future that recognizes the Dalits as equal stakeholders in our progress.

B.R. Ambedkar represented a community that, despite facing such religiously sanctioned indignities, never resorted to violence or even put forth a claim for reparations from the nation. Honest introspection would expose our lack of commitment and the incrementalistic developmental approach that continue to push the Dalits to the margins. The disproportionate focus on reservation on the part of certain vocal sections within the Dalit community has shifted the attention away from the fact that the Dalits are being left behind in a rapidly evolving economy.

That is why there is an urgent need for honest introspection, and a radical rethink in terms of how we uplift and empower the

Dalits. To that end, there are five pervasive misconceptions related to the development paradigm meant for India's Dalits that need to be reconceptualized. Addressing these are a necessary first step towards ensuring that India's constitutional promise is equitably accessible to the Dalits, and ensuring that the Dalits no longer continue to bear the disproportionate burden of the social and economic costs of a developing nation

Misconception 1: Reservations for Jobs Is the Silver Bullet to End All Dalit Problems

A significant number of Dalits in India who have managed to access the fruits of development post-Independence could do so primarily because of reservations in government jobs.

Institutional Attacks on Reservation

Reservations in public employment for the SCs and STs are guaranteed by the Constitution. But casteist elements within the state have time and again stymied reservations. Either posts are left vacant or Dalit candidates are discriminated against during the selection process,[1] or they are not promoted.[2] Today, only 11.5 per cent of the A-class administrative positions in India are occupied by SCs, while 95 per cent of the employed SCs are clustered in grades C and D.[3] Similarly, only 1.02 lakh (7.22 per cent) of the 14.1 lakh teachers in 716 universities and 38,056 colleges in the country are Dalits.[4] There have been agitations over the last seventy years demanding proper implementation of reservations across all government institutions, including public sector undertakings.

On 7 February 2020, in 'Mukesh Kumar vs the State of Uttarakhand',[5] the Supreme Court ruled that the state government cannot be directed to provide reservations for appointment in public posts, and is not bound to make reservations for SCs and STs in matters of promotions. The judgment sadly downgraded reservations from an essential mechanism for equality to a mere optional benefit.

Even if reservations are effectively implemented in letter and spirit, it will take several decades for the Dalits to come on a par with the rest of society or to gain equitable share in the nation's wealth. This is because the social, economic and political disadvantages they face have accumulated over centuries. As the scope and scale of India's state is being reconceptualized, the number of public-sector jobs are declining drastically.

Missing the Bus: Emerging Opportunities in the Private Sector

Additionally, the nation's leap into the fourth industrial revolution, of an economy based on artificial intelligence (AI) and Internet of things (IOT), has hit the Dalits the most, as employment generated by these sectors is limited to mostly white-collar and highly skilled workers. Consequently, much of the employment in these sectors has been cornered by the elite and the middle classes, who, because of previous access to education, finances and filial networks, have the skill sets and networks that the Dalits lack (since they have been historically excluded and denied these opportunities).

It is important to acknowledge that reservations in services need to be complemented by other policy interventions that can help realize the stated intent underlying India's social justice paradigm. Unfortunately, there is a misplaced notion among policymakers and the Dalits themselves that reservations are a silver bullet to eliminate caste-based discrimination and backwardness. This is fallacious because, as it has been aptly argued, 'reservations are not the answer to every social and economic problem. Caste is an important marker of socio-economic status and inequality. Reservation is only one of the anti-discriminatory policies that the Government can use.'[6] While struggling to safeguard reservations, we should not ignore numerous other development interventions that, along with reservations, can accelerate the empowerment of the Dalits and adivasis.

Misconception 2: Anti-Poverty Programmes Will Uplift the Dalits

Apart from reservations, what is also needed are policies, programmes and legislations that can secure for the Dalits their share in the nation's wealth, so that they will be on a par with the rest of the society. The discourse on Dalit welfare, in legislative assemblies and Parliament, has not led to responses aimed at addressing the key issues concerning development of the Dalits. On the few occasions when the Dalits have been able to make their voices heard on these forums successfully, the development response has been both inadequate and merely symbolic.

Poor Policy Design

A few token programmes, of the Union and state governments, are showcased to create the impression that the upliftment and empowerment of the Dalits is on the government's agenda. However, barring some notable exceptions, most of these programmes have woefully failed to secure for the Dalits their share in the nation's wealth, since they are not targeted to specifically address the multiple deprivations that the Dalits face.

Failure to Implement the Letter and Spirit of Legislations

For example, the implementation of land reform legislations was an opportunity to address landlessness among the Dalits in rural areas. But the land reforms failed the poor in general and the Dalits in particular. Specifically, the legislative assemblies of states such as Bihar and Uttar Pradesh passed the Zamindari Abolition and Land Reforms legislations within three after Independence. Yet, they have not been successful in enhancing land ownership among the Dalits.

Underinvestment in the Social Sector

Education in the government sector has failed to give quality education to the Dalits, as investments in public-sector education in general have been consistently and abysmally low. This has led to a situation where the private sector has commercialized education and institutionalized a business model that excluded the poor in general and the Dalits in particular. The pre-matric and post-matric scholarships (which Dr Ambedkar started in 1948), and social welfare hostels helped small sections of Dalit students to pursue education.

Failure to Move up the Value Chain

Despite globally connected supply chain systems, many Dalits are still stuck in hand-to-mouth economic activities, mostly in the informal sector. Similarly, while India is aggressively promoting online coding classes for children as an official policy stemming from the New Education Policy, 2020, this unfairly helps children of the dominant castes who have access to laptops, the Internet and the financial wherewithal to pay for special classes to learn coding.

Likewise, the Dalits face numerous hurdles when it comes to accessing credit for self-employment and enterprise development. Only 11 per cent of the total loans under the Pradhan Mantri Mudra Yojana went to Dalits and 4 per cent to adivasis. Reflective of pervasive casteism, the average loan size to Dalits and adivasis was a mere Rs 45,203, in stark contrast to Rs 10 lakh given to the upper castes (who incidentally cornered 88.7 per cent of the loans granted).[7] Despite the decades spent pushing for 'Dalit capitalism', there is no existing or upcoming notable Dalit enterprise that is in the list of top 100 enterprises in terms of capital and market reach.

Entry Barriers in the Private Sector

Dalit candidates are routinely excluded from employment in the private sector, since applicants are purposefully scrutinized through the lens of caste (to sift out the Dalit candidates).[8] Likewise, in a first-of-its-kind survey on the social profiles of 315 senior decision-makers in thirty-seven newspapers and television channels, it was found that 90 per cent of the decision-makers in the English-language print media and 79 per cent in television were upper caste. Not a single one of these 315 was from the SC/ST communities.[9]

Undermining Legislative and Policy Safeguards for Dalits

Even schemes that are meant to undo the deprivations faced by the Dalits (i.e., schemes specifically targeted to address the causes that lead to their socio-economic backwardness) are undermined. For example, in the early 1970s, the Planning Commission proposed the implementation of the Special Component Plan (SCP) to facilitate development across various parameters in the Dalit community, bringing them on a par with the rest of the society. The policy envisaged earmarking portions of the budgets, of both Central and state governments, to invest in the development of the Dalits. Unfortunately, the policy remained largely on paper, despite the efforts of successive governments.

Consider the case of the Union government's Scheduled Caste Sub-Plan (SCSP) and Tribal Sub-Plan (TSP), which mandate that the public resources towards SC/ST welfare must be earmarked in proportion to their share in the total population. Accordingly, the government must allocate at least 16.6 per cent of the plan component of the budget towards the welfare of the SCs and 8.6 per cent of the plan component towards the welfare of the STs. Even though five-year plans, under which the sub-plans were housed, were scrapped, the Union government issued a circular in August 2016 agreeing to adhere to the SCSP and TSP guidelines for allocations to SC/ST schemes. But both the Central government and state governments have failed to realize the objective of the SCSP and TSP policies. There are shortfalls in the allocation of the SCSP and TSP funds. The schemes funded under the SCSP and TSP don't secure direct and quantifiable benefits to the SC/ST individuals, families or habitations.

Andhra Pradesh passed a legislation—the Andhra Pradesh Scheduled Castes Sub-Plan and Tribal Sub-Plan (Planning, Allocation and Utilisation of Financial Resources) Act, 2013—providing a legal framework for the effective implementation of the SCP. The state governments of Telangana and Karnataka soon followed suit with similar legislations. However, a deeper look at the implementation of the act in these states reveals a web of deceit on the part of both the political establishment and the bureaucracy, in that they have completely diluted the spirit of the legislations.

The sub-plans of the departments were to include only schemes that have the potential to bridge the development gap between the Dalits and the rest of the society, and secure direct and quantifiable benefits for SC individuals/households/habitations. However, no tangible steps were taken to implement this. No baseline surveys were conducted through research bodies to identify the gaps in development indicators between SCs/STs and the rest of the society.

The Andhra Pradesh Scheduled Castes Sub-Plan and Tribal Sub-Plan (Planning, Allocation and Utilisation of Financial Resources) Act, 2013, prescribed a greater focus on schemes that would secure greater access to irrigated land, as well as promotion of self-employment schemes and enterprise development for the SCs. But the funds spent towards these schemes were frugal. The act mandated that the departments dealing with economics and human resource development shall prepare the SCSP to ensure equality among various social groups within the SC community. This aspect of the act was also overlooked, and no surveys were conducted to assess the inequalities among the sub-castes.

The act reposed responsibility on the nodal agency to facilitate annual social auditing of the SCSP and analyse the improvement in the human development index against the projections for the state and districts. Despite the clear mechanism laid out in the act, no social audit was conducted (in any year). Additionally, even the annual report was not submitted to the legislature for review on implementation of the act.

Misconception 3: Political Reservations Enable the Meaningful Participation of Dalits in the Political Processes

Political reservations for the scheduled castes and scheduled tribes, in legislative assemblies and Parliament, have not had a significant impact on the development of the Dalits. For example, it has been argued[10] that 'the proceedings of the 16th Lok Sabha show that barring a few Dalit MPs, no one raised Dalit issues in Parliament or spoke up on matters concerning the community in the media . . . For instance, on the Supreme Court diluting stringent provisions of the Scheduled Castes and Scheduled Tribes (Prevention of Atrocities) Act, other than Udit Raj and Ram Vilas Paswan, none spoke up.'

Similarly, 'even when the University Grants Commission (UGC) issued a notification which had a direct impact on the recruitment of SC/ST/OBC teachers in central universities and colleges, almost all Dalit MPs kept quiet.[11]

Dilution of Political Reservation

Even the 73rd and 74th Amendments, which institutionalized reservations in local self-governing bodies, were first resisted and then undermined by vested interests within the state. Numerous state governments passed laws institutionalizing education and other eligibility norms for citizens to contest at the panchayat levels. What this effectively did was exclude most Dalits, adivasis and women from the contest for panchayat posts.

Persistence of Caste Discrimination

Even when the Dalits are allowed to contest and function as elected leaders, they are humiliated. For example, in 2020, the case of a Dalit sarpanch seated on the ground while dominant caste members were seated on chairs revealed the reality of power equations in our society.[12]

Time and time again, the myth of an independent and powerful Dalit leadership has been shattered, as most Dalit leaders are symbolically included in political parties and even so, they are restrained and muted. They cannot afford to be radical or revolutionary, lest they face an internal backlash. This goes for all political parties, including those like the Bahujan Samaj Party, which were formed in opposition to what Kanshi Ram famously called *chamchagiri* (sycophancy) politics.

Lack of Political Will to Promote Assertive Dalit Leadership

A suave, smart and free-thinking Dalit is always seen as a threat in most political parties. The reserved constituency is often under the control of someone from the dominant castes who holds sway over money and muscle power and is recognized by the constituents as the real power centre.

SC/ST parliamentarians have limited authority in Parliament, as very few of them are appointed to parliamentary committees. Most of the SC/ST MPs are inducted as members of social justice or tribal affairs committees and thus, they hardly get membership of other committees. Further, a handful of SC/ST MPs have been named chairpersons of standing committees in the last decade. Since political parties field their MPs to participate in debates, SC/ST MPs rarely get the opportunity to raise their voice.

The activities of SC/ST parliamentarians—speaking up, participating in debates or raising questions—does not have a bearing on the opportunities they receive from their political parties to contest again from the same constituency. This can be an impediment to their prospects and long-term contribution as elected representatives.[13]

Misconception 4: Budgetary Allocation for Programmes Targeted at Dalits Will Further Their Interest

For over seventy years there has been no systematic approach to measure and monitor the gaps in the development indicators of the Dalits as compared to other communities. Consequently, well-designed, multi-sectoral and multi-departmental mechanisms for the overall development of the SCs have not evolved. Problems of notional allocations, diversions of funds and mis-, under- or non-utilization of funds continue to dampen the efforts of anyone working for the benefit of the SCs. Budgetary allocations in the absence of underlying data and information that could help design proper interventions prove ineffective.

As per the Annual Report 2018–19 of the Department of Social Justice and Empowerment:

> Scheduled Castes (SCs), who constitute 16.6% of our population, have historically suffered social and educational disabilities and economic deprivation arising therefrom. A number of initiatives have been taken by the Government for development of SCs, which have yielded positive outcomes, and have also resulted in narrowing the gaps between the Scheduled Castes and the rest of the population.[14]

While there can be a healthy debate on the positive outcomes based on the annual budget figures, as well as on the number of beneficiaries accessing economic and educational schemes, etc., there is absolutely no evidence to substantiate that 'narrowing the gap' claim. In fact, the very concept of 'narrowing the gap' raises the fundamental question of defining the gap itself. There is no structured checklist of various identifiable and measurable development parameters with baseline data that define the gap between the Dalits and the others. Only with such quantifiable data will the nation be able to objectively assess whether or not the mainstreaming and development initiatives are actually benefiting the Dalits.

Even if one temporarily ignores this lack of data, let us look at the allocations, for schemes meant for the development of Dalits, made by the Ministry of Social Justice and Empowerment, Government of India, in the last ten years:

- Allocations for the development of the SCs only increased a little more than twice in the last ten years, from Rs 3498 crore in 2010–11 to Rs 8198 crore in 2018–19.[15]
- Allocations for the pre-matric scholarships scheme declined to almost half, from Rs 200 crore in 2010–22 to Rs 110 crore in 2018–19,[16] whereas there still exists a gap between high-school enrolment figures (for Class 9 and 10) for the SCs and other communities.
- Special central assistance to the sub-plan increased by only 50 per cent, from Rs 600 crore to Rs 900 crore in ten years.[17]
- Allocations for pre-matric scholarships for children of parents engaged in unclean occupations (largely from the SCs) faced a drastic fall, from Rs 70 crore to Rs 4 crore,[18] whereas the number of parents in such occupations increased ever since the Prohibition of Employment as Manual Scavengers and their Rehabilitation Act, 2013, changed the definition, thereby increasing the scope, of the term 'manual scavenger'.
- Top-Class Education for SCs, a scheme meant for helping students in premier Institutes, like the IITs and IIMs, saw no increase in allocated funds, with Rs 25 crore allocated in 2010–11 as well as in 2018–19.[19]

- The allocations for the National Scheduled Castes Finance and Development Corporation (NSFDC), meant for the economic upliftment of the poor SCs, did not even double from 2010–11 to 2018–19. An allocation of Rs 137 crore in 2018–19 implies a per capita allocation of Rs 8.[20]

This data indicates that there has been little or no attention given to ensuring accelerated development of the Dalits, to bring them on a par with the rest of the society.

Misconception 5: The Trickle-Down Fallacy, or 'Dalits Will Secure a Proportionate Share of Wealth as the Nation Progresses'

Year after year, nations measure their growth by measuring one single parameter, the gross domestic product (GDP). In simple language, GDP is the wealth created in a country in each financial year. There are well-developed econometric models to determine the wealth created by a sub-set of the population. If the combined wealth of the SC population in our country is one-fifth of the GDP, then we can say that the SCs have secured their share in the nation's wealth. It is feasible to develop a methodology to measure the wealth created by the SCs, but it has never been attempted. If this figure is measured, it will not be more than 5 per cent of the GDP, while it ought to be 20 per cent.[21]

The SCs lost their wealth due to centuries of discrimination. For instance, consider this:

> . . . the disparities between high caste, OBC and SC in per capita consumption expenditure are not only due to systematic differences in the same factors, which improve income, namely in ownership of capital assets (land and enterprises), employment and education, but also discrimination faced by SC and OBC in accessing these resources. In 2012, inequality

in assets ownership (agricultural land and enterprise), and higher education explained about 60 percent of differences in per capita consumption expenditure between the high caste and scheduled caste, and 65 percent between SC and OBC . . . Alternatively about 39 percent difference between the SC and high caste, and 35 percent between SC and OBC are due to caste discrimination . . .[22]

Hypothetically, had there been no untouchability and discrimination, the SCs could have secured at least 30 per cent share of the GDP.

Recently, India's finance minister Nirmala Sitharaman emphasized the importance of ethical wealth creation as the root of economic activity and the key to India's becoming a $5-trillion economy by 2025. Dalits are the pioneers of ethical wealth creation, both directly and indirectly, and have contributed to the national economy for centuries as actual workers in fields and factories. They are endowed with skills that contributed to the growth of the nation. But the bitter reality of wealth creation is the preponderance of unethical wealth-usurpation by the dominant castes, through capture of political and economic power.

The capture of political power opens up unlimited access for the kith and kin of lawmakers to infinite reserves of public monies through low-risk-and-high-margin government contracts, particularly mega irrigation and mining projects and, in recent past, IT and telecom projects. The ubiquitous government contractor has grown in stature, to the point of yielding political power, and today, the upper house of Parliament has many members who had their humble origins in small-time government contract work.

Italian–American economist Mariana Mazzucato, in her 2013 book, *The Entrepreneurial State*,[23] completely demolished 'the narrative of innovation that omitted the role of the State, [which] was exactly what corporations had been deploying as they lobbied for lax regulation and low taxation'.[24] She sought to demonstrate the extent to which Silicon Valley's success was founded on state-funded research, with government agencies playing a critical role in many other economies. This is exactly true of the origins of big wealth creators in India as well.

The state has, directly or indirectly, always provided the groundwork for the growth of the billionaires club in India. Fugitive Indian businessmen like Nirav Modi, Mehul Choksi and Vijay Mallya have all benefitted from the liberal access to loans from public-sector banks. The diamond merchant Nirav Modi was given a loan of Rs 14,000 crore by the Punjab National Bank; Vijay Mallya had a loan exposure of Rs 9000 crore from a group of seventeen banks (and allegedly routed that money to gain 100 per cent or partial stake in about forty companies across the world). All this goes to show that it was easy access to capital that gave them the impetus to grow so rapidly. No one from the Dalit, adivasi, OBC or other minority communities has defrauded India of thousands of crores. Why are the biggest defaulters and scamsters always from the dominant castes? Their privileged access to capital and their social capital enable them to flout norms.

It is a matter of record, as reported in Credit Suisse's Global Wealth Databook for 2014, that the bottom 10 per cent of Indian society own merely 0.2 per cent of the national wealth, while the richest 10 per cent own 81 per cent of the wealth. The Dalits represent the bottom 20 per cent. And with no political power, access to wealth remains a very distant dream. Therefore, the state has to play a key role in ensuring that the Dalits secure their true share of the national wealth.

Way Forward: A Road Map for Progress

One Giant Leap of Faith for the Nation Will Be a Significant First Step for the Dalits

For decades, the Dalit story in India has been fraught with pain, misery and fear. What we need is an audacious overhaul of the Dalit script, a shift from the tragedy/horror genre to a feel-good family drama, with elements of love, happiness and, most importantly, hope. As we see the failure of a development paradigm spanning over seven decades, the only way the state can take this giant leap is by:

Dedicating one-fifth of the country's budget for the development of Dalits. It is ironic that even though the Dalits form the single largest vote bank of nearly 250 million (16.63 per cent as per 2011 Census), in a country where the crux of setting the development agenda lies in vote banks and numbers, these figures have never translated into a powerful pressure group that influences policy-making and budgetary allocations. Despite the historical and continuing prejudicial apathy, the collective conscience of the nation can be channelled positively if we as a nation resolve to set aside 20 per cent of the budget every year, for the next fifty years, as reparations—not a token policy but a gesture of gratitude towards the Dalits for enduring centuries of pain with infinite patience. The reparations must include meaningful transfer of assets and capital to the Dalits, to help them compete on a more equal footing in the new economy.

Presenting a separate Dalit Budget, one day prior to the presentation of regular Budget every year for fifty years, in both Parliament and state assemblies. Since 1924, the Rail Budget has been made separately from the general Budget, because the British deemed it necessary to focus on India's most important infrastructure network following the recommendation of the Ackworth Committee in 1920–21. The ninety-two-year-old practice effectively served its purpose in addressing a critical infrastructural need of the country. The same model can be replicated by focusing on developing a critical human resource of the country: the Dalits, the backbone of the nation.

One week prior to the presentation of the Dalit Budget, *releasing an Annual Report on the development of Dalits* across various development parameters. The Economic Survey of India is a detailed report of the country's economic performance during the past one year. A similar document can be prepared detailing the progress of the SCs over the last year along with an assessment of what is to come in the short to medium term. This can essentially lay the groundwork for the presentation of the Budget. Even though Andhra Pradesh, Karnataka and Telangana passed the SCSP Act, to give legal status to the process of identification of the gaps in development and budgetary wherewithal (equal to the population proportion) to bridge these gaps, the ground reality is a complete neglect and mockery of the spirit of the legislation. Therefore, the presentation of the annual progress on the floor of the houses of Parliament will bring about a paradigm shift in the outlook of the political and bureaucratic machinery in terms of presenting the real progress of the SCs. The broad parameters to determine the gaps of development could be:

- Livelihood enhancement: percentage of households below poverty line; percentage of households with self-employed/casual labourers; percentage of households with multiple livelihoods.
- Land ownership: percentage of land owned; average landholding per household.
- Quality education: gross enrolment ratio at secondary level, senior secondary level, college and university level; dropout ratios at all levels.
- Housing: percentage of households owning a house.
- Health: neonatal mortality, infant mortality, child mortality, under-five mortality, full immunization of children.
- Basic amenities: percentage of households with access to basic amenities, like safe drinking water, toilet, electricity, road connectivity.

Preparing five-year plans on the development of SCs. The annual Budgets of five years should envisage the realization of the five-year targets. These plans should aim to secure 20 per cent share in the nation's wealth for the SCs. The five-year plans should give projections on jobs to be secured for the SCs in both government and private establishments. It is clear that there's a need for the creation of wealth for the Dalits. The wealth and resources of this country are controlled by a minuscule number of people from socially advanced classes; one cannot dream of any long-term structural change unless some serious steps are taken towards the redistribution and creation of wealth. Giving the Dalits access to land and common resources, along with special schemes for education, employment and entrepreneurship, is crucial.

Setting up a National SC Development Commission along the lines of the erstwhile Planning Commission or the current NITI Aayog. This body would be dedicated to the empowerment of the Dalits and tasked with the responsibility to prepare annual survey reports and five-year development plans, to provide inputs to the ministries and to prepare budget proposals to realize the targets detailed in the five-year plans. Akin to the NITI Aayog, the NSCDC would function as a state-of-the-art resource centre, equipped with all the resources, knowledge and skills to enable it to act with speed, promote research and innovation, and provide strategic policy vision for the development of the Dalits. Its entire gamut of activities would be divided into four main categories:

1. Policy and programmes
2. Think tanks, knowledge and innovation hubs
3. Employment generation and wealth creation
4. Measurement and evaluation of gaps in development

Conclusion

Acknowledging the lack of progress in the development of the Dalit community in the last seventy-four years is the first step towards kick-starting the giant leap. Various statistics and annual reports on the development of Dalits in the last seventy-four years have established that the Dalits continue to languish at the bottom of the development ladder. But what they gloss over is the bitter reality that the development gap is widening. It is imperative that we as a nation resolve firmly to bring the Dalits on a par with rest of the society within the next fifty years.

Let us make #DalitLivesMatter the clarion call for a radical and disruptive change in the way we think and approach the status of the Dalits, rooted in the religiously sanctioned caste hierarchy. The proposed 'giant leap of faith' can set the ball rolling for a nationwide movement that calls for a comprehensive reform of the socio-cultural paradigm, birthing a compassionate society. As Babasaheb Ambedkar said, 'A just society is that society in which ascending sense of reverence and descending sense of contempt is dissolved into the creation of a compassionate society.'

Acknowledgements

I owe so much to Rahul Gandhiji for encouraging me to work on this volume. I would like to convey my deep sense gratitude to Pratishtha Singh, for her perceptive advice and generous support for enriching the content and narrative. I am grateful to Bharati Sekhar for her help through all the stages of editing and for the diligent research support she provided.

My heartfelt thanks to Anurag Bhaskar and Khalid Khan, for their valuable expert advice. I owe a debt of gratitude to Vinay Sitapati, who offered very useful comments and suggestions.

I would like to acknowledge, with gratitude, the invaluable assistance of Chaitanya. I am beholden to Chandrasen for his critical insights and contribution. I am grateful to Tarun Sagar for his support.

I am indebted to Pushparaj Deshpande and Aakash Singh Rathore, for their assistance and guidance from the very beginning. I deeply appreciate Elizabeth Kuruvilla and Vineet Gill of Penguin Random House India for their wonderful collaboration.

I would like to give special thanks to my family members, who have been a constant source of strength and support.

K. Raju

Notes

Introduction

1. Ishita Sengupta, 'Dakshayani Velayudhan, the First and Only Dalit Woman in the Constituent Assembly', *Indian Express*, 19 January 2018, https://indianexpress.com/article/gender/dakshayani-velayudhan-the-first-and-only-dalit-woman-in-the-constituent-assembly-5030932/

2. Nupur Preeti Alok, 'Jhalkari Bai: The Indian Rebellion of 1857 and Forgotten Dalit History', Feminism in India, 22 November 2016, https://feminisminindia.com/2016/11/22/jhalkari-bai-dalit-woman-essay/

3. Marc Galanter, 'Law and Caste in Modern India', *Asian Survey*, vol. 3, no. 11, November 1963, pp. 544–59, https://www.jstor.org/stable/pdf/3023430.pdf?refreqid=excelsior%3A3daa84ff17f988c67691bce96c2a5e60

4. 'National Commission to Review the Working of the Constitution - Summary of Recommendations', https://www.thehinducentre.com/multimedia/archive/03091/ncrwc_3091109a.pdf

5. Anindya Dutta, *Wizards: The Story of Indian Spin Bowling*, 2019, Westland Books, Chennai.

6. Ramachandra Guha, *Spin and Other Turns: Indian Cricket's Coming of Age*, 2000, Penguin India, Delhi.

The Dalit Idea of the Nation, Inspired by Ambedkar

1. B.R. Ambedkar, *Pakistan or the Partition of India*, 1946, reprint, in *Dr Babasaheb Ambedkar, Writings and Speeches*, vol. 8, Dr Ambedkar Foundation, Ministry of Social Justice and Empowerment, Government of India, New Delhi, 2014, pp. 134–94.
2. B.R. Ambedkar, *Ranade, Gandhi and Jinnah*, 1943, reprint, in *Dr Babasaheb Ambedkar, Writings and Speeches*, vol.1, Ministry of Social Justice and Empowerment, Government of India, New Delhi, 2014, p. 223.
3. B.R. Ambedkar, *Pakistan or Partition of India*, in *Dr Babasaheb Ambedkar, Writings and Speeches*, vol. 8, Dr Ambedkar Foundation, Ministry of Social Justice and Empowerment, Government of India, New Delhi, 2014, pp. 38–39.
4. Ibid., p. 38.
5. Ibid., p. 39.
6. Ibid., pp. 38–39.
7. B.R. Ambedkar, *State and Minorities: What Are Their Rights and How to Secure Them in the Constitution of Free India*, 1947, reprint, in *Dr Babasaheb Ambedkar, Writings and Speeches*, vol.1, Dr Ambedkar Foundation, Ministry of Social Justice and Empowerment, Government of India, New Delhi, 2014.
8. Ibid., p. 410.
9. Ibid., p. 9.
10. *Dr Babasaheb Ambedkar, Writings and Speeches*, vol. 1., first edition, Part IV, Chapter 10, p. 381, Education Department, Government of Maharashtra, 14 April 1979, https://www.mea.gov.in/Images/attach/amb/Volume_01.pdf
11. Ibid., p. 412.
12. B.R. Ambedkar, *Ranade, Gandhi and Jinnah*, 1943, reprint, in *Dr Babasaheb Ambedkar, Writings and Speeches*, vol.1, Ministry of Social Justice and Empowerment, Government of India, New Delhi, 2014.
13. B.R. Ambedkar, *Annihilation of Caste*, 1936, in *Dr Babasheb Ambedkar, Writings and Speeches*, vol. 1, Dr Ambedkar Foundation, Ministry of Social Justice and Empowerment, Government of India, New Delhi, 2014, p. 68.

14. B.R. Ambedkar, *Communal Deadlock and a Way to Solve It*, 1945, in *Dr Babasaheb Ambedkar, Writings and Speeches*, vol. 1, Dr Ambedkar Foundation, Ministry of Social Justice and Empowerment, Government of India, New Delhi, 2014.

15. B.R. Ambedkar, *State and Minorities: What Are Their Rights and How to Secure Them in the Constitution of Free India*, 1947, reprint, in *Dr Babasaheb Ambedkar, Writings and Speeches*, vol. 1, Dr Ambedkar Foundation, Ministry of Social Justice and Empowerment, Government of India, New Delhi, 2014, p. 427.

Ambedkar's Representational Politics: Expanding the Possibilities

1. I have used the word 'untouchables' to denote the scheduled castes, also known as the Dalits. This is to bring historical context to the present. The untouchables were also called the Depressed Classes during the British constitutional process till the time they were 'scheduled' as a 'List' in the Government of India Act, 1935, and officially came to be called the scheduled castes.

2. B.R. Ambedkar, *Pakistan or the Partition of India*, 1946, Thacker and Co., Bombay, p. 235, reprinted in *Dr Babasaheb Ambedkar, Writings and Speeches*, vol. 8, Dr Babasaheb Ambedkar Source Material Publication Committee, Education Department, Government of Maharashtra, Bombay.

3. S.K. Gupta, *The Scheduled Castes in Modern Indian Politics: Their Emergence as a Political Power*, 1985, Munshiram Manoharlal Publishers Pvt Ltd, New Delhi, pp. 188–89.

4. 'Evidence Before Southborough Committee', *Dr Babasaheb Ambedkar, Writings and Speeches*, vol. 1, Dr Babasaheb Ambedkar Source Material Publication Committee, Education Department, Government of Maharashtra, Bombay, pp. 243–78.

5. Christophe Jaffrelot, *India's Silent Revolution: The Rise of the Lower Castes in North India,* 2003, Hurst and Company, London, p. 169.

6. B.R. Ambedkar, *Pakistan or the Partition of India*, pp. 253–54.

7. 'Evidence Before Southborough Committee', *Dr Babasaheb Ambedkar, Writings and Speeches*, vol.1, Dr Babasaheb Ambedkar Source Material

Publication Committee, Education Department, Government of Maharashtra, Bombay, p. 263.

8. Raja Sekhar Vundru, *Ambedkar, Gandhi and Patel: The Making of India's Electoral System,* 2017, Bloomsbury, New Delhi, pp. 13–4.

9. S.K. Gupta, *The Scheduled Castes in Modern Indian Politics: Their Emergence as a Political Power,* p. 265.

10. 'Evidence Before Southborough Committee'.

11. Raja Sekhar Vundru, *Ambedkar, Gandhi and Patel: The Making of India's Electoral System*, pp. 25–34.

12. B.R. Ambedkar, *What Congress and Gandhi Have Done to the Untouchables*, 1945, Thacker and Co., Bombay, pp.72–3, reprinted in *Dr Babasaheb Ambedkar, Writings and Speeches*, vol. 9, Dr Babasaheb Ambedkar Source Material Publication Committee, Education Department, Government of Maharashtra, Bombay.

13. Ibid., pp.307–11.

14. Ibid., p. 307:

15. 'Claims of Minority Communities:

1. No person shall by reason of his origin, religion, caste or creed, be prejudiced in any way in regard to public employment, office of power or honour, or with regard to enjoyment of his civic rights and the exercise of any trade or calling.

2. Statutory safeguards shall be incorporated in the constitution with a view to protect against enactments of the Legislature of discriminatory laws affecting any community.

3. Full religious liberty, that is, full liberty of belief, worship observances, propaganda, associations and education, shall be guaranteed to all communities subject to the maintenance of public order and morality. No person shall merely by change of faith lose any civic right or privilege, or be subject to any penalty.

4. The right to establish, manage and control, at their own expense, charitable, religious and social institutions, schools and other educational establishments with the right to exercise their religion therein.

5. The constitution shall embody adequate safeguards for the protection of religion, culture and personal law, and the promotion of education, language, charitable institutions of the minority

communities and for their due share in grants-in-aid given by the State and by the self-governing bodies.

6. Enjoyment of civic rights by all citizens shall be guaranteed by making any act or omission calculated to prevent full enjoyment an offence punishable by law.

7. In the formation of Cabinets in the Central Government and Provincial Governments, so far as possible, members belonging to the Mussalman community and other minorities of considerable number shall be included by convention.

8. There shall be Statutory Departments under the Central and Provincial Governments to protect minority communities and to promote their welfare.

9. All communities at present enjoying representation in any Legislature through nomination or election shall have representation in all Legislatures through separate electorates and the minorities shall have not less than the proportion set forth in the Annexure but no majority shall be reduced to a minority or even an equality. Provided that after a lapse of ten years it will be open to Muslims in Punjab and Bengal and any minority communities in any other Provinces to accept joint electorates, or joint electorates with reservation of seats, by the consent of the community concerned. Similarly after the lapse of ten years, it will be open to any minority in the Central Legislature to accept joint electorates with or without reservation of seats with the consent of the community concerned.

With regard to the Depressed Classes, no change to joint electorates and reserved seats shall be made until after 20 years' experience of separate electorates and until direct adult suffrage for the community has been established.

10. In every Province and in connection with the Central Government, a Public Services Commission shall be appointed, and the recruitment to the Public Services, except the proportion, if any, reserved to be filled by nomination by the Governor-General and the Governors, shall be made through such commission in such a way as to secure a fair representation to the various communities consistently with the considerations of efficiency and the possession of the necessary qualifications. Instructions to

the Governor-General and the Governors in the Instrument of Instructions with regard to recruitment shall be embodied to give effect to this principle, and for that purpose to review periodically the composition of the Services.

11. If a Bill is passed which, in the opinion of two-thirds of the members of any Legislature representing a particular community, affects their religion or social practice based on religion, or in the case of fundamental rights of the subjects if one-third of the members object, it shall be open to such members to lodge their objection thereto, within a period of one month of the Bill being passed by the House, with the President of the House who shall forward the same to the Governor-General or the Governor, as the case may be, and he shall thereupon suspend the operation of that Bill for one year, upon the expiry of which period he shall remit the said Bill for further consideration by the Legislature. When such Bill has been further considered by the Legislature and the Legislature concerned has refused to revise or modify the Bill so as to meet the objection thereto, the Governor-General or the Governor, as the case may be, may give or withhold his assent to it in the exercise of his discretion, provided, further, that the validity of such Bill may be challenged in the Supreme Court by any two members of the denomination affected thereby on the ground that it contravened one of their fundamental rights.'

16. B.R. Ambedkar, *Pakistan or the Partition of India*, pp. 455–62.

17. For details, see Devendra Swarup and Meenakshi Jain, *The Rajah–Moonje Pact: Documents on a Forgotten Chapter of Indian History*, 2007, Books for All, Delhi.

18. Raja Sekhar Vundru, *Ambedkar, Gandhi and Patel: The Making of India's Electoral System*, 2017, Bloomsbury Publishing.

19. B.R. Ambedkar, *What Congress and Gandhi Have Done to the Untouchables*.

20. This part has been adapted from Raja Sekhar Vundru's 2013 monograph *Political Representation: Ambedkar and the Electoral Method*, NMML Occasional Paper, Nehru Memorial Museum and Library, New Delhi.

21. Ibid., pp. 134–41.

22. During this time (July 1941) the British had appointed Ambedkar to the National Defence Council. Later (1942–46), they made him a member of the viceroy's executive council. It was during this time that Ambedkar initiated the reservations for the scheduled castes in employment and introduced education grants through scholarships.

23. Wavell's letter to Gandhi on 15 August 1944. See *Dr Babasaheb Ambedkar, Writings and Speeches*, vol. 9, pp. 334–36. These were done at the instance of British war cabinet and Prime Minister Winston Churchill. For more details, see A.C. Pradhan, *Emergence of the Depressed Classes*, 1986, Bookland International, Bhubaneswar, p. 284.

24. The same plan had five seats for 90 million Muslims and one seat for 6 million Sikhs.

25. 'Note of Meeting between Cabinet Delegation, Field Marshal Viscount Wavell and Dr B.R. Ambedkar on Friday, 5 April 1946 at 12 Noon', in *Dr Babasaheb Ambedkar, Writings and Speeches*, vol. 10, pp. 484–86.

26. *Does the Indian National Congress Represent the Scheduled Castes (Untouchables) of India?*, reprinted in *Dr Babasaheb Ambedkar, Writings and Speeches*, vol. 10, pp. 525–27.

27. For details, see Raja Sekhar Vundru, 'Affirmative Action in Political Representation: Legal Framework and Electoral Methods in the Case of Scheduled Castes in India', 2011, unpublished thesis, National Law school of India University, Bengaluru.

28. As quoted by Sardar Patel in his letter dated 1 September 1946, reproduced in Sumit Sarkar (ed.), *Towards Freedom: 1946*, 2007,Oxford University Press, New Delhi, pp. 908–09. For details of the proposed plans of Ambedkar on non-territorial constituencies in that letter, see Raja Sekhar Vundru's unpublished thesis from 2011.

29. The Congress in power, headed by Prime Minister B.G. Kher and under instructions from Sardar Patel, had ensured that Ambedkar did not get elected. However, the people of the depressed classes across the country got annoyed with this move and finally, Jogendranath Mandal, a strong critic of the Congress and head of the Bengal unit of the SCF, made way to the Constituent Assembly for Ambedkar from Bengal. Mandal managed to secure the votes of six of Congress's

scheduled caste legislators in Bengal to ensure Ambedkar's nomination to the Constituent Assembly. See Masayuki Usuda, 'Pushed towards the Partition: Jogendranath Mandal and the Constraint Namashudra Movement', 1997, in H. Kotani (ed.), *Caste System, Untouchability and the Depressed*, 2003, Manohar Publishers, New Delhi, p. 254. Thus, finally, the communal composition of the Constituent Assembly, after the 1946 elections, had 161 Hindus, eighty Muslims, three Anglo–Indians, six Indian Christians, three Parsees, six tribes and thirty-one scheduled castes (twenty-eight Congress nominees; one from the Unionist Party, one Dr Ambedkar himself and one from the others). See Shekar Bandyopadhyay, 'Transfer of Power and Crisis of Dalit Politics in India: 1945-1947', 2000, *Modern Asian Studies*, 34/4, p. 918.

30. B. Shiva Rao (ed.), *The Framing of India's Constitution*, vol. 2, 1966–68, IIPA, New Delhi, 1966–1968.

31. The stipulation of the minimum number of votes for a reserved candidate, as proposed by Ambedkar, was 25 per cent, whereas the All India Adi-Hindu Depressed Classes Association had proposed 40 per cent before the Minorities Sub-Committee.

32. The Advisory Committee comprised fifty-seven members, including Sardar Vallabhbhai Patel as the chairman. The Advisory Committee submitted its report to the Constituent Assembly on 27 August 1947. See Rao (ed.), *The Framing of India's Constitution*.

33. *Dr Babasaheb Ambedkar, Writings and Speeches*, vol. 17 (part three), pp. 371–72.

34. Ibid.

35. Sardar Nagappa was a scheduled caste member of the Constituent Assembly from Andhra Pradesh. He was also the convenor of the scheduled caste members of the Constituent Assembly. For more details, see R.K. Kshirsagar, *Dalit Movement in India and Its Leaders (1857–1956)*, 1994, M.D. Publications, New Delhi.

36. 'Clause 6: No condition for a minimum number of votes of one's own community: There shall be no stipulation that a minority candidate standing for election for a reserved seat shall poll a minimum number of votes of his own community before he is declared elected.' *Constituent Assembly Debates*, vol. 5, pp. 259–70.

37. Prem Parkash, *Ambedkar: Politics and the Scheduled Castes*, 2002, Ashish Publishing House, New Delhi, p. 150–51.

38. K.K. Wadhwa, *Minority Safeguards in India: Constitutional Safeguards and Their Implementation*, 1975, Thomson Press India, New Delhi, pp. 4–8.

39. The system of double member seat in reserved seats (which would ensure non-reserved candidate to contest in a general seat of the same constituency) was changed by Nehru in 1961 to single member reserved seat.

40. For a detailed account of the subject, see Raja Sekhar Vundru, *Ambedkar, Gandhi and Patel: The Making of India's Electoral System*, 2017, Bloomsbury, New Delhi, pp. 16–17.

41. B.R. Ambedkar, Pakistan or the Partition of India, 1946, Thacker and Co., Bombay, p. 446, reprinted in Dr Babasaheb Ambedkar, Writings and Speeches, vol. 8, Dr Babasaheb Ambedkar Source Material Publication Committee, Education Department, Government of Maharashtra, Bombay.

42. Raja Sekhar Vundru, *Ambedkar, Gandhi and Patel: The Making of India's Electoral* System, pp. 134–41.

43. B.R. Ambedkar, *States and Minorities: What Are Their Rights and How to Secure Them in the Constitution of Free India, Memorandum on the Safeguards for the Scheduled Castes Submitted to the Constituent Assembly on Behalf of the All India Scheduled Castes Federation.*

44. *Dr Babasaheb Ambedkar, Writings and Speeches*, vol. 1, p. 398.

45. B.R. Ambedkar, *States and Minorities*, 1947, reprinted in *Dr Babasaheb Ambedkar, Writings and Speeches*, vol. 1, p. 415.

46. B.R. Ambedkar, *Thoughts on Linguistic States*, 1955, reprinted in *Dr Babasaheb Ambedkar, Writings and Speeches*, vol. 1, p. 168.

47. Ibid. p. 169.

48. Article 292, Draft Constitution of India, 1948.

Caste and Judiciary in India

1. *Dr Babasaheb Ambedkar, Writings and Speeches*, vol. 13, edited by Vasand Moon, published by the Government of Maharashtra, https://www.mea.gov.in/Images/attach/amb/Volume_13.pdf

2.   *Constituent Assembly Debates*, vol. 3, Secretariat, Government of India, Book No. 3, New Delhi, p. 468.

3.   T.R. Andhyarujina, 'The Evolution of Due Process of Law by the Supreme Court', in B.N. Kirpal, *Supreme but Not Infallible*, 2011, Oxford University Press, New Delhi, pp. 195–96.

4.   Constituent Assembly Debates on 14 October 1949, Part II, *Constituent Assembly of India*, vol. 10, https://indiankanoon.org/doc/54336/

5.   Shiva Rao, *The Framing of Indian Constitution: A Study,* 1968, Indian Institute of Public Administration, New Delhi, p. 194.

6.   Ibid.

7.   Anurag Bhaskar, 'Reservations, Efficiency, and the Making of Indian Constitution', *Economic and Political Weekly,* vol. 56, issue no. 19, 8 May 2021.

8.   Ibid.

9.   Ibid.

10.   Ibid.

11.   P. Radhakrishnan, 'Communal Representation in Tamil Nadu, 1850–1916: The Pre-Non-Brahmin Movement Phase', *Economic and Political Weekly*, vol. 28, no. 31, 1993, p. 1585.

12.   Eugene Irschick, *Politics and Social Conflict in South India: The Non-Brahmin Movement and Tamil Separatism, 1916–1929*, Appendix 2, 1969, University of California Press, Berkeley, pp. 368–72.

13.   'Srimathi Champakam Dorairajan and Another vs the State of Madras', AIR 1951, Mad 120.

14.   'The State of Madras vs Srimathi Champakam Dorairajan and Another', 1951, AIR 226.

15.   'B. Venkataramana vs State of Tamil Nadu and Another', 1951, AIR SC 229.

16.   'General Manager, Southern Railway vs Rangachari', AIR 1962 SC 36; 'M.R. Balaji vs State of Mysore', AIR 1963 SC 649.

17.   'T. Devadasan vs Union of India', AIR 1964 SC 179; 'C.A. Rajendran vs Union of India', AIR 1968 SC 507.

18.   'T. Devadasan vs Union of India', AIR 1964 SC 179 (see Justice K. Subba Rao's dissenting opinion).

19.   (1976) 2 SCC 310.

20. 'State of Kerala vs N.M. Thomas', 1976, 2 SCC 310 (see Justice Fazal Ali's concurring opinion).
21. 'State of Kerala vs N.M. Thomas', 1976, 2 SCC 310 (see Justice Krishna Iyer's concurring opinion).
22. 'K.C. Vasanth Kumar vs State of Karnataka', AIR 1985 SC 1495 (see Justice Chinnappa Reddy's opinion).
23. 1992 Supp (3) SCC 217.
24. Anurag Bhaskar, 'Reservation as a Fundamental Right: Interpretation of Article 16(4)', *SSRN*, 2021, available at https://papers.ssrn.com/sol3/papers.cfm?abstract_id=3868419
25. Ibid.
26. Ibid.
27. Ibid.
28. Ibid.
29. Ibid.
30. (2006) 8 SC C 212.
31. AIR 1999 SC 3471.
32. (2020) 3 SCC 1.
33. Anurag Bhaskar, 'Reservation as a Fundamental Right: Interpretation of Article 16(4)'.
34. 'General Manager, Southern Railway vs Rangachari', AIR 1962 SC 36; 'M.R. Balaji vs State of Mysore', AIR 1963 SC 649; 'T. Devadasan vs Union of India', AIR 1964 SC 179; 'C.A. Rajendran vs Union of India', AIR 1968 SC 507.
35. Ashwini Deshpande and Thomas E. Weisskopf, 'Does Affirmative Action Reduce Productivity?', a case study of the Indian Railways, retrieved from https://mittalsouthasiainstitute.harvard.edu/wp-content/uploads/2018/11/Deshpande.Weisskopf.WD_.pdf
36. 'M.R. Balaji vs the State of Mysore', 1963 AIR 649, upheld by a larger bench in 'Indra Sawhney Etc. vs Union of India and Others Etc.', AIR 1993 SC 477.
37. 'T. Devadasan vs Union of India and Another', 1964 AIR 179.
38. 'R. Chitralekha and Another vs State of Mysore and Others', 1964 AIR 1823; 'Minor P. Rajendran vs State of Madras and Others', 1968 AIR 1012. The shift in approach and emphasis of reservation is obvious. A similar view was taken by another constitution bench

in 'Triloki Nath and Another vs State of Jammu & Kashmir', 1969
AIR 1; 'Minor A. Peeriakaruppan and Sobha vs State of Tamil
Nadu And Others', AIR 1971 SC 2303; 'State of Andhra Pradesh
and Others vs U.S.V. Balram Etc.', 28 January 1972 AIR 1375;
'Janki Prasad Parimoo and Others Etc. vs State of Jammu & Kashmir
and Others', 10 January 1973 AIR 930; 'State of Uttar Pradesh vs
Pradip Tandon and Others', 19 November 1975 AIR 563; 'State of
Uttar Pradesh vs Pradip Tandon and Others', 19 November 1975
AIR 563; 'Kumari K.S. Jayasree and Another vs the State of Kerala
and Another', 1976 AIR 2381; 'K.C. Vasanth Kumar and Another
vs State of Karnataka', 8 May 1985 AIR 1495. The five-judge
benches, each treading a path of their own, held different opinions
on the period of reservation and identification tests for socially and
educationally backward classes.

39. 'Indra Sawhney Etc. vs Union of India and Others Etc.', AIR 1993
SC 477.

40. Ibid.

41. Ibid.

42. 'Virpal Singh Chauhan' (1995) 6 SCC 684 and 'Ajit Singh No. I',
AIR 1996 SC 1189.

43. 'M. Nagaraj & Others vs Union of India & Others', (2006) 8 SCC
212.

44. 'Mukesh Kumar vs the State of Uttarakhand', the Supreme Court of
India judgment dated 7 February 2020.

45. Article 16 (4)(A) and (B), providing for reservation in the services in
which the scheduled castes and scheduled tribes were not adequately
represented, and making unfilled vacancies as a separate class of
vacancies, were inserted by the Constitution (77th Amendment) Act,
1995 and the Constitution (81st Amendment) Act, 2000, respectively.
A proviso to Article 335, providing for the relaxation in qualifications
in matters of promotion to the scheduled castes and scheduled tribes
by the Constitution (82nd Amendment) Act, 2000. Article 16 (4A)
was further amended by the Constitution (85th Amendment) Act,
2001, providing for consequential seniority in promotions.

46. https://www.indiaspend.com/over-a-decade-crime-rate-against-
dalits-rose-by-746-746/

47. Judgment dated 20 March 2018, delivered in Criminal Appeal No. 416 of 2018, 'Dr Subhash Kashinath Mahajan vs the State of Maharashtra and Another'.

48. This decision/view was later overturned in 'Union of India vs State of Maharashtra', 2019.

49. *Dr Babasaheb Ambedkar, Writings and Speeches*, vol. 5, book 3, *Essays on Untouchables and Untouchability: Political*, Chapter 22: 'Held at Bay', pp. 268–69, available at http://www.mea.gov.in/Images/attach/amb/Volume_05.pdf

50. 'Fifty Years after Caste Violence Keezhvenmani Village Waiting for Daylight', *New Indian Express*, 23 December 2018, retrieved from https://www.newindianexpress.com/states/tamil-nadu/2018/dec/23/fifty-years-on-keezhvenmani-waiting-for-daylight-1915275.html; 'Khairlanji: The Crime and Punishment', *The Hindu*, 23 August 2010, retrieved from https://www.thehindu.com/opinion/Readers-Editor/Khairlanji-the-crime-and-punishment/article16149798.ece

51. Judgment dated 27 July 2017, delivered in 'Rajesh Sharma vs the State of Uttar Pradesh'.

52. https://www.thehindu.com/opinion/open-page/misuse-of-dowry-laws-and-the-failure-of-the-system/article19435399.ece

53. https://www.sbs.com.au/language/english/80-per-cent-of-all-dowry-cases-in-india-end-in-acquittal

54. http://egazette.nic.in/WriteReadData/2018/188621.pdf

55. https://main.sci.gov.in/supremecourt/2014/40984/40984_2014_Judgement_14-Sep-2018.pdf

56. 'Supreme Court Advocates-on-Record Association vs Union of India' (1993) 4 SCC 441.

57. 'Supreme Court Advocates-on-Record Association and Another vs Union of India', writ petition (Civil) No. 13 of 2015 dated 16 October 2015.

58. George H. Gadbois, 'Indian Supreme Court Judges: A Portrait', *Law and Society Review*, vol. 3, no. 2/3, 1968, p. 317.

59. Official Website of the Supreme Court of India, https://main.sci.gov.in/chief-justice-judges, accessed on 29 December 2021.

60. *Hidden Apartheid Caste Discrimination against India's 'Untouchables'*, Human Rights Watch, 2007, p. 54.

61. George H. Gadbois, Jr., *Judges of the Supreme Court of India: 1950–1989*, Oxford University Press, 2011, p. 346

62. http://supremecourtcaselaw.com/jus_hksema.htm

63. *Hidden Apartheid Caste Discrimination against India's 'Untouchables'*, Human Rights Watch, p. 54.

64. https://main.sci.gov.in/chief-justice-judges

65. *Judges of the Supreme Court of India: 1950–1989.*

66. 'Indian Supreme Court Judges: A Portrait', *Law and Society Review*, vol. 3, no. 2/3, 1968, p. 336.

67. The Wire, 10 October 2020.

68. 'For How Many Generations Reservations in Jobs, Education Will Continue: Supreme Court', Hindustan Times, 19 March 2021, https://www.hindustantimes.com/india-news/for-how-many-generations-reservations-in-jobs-education-will-continue-supreme-court-101616172304845.html

69. 'Maratha Quota Hearing: Only EWS Quota May Remain, but These Are Policy Matters, Says SC', *Indian Express*, https://indianexpress.com/article/india/maratha-quota-hearing-only-ews-quota-may-remain-but-these-are-policy-matters-says-sc-7245521/

70. 'When It Comes to Reservations, the Supreme Court Needs to Change Its Approach', Wire, https://thewire.in/law/supreme-court-caste-reservation-approach-change-social-justice

71. https://main.sci.gov.in/supremecourt/2019/23618/23618_2019_35_1501_27992_Judgement_05-May-2021.pdf

72. https://thewire.in/law/supreme-court-caste-reservation-approach-change-social-justice

73. https://thewire.in/law/supreme-court-caste-reservation-approach-change-social-justice

74. 'P.N. Duda, vs P. Shiv Shanker', 1988 AIR 1208, 1988 SCR (3) 547.

75. https://livewire.thewire.in/politics/need-for-reservations-in-the-higher-judiciary-of-india/

76. *Judges of the Supreme Court of India 1950–1989*, pp. 346–47.

77. Ibid., p. 346.

78. https://main.sci.gov.in/supremecourt/2015/23229/23229_2015_1_32_21033_Order_28-Feb-2020.pdf

79. https://theprint.in/opinion/why-all-india-judicial-service-and-reservation-in-judiciary-wont-be-a-reality-in-2019/173969/

80. https://www.livemint.com/Politics/SIaiY4YdUwYE9RL6JJR vmK/Nine-high-courts-oppose-allIndia-service-for-lower-judiciar.html

81. https://economictimes.indiatimes.com/news/politics-and-nation/all-india-judicial-service-likely-to-run-subordinate-judiciary/articleshow/37149145.cms

82. Ibid.

83. https://www.thehindu.com/archive/print/2000/10/02/

84. Committee on the Welfare of Scheduled Castes and Scheduled Tribes (2000–2001), 'Thirteenth Report on Ministry of Law, Justice and Company Affairs (Department of Justice)', https://eparlib.nic.in/bitstream/123456789/66474/1/13_Welfare_of_Scheduled_Castes_and_Scheduled_Tribes_13.pdf

85. 'A Report on Reservation in Judiciary', National Commission for Scheduled Castes, 2003, http://ncsc.nic.in/files/Reservation%20 in%20Judiciary.pdf

86. Upendra Baxi, 'Who Bothers about the Supreme Court? The problem of Impact of Judicial Decisions', *Journal of the Indian Law Institute*, vol. 24, no. 4, 1982, p. 848.

87. Anurag Bhaskar. 'Ambedkar's Constitution': A Radical Phenomenon in Anti-Caste Discourse?. *CASTE / A Global Journal on Social Exclusion* (2021), Vol. *2*(1), 109-131.

Leveraging International Institutions to Address Casteism

1. Suraj Yengde, 'Iterations of Shared Dalit-Black Solidarity', *Seminar*, 787, January 2021, p. 83–96.

2. Suraj Yengde, 'Caste Among Indian Diaspora in Africa', *Economic and Political Weekly*.

3. Hymn XC, Puruṣha, Ralph Griffith's translation, 1896, available at http://www.sacred-texts.com/hin/rigveda/rv10090.htm

4. *Arthashastra*, Book III, Wikisource, https://en.wikisource.org/wiki/Arthashastra/Book_III

5. B.R. Ambedkar, *What Congress and Gandhi Have Done to the Untouchables*, Thacker & Co., Bombay, 1945. Also, see Dr Ambedkar's interview with

the BBC in 1955, where he sums up his reservations on Gandhi: 'Dr Babasaheb Ambedkar BBC Interview 1955 Exposing M.K. Gandhi & Congress', BBC, Archive.org, 8 September 2019, https://archive.org/details/drbabasahebambedkarbbcinterview1955exposingm.k.gandhi

6. Lorna Llyod, '"A Most Auspicious Beginning": The 1946 United Nations General Assembly and the Question of the Treatment of Indians in South Africa', *Review of International Studies*, vol. 16, no. 2, April 1990, pp. 131–53.

7. Goolam Vahed, '"Nehru Is Just Another Coolie": India and South Africa at the United Nations, 1946-1955', *Alternation,* special edition no 15., 2015, 54–84.

8. B.R. Ambedkar, 'An Appeal to Join the Republican Party of India', in *Dr Babasaheb Ambedkaranchi Samagra Bhashane*, vol. 10, P. Gaikwad (ed.), Kshitij Publications, Nagpur, 2016, eighth edition, p. 197.

9. '"Scheduled Castes" case to be presented before the UNO', *Jai Bheem*, 26 January, 1947, in *Dr Babasaheb Ambedkar, Writings and Speeches*, vol. 17 (2), p. 358.

10. Goolam Vahed, '"Nehru Is Just Another Coolie": India and South Africa at the United Nations, 1946-1955', *Alternation,* special edition no. 15, 2015, pp. 54–84.

11. Ibid, p. 74.

12. Vineet Thakur, 'When India Proposed a Casteist Solution to South Africa's Racist Problem', TheWire.in, https://thewire.in/diplomacy/exploring-casteism-in-indias-foreign-policy

13. Ibid.

14. Ibid.

15. Suraj Yengde, 'Ambedkar's Foreign Policy and the Ellipsis of 'Dalit' from the International Activism', in Yengde S. and Teltumbde A. (eds), *The Radical in Ambedkar Critical Reflections* (New Delhi: Allen Lane, 2018) pp. 86–106.

16. For more on this see, Jesús Cháirez-Garza, 'B.R. Ambedkar, Partition and the Internationalization of Untouchability, 1939–47', *South Asia: Journal of South Asian Studies*, 42:1, p. 95.

17. Ibid.

18. Ibid.

19. Ibid.

20. Jesús Cháirez-Garza, 'B.R. Ambedkar, Partition and the Internationalization of Untouchability, 1939–47', *South Asia: Journal of South Asian Studies*, 42:1, p. 95.

21. Suraj Yengde, 'Ambedkar's Foreign Policy and the Ellipsis of "Dalit" from the International Activism', in Yengde S. and Teltumbde A. (eds), *The Radical in Ambedkar Critical Reflections*, Allen Lane, New Delhi, 2018, pp. 86–106.

22. Jesus Cháirez-Garza, 'B.R. Ambedkar, Partition and the Internationalization of Untouchability, 1939–47', pp. 94–5.

23. Ibid., 94.

24. Ibid., p. 93

25. 'Statement By Dr B. R. Ambedkar in Parliament in explanation of his resignation from the Cabinet', New Delhi, 10 October 1951, in Vasant Moon (ed.), *Dr Babasaheb Ambedkar, Writings and Speeches*, vol. 14 (2), Education Department, Government of Maharashtra, 1995 (2014), pp. 1315–1327.

26. Ibid., p. 1320

27. Ambrose Pinto, 'Caste Discrimination and UN', *Economic and Political Weekly*, vol. 37, no. 39, 28 September 28–4 October 2002, pp. 3988–3990.

28. Eva Maria Hardtmann, *The Dalit Movement in India: Local Practices Global Connections*, Oxford University Press, New Delhi, 2009; Balmurli Natarajan and Paul Greenough (eds), *Against Stigma: Comparing Caste and Race in an Era of Global Justice*, Orient Blackswan Press, Hyderabad, 2009.

29. Samuel Moyn, *The Last Utopia Human Rights in History* (Cambridge, MA: Harvard University Press, 2012)

30. For a list of UN Treaty bodies see, "Monitoring the core international human rights treaties" UNOHCHR, https://www.ohchr.org/EN/HRBodies/Pages/Overview.aspx

31. Alison Saldanha & Chaitanya Mallapur, "Over Decade, Crime Rate Against Dalits Up 25%, Cases Pending Investigation Up 99%", *IndiaSpend*, April 4, 2018, https://www.indiaspend.com/over-a-decade-crime-rate-against-dalits-rose-by-746-746/

32. Ibram X. Kendi, *How to Be an Anti-racist*, One World, New York, 2019, p. 18–9.

33. Constitution of India, https://www.india.gov.in/sites/upload_files/ npi/files/coi_part_full.pdf, p. 24

34. https://www.un.org/development/desa/dspd/civil-society/ecosoc-status.html

35. http://caricomreparations.org/the-global-reparations-movement/

Saffronizing the Dalits

1. 'RSS Officially Disowns Golwalkar's Book', *Times of India*, March 2006, http://timesofindia.indiatimes.com/articleshow/1443606.cms?utm_source=contentofinterest&utm_medium=text&utm_campaign=cppst

2. M.S. Golwalkar, *Vichar Navneet*, Gyan Ganga Prakashan, Jaipur, pp. 102–03, *The Unique Picture* (translation), https://www. thehinducentre.com/multimedia/archive/02486/Bunch_of_ Thoughts_2486072a.pdf

3. M.S. Golwalkar, *Vichar Navneet*, Gyan Ganga Prakashan, Jaipur, 1939, pp. 109; *Once the Glory* (translation), https://www.thehinducentre. com/multimedia/archive/02486/Bunch_of_Thoughts_2486072a.pdf

4. *The Complete Writings of Shri Guruji*, Sahitya Sindhu, Bangalore, section 9, p. 163.

5. *The Riddles of Hinduism, Collected Works of Dr B.R Ambedkar*, Government of Maharashtra, published by the Government of Maharashtra, April 1979.

6. C.P. Bhishkar, Sudhakar Raje (tr.), *Shri Guruji, Pioneer of a New Era*, Sahitya Sindhu Prakashan, Bangalore, 1999.

7. *Organiser*, 30 November 1949, p. 3.

8. *Organiser*, 6 February 1950, p. 7.

9. Runi Datta, 'Emancipating and Strengthening Indian Women: An Analysis of B.R. Ambedkar's Contribution', 22 February 2019, https:// journals.sagepub.com/doi/full/10.1177/2455328X18819901

10. L.S. Herdenia, 'When RSS Likened Hindu Code Bill to "An Atom Bomb on Hindu Society"', Sabrang India, https://sabrangindia. in/article/when-rss-likened-hindu-code-bill-atom-bomb-hindu-society

11. M.S. Golwalkar, *Vichar Navneet*, Gyan Ganga Prakashan, Jaipur, p. 355–56.

12. Ibid., pp. 364–65.

13. H.D. Malviya, *The Danger of Right Reaction*, Socialist Congressman Publication, Delhi, 1965, pp. 14.

14. M.S. Golwalkar, *Vichar Navneet*, Gyan Ganga Prakashan, Jaipur, p. 23.

15. 'Amend Constitution, Align It to Indian Values', Times of India, 12 September 2017, https://timesofindia.indiatimes.com/india/amend-constitution-align-it-to-indian-value-system-rss-chief/articleshow/60471393.cms

16. A.G. Noorani, 'Vajpayee and the Constitution', *Frontline*, 23 December 2001, https://frontline.thehindu.com/cover-story/article30252972.ece

17. https://twitter.com/Swamy39/status/1342051488562987008?s=20

18. 'Modi's Biography of Golwalkar Suggests RSS Leader Was Vital Influence', Scroll, https://scroll.in/article/669178/modis-biography-of-golwalkar-suggests-rss-leader-was-vital-influence

19. Anand Teltumbde, *Republic of Caste: Thinking Equality in the Time of Neoliberal Hindutva*, Navayana Publishing, 2018.

20. 'RSS Is a Lot More Diverse Than It Used to Be: Walter Anderson', *Economic Times*, https://economictimes.indiatimes.com/news/politics-and-nation/rss-is-a-lot-more-diverse-than-it-used-to-be-author-walter-andersen/articleshow/65273543.cms?from=mdr

21. 'Parts of Bunch of Thoughts Not Valid Anymore, RSS Chief Mohan Bhagwat', *Times of India*, https://timesofindia.indiatimes.com/india/parts-of-golwalkars-bunch-of-thought-not-valid-anymore-rss-chief-mohan-bhagwat/articleshow/65877873.cms

22. 'Know What RSS under Mohan Bhagwat Stands for and How It's Changing in This New Book', Print, https://theprint.in/india/know-what-rss-under-mohan-bhagwat-stands-for-and-how-its-changing-in-this-new-book/565424/

23. Mohan Bhagwat, *Yasashwi Bharat*, Prabhat Publications, Delhi, 2020, p. 223.

24. Ibid., p. 226.

25. https://economictimes.indiatimes.com/news/politics-and-nation/government-to-induct-3-joint-secretaries-27-directors-13-deputy-secretaries-through-lateral-entry/articleshow/81552364.cms

26. https://dopt.gov.in/sites/default/files/ewsf28fT.PDF; https://www.
     livemint.com/news/india/no-job-reservation-in-state-run-firms-
     post-privatization-11617126711306.html

27. Subramanian Swamy, 'Vaicharik Mahakumbh Keynote', *Rajasthan
     Patrika*, Jodhpur, 2017.

28. In some districts in Rajasthan, people from the Sangh attacked
     Dalit protestors, and the incumbent BJP government slapped 250
     cases against the protestors and thousands were arrested or had
     FIRs registered against them: https://hindi.caravanmagazine.in/
     politics/dalit-votes-bjp-rajasthan-elections-2018-hindi;   https://
     www.newindianexpress.com/nation/2018/apr/13/april-2-caste-
     violence-was-organised-allegedly-by-rss-and-bajrang-dal-cpim-
     report-1800847.html

29. 'Mohan Bhagwat in Overdrive to Portray RSS as Inclusive, Evolving
     Organisation', Wire, https://thewire.in/politics/mohan-bhagwat-
     views-rss-conclave

30. Mohan Bhagwat, *Yasashwi Bharat*, Prabhat Prakashan, Delhi, p. 237.

31. Ibid., p. 257.

32. Bhanwar Meghawanshi, *I Could Not Be Hindu: Story of a Dalit in the
     RSS*, 'Meeting with a Sufi Dervish', Navayana Publications, 2020.

33. Pradeep Attri, 'Appropriating Guru Ravidas – Ignorance Is Bliss for
     Hindu Education Foundation, USA', Roundtable India, 15 May 2016,
     https://www.roundtableindia.co.in/appropriating-guru-ravidas-
     ignorance-is-bliss-for-hindu-education-foundation-usa/

34. Bijay Sonkar Shastri, *Hindu Balmiki Jati* (The History of Hindu
     Valmikis), Prabhat Prakashan, 2014; *Hindu Chamar Jati* (The History
     of Hindu Chamars), Prabhat Prakashan, 2016; *Hindu Khatik Jati* (The
     History of Hindu Khatiks), Prabhat Prakashan, 2019.

35. 'The BJP Government Has Deliberately Slowed Down the Process
     of Re-publishing Ambedkar's Ideas', *Caravan*, https://hindi.
     caravanmagazine.in/history/struggle-publish-br-ambedkar-writing-
     hindi

36. 'Bombay HC Takes Suo Motu Cognisance of Stalled Govt Project
     to Publish Ambedkar's Writing', Wire, https://thewire.in/law/
     bombay-hc-takes-suo-motu-cognisance-of-stalled-govt-project-to-
     publish-ambedkars-writing

37. Anand Teltumbde, 'Saffronising Ambedkar: Why the Sangh Portrays Ambedkar as Anti-Communist and Anti-Muslim', *Caravan*, https://caravanmagazine.in/politics/saffronising-ambedkar-sangh-rss

38. 'RSS-Engineered "gharwapsi" of Ambedkar', Forward Press, https://www.forwardpress.in/2017/05/what-is-the-rss-agenda-on-ambedkar/

Hindutva and the Future of Dalit–Bahujan Politics in India

1. Abhijit Roy, 'The Middle Class in India', Asian Studies, https://www.asianstudies.org/wp-content/uploads/the-middle-class-in-india-from-1947-to-the-present-and-beyond.pdf

2. World Social Report, 2020.

3. Sandhya Krishnan and Neeraj Hatekar, Mumbai School of Economics and Public Policy based on National Sample Survey 1999–2000, 2004–05, 2011–12; https://scroll.in/article/1004102/for-the-millions-who-joined-indias-middle-class-the-pandemic-has-been-a-cruel-financial-blow

4. Report by Konrad Adenauer Foundation, 2011.

5. Badri Narayan, *Republic of Hindutva: How the Sangh Is Reshaping Indian Democracy*, Penguin Viking, Gurgaon, 2021.

6. 'How BJP Uses Gods and Icons of Marginalised Communities in Bengal and Elsewhere to Draft Them into Hindutva Politics', *Indian Express*, https://indianexpress.com/article/opinion/columns/narendra-modi-bjp-hindutva-politics-7233187/

7. Krishan Gopal and Shri Prakasha, *Rashtra-Purush Baba Shaheb Dr Bheem Rao Ambedkar*, Suruchi Prakashan, 2014.

8. Bhanwar Meghawanshi, *I Could Not Be Hindu: The Story of a Dalit in the RSS*, Navyana, New Delhi, 2020.

9. B. Narayan, *Fascinating Hindutva: Saffron Politics and Dalit Mobilisation*, SAGE Publications, New Delhi, 2009.

10. Bhanwar Meghawanshi, *I Could Not be Hindu: The Story of a Dalit in the RSS*.

11. Badri Narayan, *Republic of Hindutva: How the Sangh Is Reshaping Indian Democracy*.

12. Badri Narayan, 'Where Does Jagjivan Ram Belong?' *Indian Express*, https://indianexpress.com/article/opinion/columns/where-does-jagjivan-ram-belong/

13. 'Book Excerpt: "Republic of Hindutva" by Badri Narayan', *Outlook*, https://www.outlookindia.com/website/story/books-book-extract-republic-of-hindutva-by-badri-narayan/378269

14. Badri Narayan, *Republic of Hindutva: How the Sangh Is Reshaping Indian Democracy.*

Additional References

S.S. Jodhka, *The Indian Middle Class: Emerging Cultures of Politics and Economics*, KAS International Reports, 2011.

D. Kapur, et al., *Rethinking Inequality: Dalits in Uttar Pradesh in the Market Reform Era*, *Economic and Political Weekly*, vol. 45, issue no. 35, 28 August 2010.

C.B. Prasad, 'Fellow Dalits, Open Your Own Bank: If No One Else, Dalit Middle Class Can Fund Dalit Capitalism to Produce Dalit Billionaires', *Times of India*, 25 November 2019, https://timesofindia.indiatimes.com/blogs/toi-editorials/fellow-dalits-open-your-own-bank-if-no-one-else-dalit-middle-class-can-fund-dalit-capitalism-to-produce-dalit-billionaires/

'India Lifted 271 Million People Out of Poverty in 10 Years: UN', *The Hindu*, 12 July 2012, https://www.thehindu.com/news/national/india-lifted-271-million-people-out-of-poverty-in-10-years-un/article28397694.ece

United Nations, *Inequality in a Rapidly Changing World*, World Social Report, Department of Economic and Social Affairs, 2020.

A Blueprint for a New Dalit Politics: An Open Letter to the Dalits

1   'Anand Teltumbde: Cards and Letters for Jailed India Scholar as He Turns 70', BBC, https://www.bbc.com/news/world-asia-india-53400138

2   Saroj Giri, '"Take Your Cow": That One Slogan from Una', DailyO, 10 July 2017, https://www.dailyo.in/politics/azadi-kooch-dalits-

march-una-cow-politics-brahminism-not-in-my-name-mevani/
story/1/18274.html

New Phase in Dalit Politics: Crisis or Regeneration?

1   R.S. Morkhandikar, 'Dilemmas of the Dalit Movement in Maharashtra: Unity Moves and After', *Economic and Political Weekly*, 25 (12), 24–30 March 1990, pp. 586–91.

2   Hugo Gorringe, *Panthers in Parliament Dalits, Caste, and Political Power in South India*, Oxford University Press, New Delhi, 2017.

3   The BSP's vote share was 20 per cent. See, https://eci.gov.in/files/file/2824-state-wise-seat-won-and-valid-votes-polled-by-political-party/?do=download&r=6558&confirm=1&t=1&csrfKey=e068b29 5ed2c9d895766c028a9359b38

4   The BSP secured 22 per cent votes in 2017. See, https://eci.gov.in/files/file/3471-uttar-pradesh-general-legislative-election-2017/?do=download&r=8087&confirm=1&t=1&csrfKey=e068b295ed2c9d89 5766c028a9359b38

5   https://eci.gov.in/files/file/10961-17state-wise-seat-won-valid-votes-polled-by-political-parties/?do=download&r=30069&confir m=1&t=1&csrfKey=e068b295ed2c9d895766c028a9359b38

6   Shivam Vij, 'The Mayawati Era Is Over. Bye Bye Behenji', Print, 27 January 2020.

7   Sudha Pai, 'Changing Political Preferences among Dalits in Uttar Pradesh in the 2000s: Shift from Social Justice to Aspiration', *Journal of Social Inclusion*, 19 July 2019.

8   Ibid.

9   Ibid.

10   Sudha Pai, 'Dalit Entrepreneurs, Globalisation and the Supplier Diversity Experiment in Madhya Pradesh', in Clarinda Still (ed.), *Dalits Mobility or Marginalization? Dalits in Neo-liberal India*, Routledge, New Delhi.

11   Dalit Agenda was part of the 'Bhopal Document' adopted at the Bhopal Conference by a number of Dalit and non-Dalit intellectuals for the twenty-first century. See, Sudha Pai, *Developmental State and the Dalit Question in Madhya Pradesh: Congress Response* Routledge,

New Delhi, 2010, p. 85. The 'Bhopal Document' is available at www.ambedkar.org.

12 The Bhopal Conference: Charting a New Course for Dalits for the 21st Century, held in Bhopal, Madhya Pradesh, India, 12–13 January 2002.

13 The Dalit Agenda argued that there was need to move beyond reservations, to create Dalit entrepreneurs using programmes such as Supplier Diversity, under which the state could reserve small government contracts or purchases of required goods for the Dalits, thereby bringing them into the business arena. Over time, this would create a body of entrepreneurs who could graduate to becoming manufacturers. For details see, Sudha Pai, *Developmental State and the Dalit Question in Madhya Pradesh: Congress Response*, Routledge, New Delhi, pp. 301–06.

14 Ibid.

15 Suraj Yengde, *Caste Matters*, Penguin, Gurgaon, 2019.

16 Chinnaiah Jangam, *Dalits in the Making of Modern India*, Oxford University Press, New Delhi, 2017.

17 Sambaiah Gundimeda, *Politics in Contemporary India*, Routledge, New Delhi, 2016.

18 Badri Narayan, *Fascinating Hindutva: Saffron Politics and Dalit Mobilization*, SAGE Publications, New Delhi, 2009, p. ix.

19 Badri Narayan, *Republic of Hindutva: How the Sangh is Reshaping Indian Democracy*, Penguin Viking, Gurgaon, 2021.

20 Paul R. Brass, *Ethnicity and Nationalism: Theory and Comparison*, SAGE Publications, New Delhi, 1991, p. 75.

21 Lokniti, Centre for the Study of Developing Societies, National Election study post 2014 and 2017 polls, https://www.lokniti.org/national-election-studies

22 'CSDS–Lokniti Post-Poll Survey', *The Hindu,* 26 May 2019, https://www.thehindu.com/elections/lok-sabha-2019/post-poll-survey-why-uttar-pradeshs-mahagathbandhan-failed/article27249310.ece?homepage=true

23 Shalini Rajvanshi, 'What Is the Bhim Army?' *Indian Express*, 18 May 2018.

24   Sudha Pai and Sajjan Kumar, 'Saharanpur Protests Herald New Phase in Dalit Politics', Wire, 24 May 2017.

25   'Ambedkarite 2.0: Saharanpur's Bhim Army Signals the Rise of a New, Aggressive Dalit Politics', Scroll, 8 February 2020.

26   Gopal B. Kateshiya, 'Gujarat: 7 of Dalit Family Beaten up for Skinning Dead Cow', Indian Express, 20 July 2016.

27   'Bhima-Koregaon Violence: FIR against Jignesh Mevani, Umar Khalid for "Provocative" Speeches in Pune', Indian Express, 4 January 2018.

28   'Uttar Pradesh Dalit Girl, Victim of Brutal Gang Rape, Dies in Delhi Hospital', The Hindu, 29 September 2020, https://www.thehindu.com/news/national/other-states/dalit-girl-gangraped-by-upper-caste-men-in-uttar-pradeshs-hathras-dies-in-delhi-hospital/article32721406.ece

29   Sudha Pai, 'The BJP Is Losing the Support of Dalits in the Hindi Heartland', Wire, 4 April 2018.

30   Ibid.

31   '10 Things to Know about Jignesh Mevani, the Man Leading Gujarat's Dalit Agitation', India Today, 5 August 2016.

32   'Bhim Army Chief Chandrashekhar Azad Launches New Political Outfit – Azad Samaj Party', Print, 15 March 2020.

33   Preetha Nair, 'Willing to Join Hands with Like-Minded Parties to Defeat BJP: Chandrashekhar Azad', India Today, 6 April 2020.

34   'If Chandrashekhar Comes with Akhilesh, Mayawati's Game Will Be Spoiled, BJP Is Also Tightening the Screws of the Alliance', Jansatta Online, 29 November 2021.

35   Saurabh Shukla, 'Bhim Army's Chandrashekhar Azad Says Will Fight Yogi Adityanath in Polls', NDTV, 8 November 2021.

36   Raveedran Rehnamol, 'Bhim Army and Azad Samaj Party Mark a New Phase of Dalit Assertion', Indian Express, 18 March 2020.

37   Suryakant Waghmore, 'The Competing Armies of Bhim', India Today, 22 September 2018.

38   Hugo Gorringe, Untouchable Citizens: Dalit Movements and Democratization in Tamil Nadu (Cultural Subordination and the Dalit Challenge), SAGE Publications, New Delhi, 2005.

39   Ibid.

Dalit Cinema in India

1   Sowmya Rajendran, 'PK Rosy's Story: How Malayalam Cinema's First Woman Actor Was Forced to Leave the State, News Minute, 19 September 2019, https://www.thenewsminute.com/article/pk-rosys-story-how-malayalam-cinemas-first-woman-actor-was-forced-leave-state-109169

2   'UP: Dalit Teen Killed by 'Upper Caste' Men after Entering a Temple', Wire, June 2020, https://thewire.in/rights/up-dalit-teen-killed

Education and Dalit Liberation

1   Ghanshyam Shah, K. Sujatha and Sukhdeo Thorat, *Educational Status of Scheduled Castes*, 2020, Rawat Publications, pp. 15–28.

2   https://www.livemint.com/Politics/Dy9bHke2B5vQcWJJWNo6QK/Dalit-women-in-India-die-younger-than-upper-caste-counterpar.html

3   https://www.unicef-irc.org/article/958-the-first-1000-days-of-life-the-brains-window-of-opportunity.html

Annihilating Entrepreneurship Casteism

1   *The Rise of Asia's Middle Class*, 'Key Indicators for Asia and the Pacific 2010', https://www.adb.org/sites/default/files/publication/27726/ki2010-special-chapter.pdf

2   World Social report, 2020.

3   Anand Teltumbde, 'Globalization and Caste' (research article), *Contemporary Voice of Dalits*, Sage Journals, 1 July 2010.

4   Shoban Saxena, 'Caste and Capital Can't Co-exist', interview with Milind Kamble, *Times of India*, 2 October 2011, https://timesofindia.indiatimes.com/home/sunday-times/all-that-matters/Caste-and-capital-cant-coexist/articleshow/10202564.cms

5   Sukhadeo Thorat, 'Political Economy of Caste Discrimination and Atrocities', in, Suraj Yengde and Anand Teltumbde (eds), *The Radical in Ambedkar*, Penguin Random House, New York, 2018, pp. 255–77.

6   Fourth all India Census of Micro, Small and Medium Enterprises 2006–2007, Development Commissioner (MSME), Ministry of Micro, Small and Medium Enterprises, Government of India, 2009.

7   Sukhadeo Thorat, 'Political Economy of Caste Discrimination and Atrocities'; Surinder S. Jodhka, 'Dalits in Business: Self-Employed Scheduled Castes in North-West India', *Economic and Political Weekly*, vol. 45, no. 11,2010, pp. 41–8.

8   Sukhadeo Thorat, 'Political Economy of Caste Discrimination and Atrocities'; Ashwini Deshpande and Smriti Sharma, 'Disadvantage and Discrimination in Self-Employment: Caste Gaps in Earnings in Indian Small Businesses', *Econ Papers*, vol. 46, issue 2, no. 9, 2016, pp. 325–46; Aseem Prakash, 'Dalits Enter the Indian Markets as Owners of Capital: Adverse Inclusion, Social Networks, and Civil Society', *Asian Survey*, vol. 55, no. 5, 2015, pp. 1044–169; S.S. Jodhka, 'Dalits in Business: Self-Employed Scheduled Castes in North-West India'.

9   S.S. Jodhka, 'Dalits in Business: Self-Employed Scheduled Castes in North-West India'.

10   Aseem Prakash, *Dalit Capital: State, Markets and Civil Society in Urban India*, second edition, Routledge India, 2020.

11   Ashwini Deshpande and Smriti Sharma, 'Disadvantage and Discrimination in Self-Employment: Caste Gaps in Earnings in Indian Small Businesses'; Stephen Coate and Sharon Tennyson, 'Labor Market Discrimination, Imperfect Information and Self Employment' *Oxford Economic Papers*, vol. 44, no. 2, 1992, pp. 272–88.

12   '55% Of PM's Small Business Loans to Backward Classes: BJP Claim Masks True Picture', Fact Checker, 21 June 2018, https://www.factchecker.in/55-of-pms-small- business-loans-to-backward-classes-bjp-claim-masks-true-picture/?infinitescroll=1; 'Dalits, Tribals, OBCs, 78% of India, Get 37% of Loan Under Modi's MUDRA Scheme for Marginalized', Counterview, 21 June 2018, https://www.counterview.net/2018/06/dalits-tribals-obcs-78-of-india-get-37.html

13   Shoban Saxena, 'Caste and Capital Can't Co-exist'.

14   'State Government to Introduce Welfare Schemes for Taxi Drivers, *The Hindu*, 9 March 2019, https://www.thehindu.com/news/national/karnataka/state-government-to-introduce-welfare-schemes-for-taxi-drivers/article26476313.ece

Redesigning the Dalit Development Paradigm

1   National SC Commission report 2011–12.
2   Ibid.
3   Pushparaj Deshpande, 'Revisiting Ambedkar, Gandhi and India's Unfinished War', Wire, 14 April 2016, https://thewire.in/politics/revisiting-ambedkar-gandhi-indias-unfinished-war
4   https://www.gservants.com/2012/12/28/employment-of-other-backaward-classes-obcs-and-scsts-in-central-government-jobs-groups-a-to-d/
5   'Mukesh Kumar vs the State of Uttarakhand – Right Of Promotion Is Contingent upon the Discretion of the State Government', https://viamediationcentre.org/readnews/NjA=/Mukesh-Kumar-Vs-The-State-Of-Uttarakhand-Right-of-Promotion-is-contingent-upon-the-discretion-of-the-State-Government#:~:text=Latest%20News-,Mukesh%20Kumar%20Vs%20The%20State%20Of%20Uttarakhand%20%2D%20Right%20of%20Promotion,discretion%20of%20the%20State%20Government&text=The%20Supreme%20Court%20ruled%20that,SCs%2C%20STs%2C%20and%20OBCs.
6   Shreehari Paliath, IndiaSpend.com, 'Job Losses among SCs Were Three Times Higher Than for Upper Castes: Economist Ashwini Deshpande', Scroll, 8 September 2020, https://scroll.in/article/972357/economist-ashwini-deshpande
7   'Narendra Modi Govt Claims 55% of Mudra Loans Given to Backward Classes, Data Tells a Different Story', Firstpost, 21 June 2018, https://www.firstpost.com/business/narendra-modi-govt-claims-55-of-mudra-loans-given-to-backward-classes-data-tells-a-different-story-4558711.html
8   Surinder S. Jodhka, *Caste in Contemporary India*, chapter 'Caste Blinding and Contemporary Hiring', Tailor and Francis, second edition, 2018.
9   Ibid.
10 Dilip Mandal, '17th Lok Sabha Looks Set to Confirm Ambedkar's Fears: No Vocal Dalits in Parliament', Print, 8 May 2019, http://theprint.in/opinion/17th-lok-sabha-looks-set-to-confirm-ambedkars-fears-no-vocal-dalits-in-parliament/232383/

11 Ibid.

12 E.T.B. Shivapriyan, 'Dalit Panchayat President Made to Sit on Floor during Meetings in Tamil Nadu', *Deccan Herald*, 10 October 2020, https://www.deccanherald.com/national/south/dalit-panchayat-president-made-to-sit-on-floor-during-meetings-in-tamil-nadu-899973.html

13 'Reservations Take SC/STs to Parliament, but Not to Positions of Influence', *Business Standard*, 27 June 2021, https://www.business-standard.com/article/economy-policy/reservations-can-take-sc-sts-to-parliament-but-not-in-key-positions-121061600147_1.html

14 Ministry of Social Justice and Empowerment, Government of India Annual Report, 2018-19, P. 33

15 Expenditure Budget Documents, 2010–11 to 2019–20, Ministry of Finance, Government of India, https://www.indiabudget.gov.in

16 Ibid.

17 Ibid.

18 Ibid.

19 Ibid.

20 Ibid.

21 'Upper Caste Hindus Own 41 Per Cent of India's Total Wealth: Study', *Business Today*, 14 February 2019, https://www.businesstoday.in/latest/economy-politics/story/upper-caste-hindus-own-41-per-cent-india-total-wealth-study-170486-2019-02-14

22 Sukhadeo Thorat, 'Graded Caste Inequality and Poverty', LSE Blogs, https://blogs.lse.ac.uk/inequalityandpoverty/files/2017/12/Graded-Caste-Inequality-and-Poverty.pdf

23 Mariana Mazzucato, *The Entrepreneurial State: Debunking Public vs Private Sector Myths*, Public Affairs Publications, 2013.

24 João Medeiros, 'This Economist Has a Plan to Fix Capitalism. It's Time We All Listened', *Wired*, 8 October 2019, https://www.wired.co.uk/article/mariana-mazzucato

About the Contributors

Sukhadeo Thorat served as faculty and researcher at Jawaharlal Nehru University, Delhi, from 1980 to 2014, for about thirty-four years. Since 2014, he has been a professor emeritus at the same university. So far, he has published twenty-two books, mainly with Oxford University Press and SAGE International. The themes of his research include subjects like agricultural development, poverty, wage labour, economics of caste, labour market discrimination, inter-caste inequalities and the impact of caste discrimination and poverty.

Raja Sekhar Vundru is the author of *Ambedkar, Gandhi and Patel: The Making of India's Electoral System* (2017), which has been translated into Marathi, Telugu and Hindi. He studied at the University of Hyderabad, Jawaharlal Nehru University and the National Law School of India University. He is a senior civil servant, and he joined the Indian Administrative Service in 1990. He has written extensively on Ambedkar, caste, Dalit history and literature. He is a recipient of Dr B.R. Ambedkar Ratan Award 2016 (Delhi government); the India International Excellence Award, 2019 (UAE); and Dr Ambedkar Prabuddha Bharat Peace Prize 2019. He has been invited to speak at the Chandigarh, Kalinga and Dehradun literary festivals.

Kiruba Munusamy is an advocate practising in the Supreme Court of India. She extensively works against caste-based discrimination and related violence. She founded Legal Initiative for Equality to render legal assistance to the victims of human rights violations. She was the first Indian guest to be invited by Justice and Peace Netherlands and the Dutch Ministry of Foreign Affairs, the Netherlands. She is the only Indian to be portrayed in the Cobra Museum of Modern Art, the Netherlands, among hundred human rights defenders from across the world. She is a recipient of the Lawyers for Lawyers Award (2019); Eliasson Global Leadership Prizes (2018); Front Line Defenders Award (2018); and Human Rights Tulip Award (2017).

Suraj Yengde is one of India's leading scholars and public intellectuals. He is the author of the bestseller *Caste Matters* (2019) and co-editor of the award-winning anthology *The Radical in Ambedkar* (2018). He holds a research associate position with the Department of African and African American Studies and is a non-resident fellow at the Hutchins Center for African and African American Research. He is part of the founding team of Initiative for Institutional Anti-Racism and Accountability (IARA) at Harvard University. He was recently appointed as a senior fellow at the Harvard Kennedy School.

Bhanwar Meghwanshi is an award-winning writer, journalist and social activist. He was born in 1975 in a small village in Rajasthan. As a teenager, he became a member of the Rashtriya Swayamsevak Sangh (RSS), which he later quit, associating instead with several grassroots organizations working for social and economic justice. He was formerly founder and editor of *Diamond India*, a monthly journal about issues from a grassroots perspective. His most recent book, *I Could Not Be Hindu: The Story of a Dalit in the RSS*, has caught the attention of people from all over the world. He runs the award-winning news website Shunyakal.

Badri Narayan, is a social historian and cultural anthropologist, and the director of G.B. Pant Social Science Institute, Allahabad. His interests lie in popular culture, social and anthropological history, Dalit and subaltern issues, and the relationship between power and culture. Besides having written a number of articles, both in English and Hindi, he has authored *Republic of Hindutva* (2021); *Fractured Tales: Invisibles in Indian Democracy* (2016); *Kanshiram* (2014); *The Making of the Dalit Public in North India: Uttar Pradesh 1950–Present* (2011); *Women Heroes and Dalit Assertion in North India* (2006); *Fascinating Hindutva: Saffron Politics and Dalit Mobilisation* (2006).

Jignesh Mevani is an independent MLA from the Vadgam constituency of Gujarat. He is also the convener of the Rashtriya Dalit Adhikar Manch, an organization fighting for the rights of the Dalit community. He rose to national fame in 2016 after issuing a state-wide call asking Dalits to march to Una, where cow vigilantes had publicly thrashed and assaulted seven Dalit men with sticks and knives. He has been a lawyer and an activist fighting for land rights of the Dalit community, and is a staunch advocate of a caste-free society.

Sudha Pai retired as professor at the Centre for Political Studies, and the pro-vice Chancellor (2011–2015) of Jawaharlal Nehru University. She was a national fellow, ICSSR, New Delhi (2016–2017), and a senior fellow at the Nehru Memorial Museum and Library, New Delhi (2006–2009). She is the author of *Dalit Assertion and the Unfinished Democratic Revolution: The BSP in Uttar Pradesh* (2002); *Developmental State and the Dalit Question in Madhya Pradesh: Congress Response* (2010); *Everyday Communalism: Riots in Contemporary Uttar Pradesh* (2018); and *Constitutional and Democratic Institutions in India: A Critical Analysis* (ed., 2019).

Pa. Ranjith is an Indian film director and producer who makes films in Tamil. He directed *Attakathi* (2012), *Madras* (2014),

Kabali (2016) and *Kaala* (2018), and produced *Pariyerum Perumal* (2018). Apart from writing and directing films, he is also a socially committed artist who has produced documentaries on social issues, including *Ladies and Gentlewomen* (2017); *Dr. Shoe Maker* (2016); and *Beware of Caste: Mirchpur* (2016). He is the founder of the Casteless Collective, an energetic gaana-rap band; Koogai, a film movement and library; and the Neelam Cultural Centre.

R.S. Praveen Kumar joined the Indian Police Service (IPS) in 1995, and in a career of twenty-six years, he showed commendable leadership, initiative and industry in both law enforcement and welfare sectors of public administration. He has received several prestigious awards from the Government of India and the Government of Telangana, and from non-governmental organizations. He was also awarded the Police Medal for Gallantry by the President of India. He transformed the lives of lakhs of marginalized children through quality education in Telangana. In 2021, he quit the IPS to join the Bahujan Samaj Party (BSP) and pursue the unfulfilled dreams of Mahatma Jyotirao Phule, Babasaheb Dr B.R. Ambedkar, Manyavar Kanshi Ram and many doyens of the social justice movement.

Priyank Kharge is a politician from the Indian National Congress. He is a second-time legislator from Chittapur, Karnataka, and was the youngest cabinet minister in the government led by Siddaramaiah (he served as minister for IT, BT and tourism). In the next coalition government, he was given the all-important responsibility as the minister for social welfare. He was also a design professional (graphics and animation) and had worked extensively for corporations in India and abroad before joining politics. A keen observer of future technologies, he has co-founded and mentored a few start-ups that have broken new ground in their verticals.

Neeraj Shetye is a candidate for MSc Politics of Conflict Rights and Justice, and works as a graduate research associate at the Centre on Conflict Rights and Justice at SOAS University of London (2021–22). Before this, he worked as the public policy research lead and programme manager at Khaana Chahiye Foundation, contributing towards their COVID-19 hunger-relief operations. He completed his BA (research) in sociology, with a minor in international relations and public affairs, from Shiv Nadar University. His research interests are in social policy, with focus on social justice measures and sustainable livelihoods.

Budithi Rajsekhar is an Indian Administrative Service (IAS) officer from the Andhra Pradesh cadre, 1992 batch, and has worked mostly in the social sector in the domains of tribal welfare, social welfare, poverty alleviation, empowerment of marginalized communities and community mobilization. He distinguished himself as an officer who empowered the poor by making them partners in development. He is acclaimed for his outstanding work in reforming schools in the government sector in Andhra Pradesh. He did a three-year stint in the Government of India, and to reinvent himself with newer skills and perspectives, he took a sabbatical and went to Harvard University to pursue a master's degree in public administration.

About Samruddha Bharat Foundation

Samruddha Bharat Foundation is an independent sociopolitical organization established after the Dr B.R. Ambedkar International Conference held in July 2017 to:

1. Further India's constitutional promise
2. Forge an alliance of progressive forces
3. Encourage a transformative spirit in Indian politics and society.

Addressing both the symbolic and the substantive, SBF works to shape the polity, serve as a platform for participatory democracy, shape public discourse and deepen engagement with the diaspora.

In doing so, SBF works closely with India's major secular political parties on normative and policy issues. It has also created a praxis between India's foremost academics, activists and policymakers, as well as people's movements, civil society organizations, think tanks and institutions. Finally, it has established Bridge India as a sister organization in the United Kingdom to do similar work with the diaspora.

For further details, see:

www.samruddhabharat.in

 @SBFIndia

Samruddha Bharat Foundation

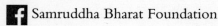 @SBFIndia